This Day . . .

A Daily Guide to Living

To my friend
and neighbor Osten —
May This Day and
every day be really blessed.

J. J. Jones

This Day . . .

A Daily Guide to Living

J.T. JONES

Pleasant Word
A Division of WINEPRESS PUBLISHING

ISBN 1-57921-636-6
Library of Congress Catalog Card Number: 2003102893

Special Thanks

We are the sum total of our experiences.

—Unknown

This Day . . . is a collection of some of my life's experiences that could only have come from God's omniscient mind for time and place. Thanks to God's providence and to all those who have added to my sum total to date.

A special thanks goes to my mother, Lois Jones, and to my Aunt Elaine Angell. Both encouraged my work and their keen eyes proofread my drafts. When I was growing up, their critical ear for grammar was an annoyance. Today it is valued and welcomed.

The same deep appreciation goes to Bette Houle and Eloise Johnson who spent many hours helping to organize this material. They lovingly took on a far bigger project than anyone could estimate. When such kindness is shown, a mere "thank you" is woefully inadequate.

Thanks to the cover artist, Dotti Rackliffe, whose artistic talent brought life to a vague idea that floated in my mind. Dotti generously shared her talent, encouragement, and rich experience from the world of printing. The same indebtedness goes to Don Gibbs who tuned portrait into cover. There are no words to ever fully thank Don for his longstanding role as willing listener, mentor, and reality checker.

And to Marilyn, who tops the list of my sum total.

Introduction

Why invite a daily devotional along as a companion and guide of your faith journey? That is a fair question that does not have a single answer.

First, a daily devotional helps with the discipline of everyday meditation and prayer. The busyness of life robs good intentions of becoming realties. A devotional is an aid in keeping your best intentions in good repair. It will help keep you focused. The array of distractions that every one of us is obliged to face every day has a way of blurring our focus. A one-page daily meditation followed by a two—or three-sentence prayer is doable for the busiest of lives. The two or three minutes a day that you spend with *This Day* . . . will exponentially grow your faith. Recognizing the busy reader's need for efficiency and the challenges that developing a daily discipline entails are part of the "why bother?" question.

Second, we have a tendency to live in the past or in the future at the expense of the present. Often we try to replicate the past. We rewrite its idyllic calm. We sort out what is pleasing and reject, or quietly forget, the unpleasant episodes of long ago. Or, we can be so absorbed in past hurts, historic wrongs, or childhood abuse that we carry a suitcase of ancient wounds with us. By living in the past, we allow the past to negatively inform our today or trivialize our present being.

The inverse of living in the past is just as toxic to the present. If we constantly look beyond the present as a time of fulfillment, then the present moment is understood as less-than-fulfilling. We plan for that one distant day when we will have the perfect mate, the dream house, the fulfilling job, the right compensation, the bigger boat, the faster snow-mobile, or the children who suddenly realize our true worth. That one day of elusive wholeness, when we will be truly happy, is always in the distant future. By living in the future, we allow the dissatisfaction of the present to rule our lives.

The hope of a balanced life is to live in the present. The past is gone—never to be seen again. The future is an ever-changing mirage that will always remain elusive and distant. We may not live to see the future. We surely will not revisit the past. All we have is this very moment. Spiritual growth lives and has its being in the present moment. Thus, the reason for the title: *This Day* . . .

The hope for the reader is to help establish the daily discipline of spiritual growth by redoubling his or her focus on the present. By fully living in this day, the past and the future take on a new essence in our lives. For today, well lived, is our only opportunity to make all of our yesterdays fond memories and every tomorrow a living hope.

Alongside the reader's purpose in pursuing a daily devotional, are a whole set of questions regarding its origin. Where did this come from? Why was it compiled in this format? What was the moving force behind the effort, and what is the ultimate hope for the reader?

Again, a single answer will not suffice.

First, I wanted to give a lasting gift to the people in my life whom I love most—my family and the congregation I serve as their pastor. If my daily spiritual musings lighten another's load, even for a moment, then the effort is worthwhile. If I can help another form the habit of daily mediation, even for two or three minutes a day, I will have helped nurture spiritual growth. If these pages draw the reader into a new understanding of how to deftly live one day at a time, then the labor has yielded the essence of *This Day* . . .

My second hope was to chronicle a farming culture that is rapidly slipping away. I lived on dairy/hog/grain farm in the upper Maumee Valley on the Michigan/Ohio border for more than four decades. Men and women, who were shaped by the Great Depression and World War II, in turn shaped my life. Many of these were men and women who were educated in one-room schools—some for no more than eight years. All of them had agrarian roots. They lived on and from the land. They lived in a harmony with the seasons, the markets, and the fortunes that befell their kind and neighbors. They lived in a vibrant sense of community that saw the wellness of the whole was predicated on the health of every part. Above all else, they were grand storytellers, and they passed on to me the tradition of storytelling.

The pressures of corporate farming, dismal commodity prices, market and weather uncertainties, and the need for ever more efficiency have drawn the final curtain on family farming. The last act is now on stage. The cast will soon make its final bow. A kindly commentator, whose heart will forever love these kind and wise people, must document the passage. I see my role as keeper and teller of their story. Their wisdom, wit, and sense of community must be told with respect. A monthly magazine of reminiscence dare not do the job of retelling their story in a sappy fashion. Their story needs to be retold, and it must be told lovingly with its warts, smells, and bruises intact. My endeavor is chronicler and not redeemer or one who wants to reestablish the past.

In the pages of *This Day* . . . the reader will encounter many of these stout characters. These folks were kind and tough rolled into one. They swore a lot, and often had good reason to do so. They were brave risk takers who had insurmountable faith. They were fiercely patriotic. They were believers in Jesus Christ and saw no hypocrisy in smoking and chewing too much tobacco. They were staunch moralists. They were wise, yet they had no letters that followed their names. These were good, yet flawed and complicated people who simply did their best.

My final hope is to pass on preachable stories to my peers in the pulpit. We come from a tradition of storytellers. Jesus Christ was a storyteller. The gospels are filled with passages that begin with: "He told them the story of . . ." Jesus used parables and stories to convey meaning, truth, and understanding. Stories are portable. The listener can tell and retell them. They cut to the heart of the matter.

Good stories have a lasting quality about them. They transcend generational and cultural boundaries. The worth of story never fades or goes out of style. Every preacher I have met is constantly filtering what he or she hears through a filter that is labeled, "That will preach!" An index has been added for your convenience and for a more efficient use of this text as a preaching resource. All biblical references are from the New International Version (NIV).

These stories will preach, because they speak to the heart of the human condition. The intent is to be readable and retellable. Though not presented in a scholarly fashion, the theology is not thin soup that lacks integrity or Christian focus. Neither is it denominationally specific. These are stories of flawed people who seek a loving God. Nearly always they were successful in achieving that end. That is the good news within the Good News!

My prayer for each of you is that you read, pray, and live in This Day . . .

J. T. Jones

> Look to this day,
> For it is life,
> The very life of life.
> In its brief course lie all
> The realities and verities of existence,
> The bliss of growth,
> The splendor of action,
> The glory of power—
> For yesterday is but a dream,
> And tomorrow is only a vision,
> But today, well lived,
> Makes every yesterday a dream of happiness
> And every tomorrow a vision of hope.
> Look well, therefore, to this day.
>
> —A Sanskrit Proverb

Why This Day? The answer is simple: This particular day matters because it is all we really have. Yesterday is gone and tomorrow may never be. This very day, this moment, indeed, the immediate present is where we live. Yesterdays color our today. The dreams of tomorrow help to shape this day. But this day is the only place where life is lived out.

The psalmist put it this way:

> Today is the day that the Lord has made; Let us rejoice and be glad in it. (Psalm 118:24)

Jesus said:

> Give us today our daily bread. (Matthew 6:11)

Paul wrote to the Corinthians:

> Today is the day of salvation! (2 Corinthians 6:3)

This day is God's gift to you. What you do with this day is your gift to God. Make the most of it, for it is the only day you have.

Prayer: This Day I will need some help in not trying to replicate the past or living in a time yet to come. I will not fritter away the present on disappointing yesterdays or one day in the future when I supposedly have it all together. I will live this day!

'Tis well an old age is out, and time to begin anew.
—John Dryden

As we stand at a new beginning, a brief outline of what really matters makes good sense. Here are twelve points that lead to living a life of contentment you may want to consider:

LIVING CONTENTEDLY

1. Keep first things first.
2. Dream big dreams.
3. Live with a sense of passion.
4. Never settle for easy answers. Keep on questioning.
5. Be a person of hope, even when it is easier to cave in to hopelessness.
6. Refuse to just go along to get along.
7. Always put community above individuality.
8. Think, act, and live inclusively.
9. There are some things you will never be able to fully explain (Things like prayer, love, hope, faith, heaven, or for that matter, even God). Just remember that prayer, love, hope, faith heaven and even God do not need your explanation in order to exist.
10. Live so your life has significance.
11. Seek to be a more spiritual being rather than more religious.
12. Look for God in the crowd when you cross the finish line first.
13. Look beside you for God when you stumble and fall.

There, that ought to help with a new beginning. Have a happy and contented new year.

Prayer: This Day is poised at a new beginning. Help me put down the baggage of the past, to travel light, and to live contentedly.

RUTH
IVAN
PATTI
SHAROLYN
GODFREY
LYNN
VASILY
APE
KBARRET

969-1139
-917

page 516
in Encyclopedia
cook Book

Vegetable
        Casserole

2 mild onions
4 large tomatoes
2 cups diced
        Potatoes
1 cup chopped
        celery
1 cup sliced
        carrots
1 tsp salt
1/4 tsp pepper
1 tsp Paprika
4 tBs fat

MEAT LOAF

Do not be afraid; do not be discouraged.
—Deuteronomy 1:21

My friend, Denny Pressler, keeps me supplied with an assortment of clippings that could be called nuggets of wisdom, bits and pieces of humor, and general good advice. I am grateful for his careful eye and willingness to pass on the following tidbit.

Consider this bumper sticker:

You can tell how big a person is by what it takes to discourage him.

How true! One's spiritual depth is in direct proportion to one's ability to press on in a spirit of hope. The same is true for businesses, institutions, sports teams, nations, and even churches. To be easily discouraged is to have little resolve. To be easily dissuaded is to have small faith.

Thinking that the enormity of a happening is just too big for our meager ability is *not* consistent with the gospel of Jesus Christ. The Good News can be understood in many ways. It can be seen through many different lenses. But, the one certain truth of Jesus' teachings is that nothing is impossible for the believer. Thus, there ought not be a Christian who is easily swayed from his or her chosen course. To be easily dissuaded is incompatible with Christ's hope and is positive evidence of puny or lukewarm faith

To be sure, there are challenges that cause us to say, "Wow, that is going to take some doing!" For the community that is grounded in faith, the impossible becomes possible, the improbable is made probable, and the out-of-the-ordinary is achievable. Beyond that, the discouraged find more than enough courage in Christ.

Prayer: This Day I will seek new courage as I meet its challenges. Knowing that I belong to the One of indisputable courage gives me hope even in the face of trial.

And when you pray, do not keep babbling like the pagans,
for they think they will be heard because of their many
words. Do not be like them, for your Father knows
what you need before you ask him.

—The words of Jesus as recorded
in Matthew 6:7–8

My friend, Denny Pressler, passed the following clipping to me. Consider the number of words it takes to convey an important thought. Consider these:

Pythagorean Theorem:	24 words
Pledge of Allegiance:	31 words
The Lord's Prayer:	66 words
Archimedes' Principle:	67 words
The 10 Commandments:	179 words
The Gettysburg Address:	286 words
The Declaration of Independence:	1,300 words
The U.S. government regulations on the sale of cabbage:	26,911 words
Eternal Hope:	26 words

Denny's clipping seems to prove that wordiness is all a matter of perspective. Sometimes heaping on more words does not necessarily convey more wisdom. Perhaps this is a strong argument for shorter sermons.

The gospel of Jesus Christ has an economy of words. It is likely that the conservation of words is what the Gospel writer, John, had in mind when he penned the heart of the Easter message: *For God so loved the world that He gave His one and only Son that whoever believes in Him shall not perish but have eternal life.* (John 3:16).

Prayer: This Day I will practice an economy of words in thanking God. Thanks, God. Amen.

Provide purses for yourselves that will not wear out,
a treasure in heaven that will not be exhausted,
where no thief comes or moth destroys.
—The words of Jesus as recorded
in Luke 12:33

According to an article in the *Antique Trader*, the estate of the King of Cowboys has fallen on hard times. Roy Rogers' family was forced to auction a number of Rogers' memorabilia to pay the inheritance tax that had been levied on the estate. The top item in the auction was Roy Rogers' custom-made saddle. It brought an amazing $412,500.00! That's a lot of money for a saddle. Especially when it only cost a fraction of that amount when Roy Rogers had it commissioned in 1950.

The family said they hated to see the "King of the Cowboys'" stuff having to go under the gavel. They spent some time evaluating what to offer and what to keep. Finally, after much heart-rending thought, they selected forty-four items to list in the public auction. The family felt some measure of relief that they were able to save Roy's horse, Trigger, from the sale. You see, Trigger went to the taxidermy shop after his death. Roy had him stuffed. So, there they are—a saddle-less stuffed horse and a half million bucks in tax receipts.

Keeping a stuffed horse and selling a $400,000+ saddle seems like a dubious choice. What are you going to do with a stuffed horse and no saddle? And, even more puzzling is the saddle itself. Roy's side of the saddle was beautifully tooled and studded with rubies. But, what about Trigger's side of the saddle, was it ,tooled? Or, was the horse's side of the saddle left rough?

And, what about the winning bidder? The article said that he bought it as a surprise for his wife. Now, that would be a surprise if one of us came home with a half-million-dollar saddle and said, "Honey, look what I got for your pony!" Most likely, most of us would be stuffed and standing right beside old Trigger if we pulled such a stunt.

Fame and fortune is not all that it is cracked up to be.

Prayer: This Day I will weigh up what really matters. I will inventory my holdings in heaven and keep them in good order.

The stone the builders rejected has become the capstone,
the Lord has done this, and it is marvelous in our eyes.
—The words of Jesus as recorded
in Matthew 21:42

When we finished the new log cabin on the Clam River, we had a large pile of knotty pine left over. It was scarred, twisted, and warped. The boards were too flawed to use. The problem was that these boards had been finished with a wood preservative, so they could not be returned to the supplier. What do you do with a pile of warped boards?

My Scottish blood would not allow these boards to be the guest at a hot dog roast. And I had already moved the pile a half dozen times. Something had to be done, but what?

First, I cut out all the bad spots. If there was a serious blemish, a deep scar, or busted edge, it was cut out and thrown away (hot dog roast material). I then had an even larger pile of shorter boards. But I made a surprising discovery. The twisted and warped boards were manageable in shorter lengths. It took some time and much fitting, but the once-warped boards created a respectable wall in the basement.

As I was building that wall with what was once rejected material, it dawned on me how much that pile of boards is like life. Get rid of the garbage and it becomes manageable. Beyond that, taking life in smaller bites makes the overwhelming doable. The shortened, once-warped boards are a metaphor for "One day at a time." Like any intentionally-lived life, the twisted boards did not make a perfect wall, but one that has worth and value.

From a pile of flawed lumber, I discovered that if you get rid of the junk and take life in small pieces, great things happen!

Prayer: This Day I will offer the lumber of my life to be used as material to build a temple to God. Today, in the hands of the Master Carpenter, I will gladly be God's less-than-perfect raw material.

The greatest poverty in the world lives between your ears.
—Paul Bradley

One day a father of a very wealthy family took his son on a trip to the country with the firm purpose of showing his son how poor people can be. They spent a couple of days and nights on the farm of what would be considered a very poor family. On return from their trip, the father asked his son, "How was the trip?"

"It was great, Dad."

"Did you see how poor people can be?" the father asked.

"Oh yes," answered the son.

The son went on to say, "I saw that we have one dog and they have four. We have a pool that reaches to the middle of our garden, and they have a creek that has no end. We have imported lanterns in our garden, and they have the stars at night. We have a small piece of land to live on, and they have fields that go beyond our sight. We have servants who serve us, but they serve others. We have walls around our property to protect us; they have friends to protect them."

With this, the boy's father was speechless. Then the son added, "Thanks, Dad, for showing me how poor we are."

Prayer: This Day I will take inventory of my wealth with the knowing that it cannot be tallied on a balance sheet. Today, I will realize that poverty of the spirit is the greatest deprivation of all.

*The spirit of the Lord is on me, because he has anointed me to preach
good news to the poor. He has sent me to proclaim freedom for the
prisoners and recovery of sight for the blind,
to release the oppressed, to proclaim the year of the Lord's favor.*
—The words of Jesus as recorded
in Luke 4:18–19

My father believed in people. He was a caring man with an inexhaustible sense of optimism. He believed that no matter how far down the ladder of decency one had descended, given the right opportunity, that wasted life could be salvaged. He thought anyone could change for the better if just given the chance. In that spirit, my father negotiated a work-release contract with the Jackson State Penitentiary that brought a prison parolee to work on our farm.

My father's responsibility in all this was to provide room and board, transportation to his weekly visit with his probation officer, and a wage. But, I know that he quietly wished for more for this man than just another farm hand. The man's name was Chet. I do not recall what led to Chet's conviction. He was well groomed and polite enough, but he was the biggest whiner I have ever met!

Chet never let up. He complained incessantly about everything. He was about as miserable as a man could be. He wanted a car, a home, an expensive suit, a gold watch, and a bankroll. He wanted to visit his old watering holes. Chet had a bad case of the "wants." He wanted it all and he wanted it now. Chet's constant whining grew weary. His tenure as a farm worker was short and unpleasant for both Chet and all of us. Though I do not know the exact circumstances of his dismissal, one day when I came home from school, Chet didn't live there anymore.

Chet showed me that there are prisons with bars and prisons without bars. He had done his time, but he was still incarcerated in the prison of "want." Perhaps his personal prison was as confining and constraining as the walled "palace" he had left behind in Jackson. I never knew what happened to Chet. My guess is that the prison of "want" was harder time than the cold gray walls of Cooper Street.

Prayer: This Day I will give thanks for the freedom that only Christ can bring. For in Christ I am paroled from the prison of "want."

Consequently, faith comes from hearing the message, and the message is heard through the word of Christ.

—Romans 10:17

A number of studies have shown that hearing is the last sense that leaves a dying person. That is important because there may be a time when we still have something important to say to a loved one who is near death. When a loved one is close to crossing over into the new life God has prepared for him or her, they do not go in total silence. It brings a good measure of comfort to us in the knowing that what we say can still be heard. It gives us the opportunity to attend to our unfinished business. What we have kept in our hearts for perhaps decades can still be said with the certain knowing that it will be heard.

Based on this knowledge, a study was designed to determine if surgical patients had this same capacity of unconscious hearing. It seems they do. Anesthetized surgical patients who heard doctors, nurses, and other operating room staff talking in a positive or cheerful manner during surgery had shorter recovery times. Moreover, these patients had fewer post-operative problems. Patients who heard angry debates, hostility, or negative talk have significantly more post-operative problems.

Given the facts that anesthetized people respond to positive talk, it changes everything for a preacher. Even if hearers doze off, the Good News must be kept affirming, uplifting, and pointing toward new wholeness!

Prayer: This Day I will listen to God's voice in my life. Today, I will deliberately take the cotton out of my ears and put it in my mouth.

"Peace be with you!"
—The words of Jesus as recorded
in John 20:21

Ever say to yourself, "Who am I to make a difference? I am just one person."

One person can make a huge difference.

In 1985, a pastor from Pennsylvania, the Reverend Mooney, took a group of Christians to the Soviet Union. The group toured the countryside, visited several museums and the remains of a number of unused cathedrals. Their tour was closely scrutinized by Soviet authorities and was no more than a token view of communist life. But, it was a goodwill gesture in a time when American and Soviet relations were in a sorry state of disrepair.

As the group was about to leave Russia, an elderly, wrinkled-faced woman reached out to the Reverend Mooney and pressed three rubles into his hand. In her broken English she said one word: "peace." Pastor Mooney took the three rubbles home with him and spent some thoughtful time mulling over what a few pennies could do to bring about world peace. In the face of hundreds of billions of dollars in expenditures for arms, the three rubles looked pretty puny.

Pastor Mooney decided to purchase a votive candle with the Russian woman's pennies. He would call the votive candle a "Peace Candle." His church's missions committee added to the "Peace Candle" fund and made it an outreach of this Pennsylvania church by sharing these candles with other churches. The idea spread. Today there are thousands of churches across America where the direct descendants of the Russian woman's pennies still flicker with the hope for peace. The "Peace Candle" continues to illumine the darkness of global war. It sheds its warming glow on countless worshipers who pray for peace.

You are just one. But, in the spirit of that one word that came from the lips of a forever-unknown woman, ten thousand "Peace Candles" still light the way.

Prayer: This Day I will not allow my oneness to be silent. Today, my voice, my prayers, and my caring will add to God's light.

And lead us not into temptation, but deliver us from the evil one.
—The words of Jesus as recorded
in Mathew 6:13

What does it mean to ask God not to lead us into temptation? It is one of the most often asked questions by vicinage councils and ordination credential committees. It is the most feared question any seminarian can face. It has sent chills up the spines of candidates who seek the blessing of ordination. It is one of those tough sayings that the Bible presents. It is one we would prefer to avoid. But, avoidance and fear will not make it go away. What do we mean when we say, "God, please do not lead me into temptation?"

Does it imply that God is in the business of tempting us? Does it mean that God wants to test our resolve? Does it mean that God and Satan have formed a curious partnership that toys with our ability to stand tough in the face of temptation? Surely not! God does not tempt. And it is lousy theology to even think that a loving God would find pleasure in dipping us into harm's way just to see if we have the stuff to say, "No!" God does not behave like that.

"Lead us not into temptation" means do not allow us to be so led. It means keep us safe. It means as life tests us, give us the resolve, the wherewithal, and the determination to avoid sin. It means that we readily acknowledge our vulnerability to temptation and God's ability to keep us out of harm's way. It is saying, "In my powerlessness, may your power keep me safe."

God does not tempt. In the words of James it says: When tempted, no one should say, *"God is tempting me." For God cannot be tempted by evil, nor does he tempt anyone . . . (James 1:13)*

Believing that God tempts and leads us to sin is like believing that sun causes darkness.

Prayer: This Day I will pray out of my sense of vulnerability. Today, I will make no excuses or pretend I have found a better way.

"There are only two things I want to know: Does God speak, and what does He say?"
—An unidentified Puritan author

We Congregationalists take great pride in our Pilgrim heritage. We delight in the fact that our forebears breathed life into both a democratic form of government and freedom of religion. The other side of our family tree, the Puritans, we prefer not to mention. Theirs was a staunch morality that deplored anything that resembled having fun. The Puritans brought us one of history's sorriest chapters—the Salem Witch Trials. It is no wonder that we like to omit Puritanism from our pedigree. Yet, occasionally a bit of Puritan wisdom pokes through the easily forgettable past and speaks to the richness of our heritage.

The Puritan forbearer asked, "Does God speak?" The answer is a resounding, "Yes!"

"What does He say?" is not as simple to discern. What does God have to say? There are some broad and obvious generalities. For example, to the fearful, God says, "Be brave." To the weak, God says, "Let me give you a hand." To the confused, God might say, "Let me help you decide." To the downtrodden, God says, "You matter to me." To the grieving, God says, "I care." To the hurried, God says, "Whoa, Big Fella! Slow down!"

God has much to say when He speaks to our inner spirit. It is there that God comforts, encourages, reveals possibilities, and gives each of us an intuitive knowing of His will. To know what God has to say demands a bit of silence in the presence of God. Asking God to do this and that is a common prayer. But to be still in the presence of God seems to go against our impatient spirits. Speaking to God is the easy part. Listening to God takes a bit of effort.

Prayer: This Day God will hear my stillness and the longing of my soul to hear His voice. His speaking is a given; my listening will take some effort.

> *It may be called the Master Passion,*
> *the hunger for self-approval.*
>
> —Mark Twain

We hear a lot about the destructive nature of our competitiveness. It is hard to deny that overt competitiveness can be destructive. We have all watched someone turn what ought to be a leisurely sport into a matter of life and death consequences. A friendly game of cards, pool, golf, or bowling becomes the Super Bowl of human worth. There are those who must have the deer with the biggest rack of horns and the largest fish hanging on the wall. It matters little if the sport is collecting baseball cards or Beanie Babies; the urge to have the most and the best drives the collector. For these overtly competitive souls, it is as if the axis of the world turns on winning.

Some have cried that competitiveness ought be incised from our spirits. They have suggested that we nurture our children with the desire to win through Little League statistics, dance recitals, and awarding scouting badges. They push to have Little League games without scoreboards. In their myopic naiveté, these reformers believe that we can remove competitiveness from the human spirit.

To remove our drive to win is neither possible nor desirable. What really needs to change is how our passion to be remembered is lived out. If we are remembered only for the most home runs, the biggest collection of jam jars, or the most Beanie Babies on the shelf, we have lived a sorry life. However, we will be long remembered if we are able to come to a delicate balance of living with passion. Ours must be a checked passion that does not control us or the quality of our relationships. Be competitive, but do not let your passion to win be all that defines you.

Remember this: our competitiveness is a good thing; our unchecked passion to be recognized is toxic.

Prayer: This day I will be all I can be. I will live with passion, but one that is channeled not for recognition, trophies, or wealth, but rather a passion to use my God-giftedness in ways that are pleasing to God, to others, and to myself.

> *It's them that take advantage that get advantage*
> *in the world.*
>
> —George Eliot

Sarah was born with a muscle missing in her foot. She had to wear a special brace all the time.

One day Sarah came home from school to tell her father that she had competed in an indoor track meet. Because of her leg support, the father was a bit puzzled. In fact, his mind was racing to think of some kind words to soothe his daughter's disappointment. Before he could get a word out, she said, "Daddy, I won two races!"

He could not believe what his daughter was saying. And then she said, "I had an advantage."

Inwardly the father sighed. Now he knew what had happened. The race officials must have given her a head start or some other advantage.

But again Sarah spoke before he could say anything. She said, "Daddy, I didn't get a head start. My advantage was I had to try harder!"

Prayer: This Day I will try harder. Today, I will understand that my head start is measured in heart, not in feet, dollars, or seconds.

I keep six honest serving men (They taught me all I knew);
Their names are What and Why and When and How
and Where and Who.

—Rudyard Kipling

I am not sure if "*Whyness*" is a word. It is not to be confused with highness, nor is it a root of whinny or whiny. Whyness sounds like a word, and it seems to have the ability to stand on its own terms. If the governing body that validates and certifies words does not already recognize "whyness" as a useable word, I think it ought to be nominated as a new word.

The "Why?" question is central to being human. We are born as whyness seekers. Anyone who has lived through the first half dozen years of parenthood understands whyness. A child's inquisitive mind is a perpetual whyness machine. Sometimes that constant barrage of "Whys" wears on a parent's patience to the point of saying, "Don't ask why again!" A child whose whyness is squelched tragically begins to believe that it is somehow wrong to ask, "Why?" Added to the childhood taboo of asking why, we soon discover that many of life's important questions defy a clear answer. It is easier to avoid seeking the whyness of an idea. Still another whyness barrier is that by asking "Why?" we appear to be uninformed, or, worse yet, look a bit foolish.

Whyness is the fearless look at the reasons that underpin a belief or an idea. I suspect that we misidentify or confuse the whyness that drives an idea more often than we would like to believe.

So, why is it so important to be able to ask the "Why" question? Plato said, "The life that is unexamined is not worth living." Asking "Why?" is the ultimate examination. It is good that God is confident and big enough to allow our whyness to shine. Who would want to put faith into a puny God who squashed our deepest yearnings with, "Don't ask, 'Why?'"

Praise God for "Whyness."

Prayer: This Day I will fearlessly seek my soul's deepest yearnings. Today, I will put aside anxiety, fear of ridicule, and all other petty barriers.

In the last days, God says, I will pour out my Spirit on all people. Your sons and daughters will prophesy, your young men will see visions, your old men will dream dreams.

—Acts 2:17

Dreams are important. They are vital to living fully. A life void of the ability to dream dreams cannot live up to its potential. I am not speaking about the dreams we have when we are asleep. They, too, are vital to our emotional and physical wellness. The dreams I am speaking of are the visions and hopes that dwell in our minds and souls—the ones that make us possibility thinkers.

A life void of dreams is one of monotony. It is one that can never imagine that which is beyond the seen. It is a life that settles for the empirical, the mundane, and the lowest measure of hope. Dream puny and live little. Dream big and your life is only limited by your imagination.

Not every dream has to be achieved to make it worthwhile. A dream that plays only in the theater of your mind has its value. Dreams come in all sizes and shapes. Some are silly. Some are impractical. Some would make us look a bit foolish if we shared them with others. Some will never be. But, just because a dream may never become reality, it does not invalidate a dream's worth.

If you think your most quiet dream is silly, then consider this: My dream is to drive the Zamboni Machine at an NHL hockey game. I want to resurface the ice between periods while the teams are in the locker rooms. I want to hear the roar of the Zamboni. I want 12,000 fans to sit and watch me deftly maneuver the massive Zamboni into the arena's corners and lay down a new surface of ice. There, I have said it—I want to drive the Zamboni Machine!

Dreams do not have to be achievable, realistic, or even practical. Dreams have great worth simply because they validate our imaginative selves. Who knows? Maybe a few of them will actually happen.

Prayer: This Day I will dream big, for I know that my dreams are the stuff of reality.

> *The fool doth think he is wise, but the wise man*
> *knows himself to be a fool.*
> —William Shakespeare

Consider these curious and humorous inconsistencies:
Only in America:

. . . can a pizza get to your house faster than an ambulance.

. . . are there handicap-parking places in front of skating rinks.

. . . do drugstores make the sick walk all the way to the back of the store to get their prescriptions while healthy people can buy cigarettes at the front of the store.

. . . do people order double cheeseburgers, large fries, and a diet coke.

. . . do banks have both doors open and chain the pens to the counters.

. . . do we have cars worth thousands of dollars in the driveway and put useless junk in the garage.

. . . do we use answering machines to screen calls and then have call waiting so we won't miss a call from someone we didn't want to talk to in the first place.

. . . do we buy hot dogs in packages of ten and buns in packages of eight.

. . . do we use politics to describe the process so well: "Poli" in Latin means "many," and "tics" means "bloodsucking parasites."

. . . do they have drive up ATMs with Braille lettering.

. . . do we spend millions to subsidize tobacco farmers and hundreds of millions to educate our citizens about the harm of smoking.

Prayer: This Day I will take a brave look at my inconsistencies. Some may be humorous. Some may need my attention.

Be still and know that I am God.

—Psalm 46:10

When I was a child it often occurred to me that God certainly had a lot to do. For example, if God heard every prayer, how did he keep them all straight? Suppose a man in Ceylon prayed for his water buffalo to live forever. And, at exactly the same time, a mother in Buffalo prayed for her children to have enough hamburger for a meatloaf. Did God ever get mixed up? Or what about the farmers who prayed for rain and the city dwellers who just as fervently prayed for a sunny weekend? Curious how young minds worry about such things.

Of course my dilemma as a child was the same one we encounter all of our days—attempting to comprehend the infinite with a finite mind. Just growing up does not put an end to this dilemma. We still want to understand the scope of and the mind of God.

Indeed, such pondering is not limited to children. The story is told of Galileo's astrological investigations receiving much criticism. Some felt that his concepts of the vastness of the universe left no place for humans. If indeed the universe was as big as Galileo suggested, then how could God keep track of each tiny detail?

Galileo's answer was simplicity itself. He pointed to a bunch of grapes and said, "The sun will ripen one small bunch of grapes as though it had nothing else to do."

We all need that same assurance of a personal God in this vast world. Aren't you glad God is God and all we have to do is live in that assurance?

Prayer: This Day I will stand in awe of the vastness of God, knowing fully well that I will never fully comprehend. And knowing just as fully that God can be God quite nicely without my comprehension.

And surely I am with you always, to the very end of the age.
—The words of Jesus as recorded
in Matthew 28:20b

Jesus was walking down the road one day and came upon a man who was crying. The Lord said, "My friend, what's wrong?"

The man replied, "I'm blind. Can you help me?"

Jesus healed the man and went on his way. As he continued his journey, he came upon another man who was sitting beside the road weeping. "Good friend, what is wrong?"

The man answered, "I'm lame and cannot walk. Can you help me?" Jesus healed the man and he, too, went down the road.

Presently, the Lord came upon a third man who was sobbing. "Good friend, what is wrong?" the Lord asked.

The man said, "I'm a minister."

And Jesus sat down and wept with him.

We are not all pastors, but we are all ministers. We are the hands and the arms of the living Christ. We are the servants and the doers of Christ. We are ministers because we move among the needy, bring hope, and labor for peace and justice. In short, we are the body of Christ that lives and has its being in the world.

That sounds like a tall order. Surely it is more than any one of us can bear. Take heart. In Jesus' own words he said, "I will be with you always." Christ knows the scope of the job we have as ministers. Therefore, he walks with us, heals us, gives us new vision, and encourages us. Perhaps he even weeps with us from time to time, for he surely knows the magnitude of the job.

Prayer: This Day I will recognize the awesome task that is mine as a minister of Christ. I will not be timid or fearful, for I know I am not alone on this journey.

"Is it 'When all Else Fails, Pray' or is it
'Pray Before all Else Fails?'"

—Unknown

Plague. Epidemic. Pandemic. Frightening words aren't they? Consider anthrax. It is a disease that spreads rapidly, causes much harm, and leaves death in its wake. The very mention of anthrax sends a shudder through us. The idea of an epidemic is truly frightening.

The wandering band of Israelites was faced with a different sort of plague. It, too, was an epidemic, though slightly different kind of plague. This plague did not cause high fever, skin rash, flu-like symptoms, or shortness of breath. Yet this epidemic caused suffering, great harm, and much destruction. The Israelites were suffering from a bad case of complaining. Their symptoms were whining, moaning, and complaining. They had fallen victims to the plague of complaining.

"Why have you brought us out here?" "I'm thirsty!" "My feet hurt." "The sand is hot." "My sandals are too tight." "My goats and sheep are thirsty." "Where is God in all my misery?" "We had it better when we were slaves in Egypt." Whine, whine, whine, and moan. They complained incessantly. They were plagued with relentless complaint.

They were a miserable lot. The hot sun beat down on them. They were thirsty, their feet hurt, and their livestock must have also been miserable. This had been a tough journey. The desert heat, the lack of water, and the arduous trudge had taken its toll. The people were weary. But, the plague of complaining, whining, and moaning was not helpful to their situation.

Incessant complaining and the whining and moaning that goes with it may be the most crippling and deadly of all diseases.

Here is the good news: The cure is simple—just listen to yourself.

Prayer: This Day I will listen to the lament that others are obliged to hear from my mouth. Justifiable or not, my complaining usually has an audience of one. I will begin the healing within through my grateful conversation with God.

"He who has ears to hear, let him hear."
—The words of Jesus as recorded
in Luke 14:35

Pete Gould was an elderly neighbor of mine when I was a child. Old Pete had a little Fordson tractor that was the cutest little tractor you have ever seen. Pete's Fordson was badly undersized for the 80-acre farm Pete owned and operated. Pete nearly ran the wheels off this little tractor to get his work done. It had seen so much use that the sheet metal had worn around the screws from the constant vibration of the little engine that constantly ran at full throttle. The result was that the sheet metal hood began to rattle around the loose screws. Listening to that rattling hood all day long was about as unnerving as the Chinese water torture.

Pete fixed the situation and silenced the constant rattle with a piece of felt that he jammed under the tractor's hood. Pete called that piece of felt his A.R.D. It was a fancy term for Anti Rattling Device. By stuffing the A.R.D. under the tractor's hood, the annoying sound was stilled. Pete's A.R.D. worked. The tractor hood did not rattle, but the problem was just silenced. The incessant racket was only stilled, and the real problem was not solved. There are people for whom an A.R.D. would be helpful. If we could just stuff a piece of felt in the din of their racket, all would be well.

But, sometimes complaining is more than just an annoyance. A real problem exists, and just ignoring it or covering it up is not a healthy solution. Sometimes another's concerns need more attention than Old Pete's A.R.D. We need to be good listeners.

Prayer: This Day I will avoid complaining for this complainant's sake. I will also make a sincere effort to listen to the lament of others.

A good name is better than fine perfume . . .
—Ecclesiastes 7:1

Fred Craddock is a prolific writer, a preaching professor, and one of America's best preachers. Dr. Craddock has a keen insight that sees truth in the simplest of life's happenings. He tells the story of the importance of one's name.

When Dr. Craddock was a child, he and his four siblings attended church every Sunday with their mother. The minister would say, "How are you, Miz Craddock?" And to the five youngsters who followed along like little ducks in a row behind their mother he would say, "How are you, sonny? How are you, honey? How are you sonny? How are you honey? How are you, honey?"

Another minister came to serve that church, and on the fifth or sixth Sunday he said, "Fred, how are you doing?" Craddock says he was the best minister who ever served that church, because there is a big difference between "sonny" and "Fred."

What is in a name? Everything.

Prayer: This Day I will do whatever it takes to keep my name healthy and in good repair. I will honor others with the same respect.

We have learned that we must live as men, and not as ostriches, nor as dogs in the manger. We have learned to be citizens of the world, members of the human community.
—Franklin D. Roosevelt

We have seen a great rise in individualism. This spirit of individuality comes at the expense of our sense of community. It is hard for any culture to embrace both individuality and community. Perhaps our individuality shows its sorriest and most absurd side in frivolous lawsuits. It seems that gone is any sense of personal responsibility, because we have individual rights. The solution is to sue someone because we have been wronged.

Jim Shea, who is a columnist for the *Hartford Courant*, offers his imaginary and wildly absurd list of pending lawsuits. Among others, he is considering suing the following:

- His barber for his gray hair.
- Maxwell House for making him nervous.
- The trouser industry for not making 31-inch inseams.
- The potato-chip industry because he can't eat just one.
- His former teachers because he is not smarter.
- John Madden for doing hardware commercials that made him buy the hammer that hit his thumb.
- All the girls who dumped him.
- Movie theaters for the size of their sodas.
- The Boston Red Sox for pain and suffering.

Personal responsibility ought be enhanced by individualism. However, the more we celebrate self, the more wronged we feel by life. Go figure!

Prayer: This Day will be one of personal responsibility. The greatest responsibility I will have today is to be a responsible and contributing member of my greater community.

*You see things and say, "Why?" But I dream things
that never were; and I say, "Why not?"*
—George Bernard Shaw

Wendy Booker and Clay Roscoe both live with the disease, Multiple Sclerosis (MS). Wendy and Clay may be as determined as any two people you will ever meet. They joined a group called "Climb for the Cause" and attempted to climb one of North America's highest peaks, Mt. Denali. The summit of Mt. Denali is 20,320 feet. Wendy and Clay did not reach the summit. High winds turn the two MS mountaineers back at 17,200 feet.

What is remarkable about this is not that they came within nearly 1,000 yards of the summit. What is remarkable is that they even attempted such a feat. It would have been reasonable for them to just say, "I can't do that!" Who would have ever suggested that they were somehow wimps for not trying? After all, everyone knows that MS is a debilitating muscular disease. Sitting on the sidelines would have been both expected and reasonable. Wendy and Clay are not about to settle for the reasonable or the expected.

The Wendy Bookers and the Clay Roscoes of the world help stretch our imagination. They have turned the "Why mes?" of life into "Why nots?" They have shown us guts, determination, and imagination that go beyond the ordinary.

Both Wendy and Clay plan to try Mt. Denali on for size another time. It matters little if they ever reach the summit, because they have already conquered the highest peak of all by just trying.

Prayer: This Day I will put a lid on my whining. Today, I will allow my determination and my imagination to run wild.

Do not let your hearts be troubled.
Trust in God, and also in me.
—The words of Jesus as recorded
in John 14:1

Each year at Christmas time, it is the tradition of the ministerial association to jointly rent a large billboard on the outskirts of town. A dozen or so churches share the cost in bringing the Christmas message to our community. It is our way of offering the community a Christmas greeting from the Christian perspective.

One recent year the billboard featured a picture of the holy family accompanied by the familiar words: *Jesus is the reason for the season.* It was an appropriate message and a good reminder for a materialistic world to remember that our Savior's birth is the reason for Christmas joy.

Apparently the billboard company did not get the space rented immediately after Christmas. The New Year lagged into mid-January, and I noticed that the holy family was still greeting the community. Then one day in late January, the sign changed. It now featured a popular sports utility vehicle with the slogan: *"A little security in an insecure world."*

Tragically, they had pasted over the world's only real security with populism and materialism. The message to buy a new sports utility vehicle and to have a little security proclaimed that Christmas was over and it was now business as usual.

Prayer: This Day I will hold on to the world's only real security. For the hope of Christmas is not about a season. It is total security in an insecure world.

> *Not what we give, but what we share—*
> *For the gift without the giver is bare;*
> *Who gives himself with his alms feeds three—*
> *Himself, his hungering neighbor, and me.*
> —James Russell Lowell

Many years ago in a California desert, there stood a rundown hut. Nearby was a well. In this parched land, this was the only source of drinking water for miles around. Attached to the pump handle was a tin baking powder can with a message inside, written in pencil on a sheet of brown wrapping paper.

The message read:

> *This pump is in good repair. I just put new leathers and washers in it that should last another five years or so. But, the leathers dry out, and to get the bloom'n thing to work, you have to prime the pump with water. Under the white rock I buried a bottle of water so that it was out of the sun. There is enough water to prime the pump if you don't drink any of it first. Pour some in and then pump as fast as you can. The well has never run dry. Have faith.*
>
> *When you get all the water you want, be sure to fill the bottle up and put it under the white rock for the next person who needs water.*
>
> *Signed: Desert Pete*
>
> *P.S.*
> *Don't go drinking the water first! Prime the pump and you will get all you can hold. And the next time you pray, remember that God is like the pump. He has to be primed. I have given my last dime away a dozen times to prime the pump of my prayers, and I have never failed to get an answer. You got to get your heart fixed to give before you can get.*

Prayer: This Day I will take the time to get my heart fixed to give. For it is when I share with another that I am doubly blessed.

> *Winter lies too long in country towns; hangs on until it is*
> *stale and shabby, old and sullen.*
>
> —Willa Cather

Winter! Had enough by now? Somehow those idyllic Christmas cards with the lovely old Currier and Ives prints showing a horse and sleigh slipping over a frozen farm scene is not what you see outside your kitchen window. What you see is slush. You see snow piled up in ugly, frozen piles that look like off-white haystacks. You feel the biting cold. Oh, just to be able to go after the mail once more in stocking feet.

Every one of us has a winter story. We Northerners are winter warriors. You have a bare-feet-on-cold-linoleum story. You have a tongue on a frosty flagpole story. You have a pre-central heating story, a frozen pipes tale, or a saga of a snowbound week. You have leaky boots, itchy woolen underwear, no mittens, lost cap, car won't start stories. We are winter warriors with the badges of courage that attest to our campaigns of suffering. We wear those badges proudly. The retelling of long suffering is a privilege that goes with many winters. Every one of us has a story that begins with: "Let me tell you about the winter of . . . ."

Here is a winter story of a different sort. Don Adams was a Maine potato farmer. He drove a school bus to supplement his income. Don said he had known many sleepless nights thinking about the children who got on the bus every morning without mittens. Mittens and children seldom stay together for an entire winter. After retiring from farming and driving a bus, he had his wife teach him how to knit. Don spent his days knitting children's mittens.

Don lived to be well over ninety years old. Every Christmas, Don would bring a half dozen grocery sacks of woolen mittens to a local church to be given to children. Don Adams knitted thousands of pairs of woolen mittens. His mittens were of every size and every imaginable color. Don quit moaning about winter's harshness. And in doing so, he helped ease a few suffering tales that begin with: "Let me tell you about the winter of . . . ."

Prayer: This Day I will leave the whining behind. Knowing that spring will come, and that my moaning will not hasten it, I will be silent and delighted to be alive on this winter day.

Jesus was in the stern, sleeping on a cushion. The disciples woke him and said, "Teacher, don't you care if we drown?"

He got up, rebuked the wind and said to the waves, "Quiet! Be still!!" Then the wind died down and it was completely calm.

He said to his disciples, "Why are you so afraid? Do you still have no faith?"
—The words of Jesus as recorded
in Mark 4:38–40

Fred Craddock tells the story of a man who moved into a small cottage that was equipped with a wood stove and a few simple furnishings. As the sharp edge of winter crept across the landscape, the cottage grew cold and inhospitable. The man was miserable.

He went out and pulled a couple of boards off the back of the cottage to kindle a fire in the wood stove. The fire was warm, but the house seemed as cold as before. More boards came off for a larger fire to warm the now even colder house, which, in turn, required an even larger fire to warm it against the winter blast. More boards, a bigger fire, and a colder house became the routine. The more boards he tore loose, the bigger the fire it fueled, the colder the house grew, and the more miserable the man became.

In a few days the man cursed the weather, cursed the cottage, cursed the stove, and moved away.

Some of life's ill-planned solutions only fuel the fire of discontent. We need more than our own sorry devices in times of challenge. We need faith to fuel the fires of life.

Prayer: This Day I will carefully consider how God and I can meet life's challenges. For I know that left to my own devices, I can only make matters worse.

When living out Christ's call to love one another,
we always need to ask ourselves the question:
whose needs are being met here?
—The Reverend Robert T. Carlson

Have you overheard someone who was leaving a service of worship say, "Well, I sure didn't get anything out of that!"?

Who is the consumer of worship? Is it you? Or, is worship intended for God? It is a fair question: who is the intended recipient of worship? Is the focus of worship on spiritual growth, fostering a sense of affirmation, and bringing a new sense of wholeness to the individual? Or, do we gather to lift our praises to God? Which is it? Whose needs are being met?

The answer may surprise you. It is both!

In some ways, corporate worship is like loving another. The more you care for that person, the more affection you get in return. It is a giving-to-get kind of arrangement. So, when one says, "I didn't get anything out of that!" it may be just another way of saying, "I didn't bring much to God today."

It happens to every one of us sometime. We think that worship is especially designed just for us. The hymns are our favorites. The Scripture reading is exactly what we need to hear. And the message of the Good News is speaking directly to us. One man said he could always tell when the preacher was saying something he needed to hear, because his wife would poke him in the ribs. He said, "Today the preacher was really on target. My wife poked me four times!"

Whose needs are being met in your worship time? The good news within the Good News is that God already knows our needs and is anxious to meet those needs. For it is in worship that God hears, the heart of God is moved, and God responds. The consumer is both God and God's own!

Prayer: This Day will bring a renewed sense of both who I am and whose I am. Today, I will carefully consider whose needs are being met.

> *"I tell you the truth, the tax collectors and the prostitutes*
> *are entering the kingdom of God ahead of you.*
> —The words of Jesus as recorded
> in Matthew 21:31

A friend of mine suggests that if Jesus were to use a modern consulting firm to help him start his ministry, it might look like this:

We have carefully screened the twelve resumes you submitted to us. All twelve candidates have now taken our battery of tests and have been personally interviewed by our team of psychologists and vocation aptitude consultants. It is our opinion that most of your nominees are unsatisfactory. They do not have the team concept and they are lacking in educational background. We would recommend you continue your search for proven persons of experience. To summarize our assessment please review the following:

Simon Peter is emotional, unstable, and given to fits of temper.

Andrew has absolutely no quality of leadership.

The two brothers, James and John, the sons of Zebedee, place personal interests above company loyalty.

Thomas demonstrates a questioning attitude that would tend to undermine morale.

We believe it is our duty to tell you that Matthew has been blacklisted with the Greater Jerusalem Better Business Bureau.

James and Thaddeus definitely have radical leanings.

Judas Iscariot does show potential in fiscal matters and has demonstrated a keen business mind. We highly recommend him.

What if Jesus had chosen the twelve disciples based on modern methods of leadership selection? Most of them would have failed miserably before they had a chance to participate. God chooses people not for who they are, but for what they can become. As my friend pointed out in this improbable piece, the Good News is based on the fact that God chooses imperfect and unremarkable people to build the kingdom of God. Aren't you grateful for that?

Prayer: This Day I will not hide my imperfection, for I know that my brokenness does not exclude me from God's love.

*For whoever wants to save his life will lose it, but
whoever loses his life for me will find it.*
—The words of Jesus as recorded
in Matthew 16:25

So how is your New Year's resolution going? Is it still intact? If it is, you are among a tiny fraction of resolution makers. Most New Year's resolutions fail in the first week. Only a few—perhaps five percent—make it until the end of the month. But, here is the good news: if you have stuck it out this long, there is a good chance you will succeed for the rest of the year. The tough part is behind you!

There is another layer of good news in resolution keeping. Suppose you have not been successful. What is keeping you from trying again? If you fail again, there is nothing stopping you from trying a third time. And if that does not work, then keep starting over and over and eventually you will succeed. It does not matter how many times you have tried to do or to stop doing whatever it is you have resolved. After all, who is keeping track of the number of times you start over again? The point is that you have a desire to change.

There is a huge help in resolution keeping. It is called surrender. "Surrender?" you ask.

Yes, surrender. It is exactly what Jesus was talking about when he said, "You find your life by giving it away." It is the notion of victory through defeat, success through failure, and having through giving. Leave how it works up to the psychologists. Just bask in victory regardless of how it happens!

Prayer: This Day I will gladly accept surrender if it means winning. For changing what I do not want to be is a victory at any price.

> *… he humbled himself and became obedient to*
> *death—even death on a cross!*
>
> –Philippians 2:8

My grandmother was silent on our way home from church one Sunday morning. She wore a determined scowl and bit her lip as she drove along. Finally, she turned to me and said, "Don't you ever laugh at anyone's singing again!"

Grandmother had caught me trying to choke back my mirth. I had not busted out laughing, but Grandmother had seen me cover my mouth as Mrs. R. was singing *The Old Rugged Cross*.

Mrs. R. was the kindest and gentlest soul I have ever known. She was a devout Christian woman who quietly lived her faith. She had a generous heart and a compassionate spirit. However, Mrs. R. was not musically gifted. The kindest thing I can say about Mrs. R's singing was that it was loud. I sat beside Mrs. R. in worship that morning and I had the full benefit of her musical aptitude. It was more than I could bear. I bit my lip, focused on my new shoes, and did everything I could to avoid laughing. However, for a mere instant I lost control. It was not a guffaw laugh, but my snicker was enough. Grandmother was ticked, and my bad manners were the object of her wrath.

As I endured my grandmother's reprimand, I remained silent and did not contest my case. Grandmother never knew the whole story. In the midst of Mrs. R's scratchy and screechy singing, I looked up at her. As she sang, "I will cling to that old rugged cross, and exchange it someday for a crown", there were tears streaming down her cheeks. The sorry music was one thing, but the joy that spilled over as this gentle soul proclaimed her love for Christ quelled my laughter. A few decades have passed since I last heard Mrs. R. sing *The Old Rugged Cross*. However, I cannot hear that familiar tune without seeing her tear-stained cheeks and the joy that was more than her heart could contain.

Prayer: This Day I will endeavor to make a good match of the words from my mouth and the compassion I show the world. Today, I will try to make a harmony of the prayer I pray and the life I live.

*Here I am! I stand at the door and knock. If anyone
hears my voice and opens the door, I will come in
and eat with him, and he with me.*
—The words of Jesus Christ as recorded
in the Book of Revelation

Consider this prayer of entrance:

Loving God, your holy Word says that if we knock on the door, we will be invited in. If we ask, we will receive. So, we ask for peace and tranquility to begin in our homes and move throughout the community. We pray that that peace would prevail in our schools, our churches, our nation, and in every village and capital in the world. We ask for good health—physical, emotional, and spiritual—to be part of every life. We ask that old hurts and worn out grudges would be forgotten. We ask that words like hunger, abuse, rage, and poverty would seldom be backed up by evidence.

Your Holy Word says that if we seek, we will surely find. So, we seek wisdom to know how you would have us live. We seek solidarity to know how you would have us live together. We seek community so that together our living matters to every citizen. We seek, solace, peace, equality, and above all else, hope.

Your holy Word says that if we knock, the door will be opened to us. So, we knock on the door of opportunity that we might serve in ways yet unseen. We knock to be welcomed into your eternal household. We knock on the door of justice, longing for equal integrity in our realm, and expecting you to be the final judge in your realm.

We ask, we seek, and we knock. We willingly give you the very essence of our being, knowing that fullness in life comes from the abandoning of self; that full lives grow from tiny seeds of faith that are well cultivated; that wholeness is the mending of brokenness that only you can give.

Prayer: This Day we ask, we seek, and we knock, not only for ourselves, but also for all—the just and the unjust, the strong and the weak, the youthful and the seasoned, the present and the forgotten.

> *Love never ends . . . Now faith, hope and*
> *love abide these three, and the*
> *greatest of these is love."*
> —1 Corinthians 13:8,13

One of my favorite authors is Robert Fulghum. He is a master storyteller who has the ability to fashion a story from the simple and everyday happenings of life. He deftly turns out a story like a potter turning a fine vase out of clay. His medium is the mundane. His finished product is sublime.

Fulghum weaves his stories within the bounds of a solemn creed that he calls the Storyteller's Creed. Fulghum's Storyteller's Creed says:

I believe that imagination is stronger than knowledge.
That myth is more potent than history.
That dreams are more powerful than facts.
That hope always triumphs over experience.
That laughter is the only cure for grief.
And I believe that love is stronger than death.

The Storyteller's Creed is the heart of the gospel for it, too, proclaims that knowledge, facts, experience, and death are all insignificant beside faith, hope, and love. Stories that inspire us, define our passions, and show us that the extraordinary is within the grasp of the ordinary are the blocks of life that are bound by the mortar of faith, hope, and love. In an endurance race, death, grief, hopelessness, and despair always finish well behind, hope, love, and laughter.

Fulghum's Storyteller's Creed would work well as the model for a Believer's Creed. One in which we live out that faith, hope, and love rather than to merely tell of it.

Prayer: This Day I will create my story as one of peace, faith, hope, and love. With God's help, I expect it to be a grand tale worthy of telling!

For we walk by faith and not by sight.
—2 Corinthians 5:7

There was once a pair of twin sisters who were both musically talented and privileged enough to have the finest instructors available. One of the twins was a pianist, while the other played the harp. Quite unexpectedly, the sixteen-year-old harpist fell ill and died. Naturally, the family was strickened with grief. The bereaved family was driven by sorrow rather than reason, and so they put the girl's harp in the attic where it remained for the next eight decades.

The surviving twin had a brilliant career as a classical musician. She never married, nor did she ever mention her sister's harp that gathered dust in the attic. Upon the elderly woman's death, the old harp was discovered. The years of sitting in the dusty attic had not been especially kind to the harp. It was in need of major restoration. The professional who restored the harp said it was one of the finest he had ever seen. He said it was among a handful of the finest harps ever made.

The rare instrument was donated to a local convent. The Nuns were delighted with the gift of the expensive harp. However, the harp's tone was a sorry disappointment. At first, its voice was no sweeter than an ordinary harp. Then a strange evolution began to take place. The more the harp was played, the sweeter its sound became.

Faith is like a harp in the attic. Faith kept out of sight grows flat. Faith has to be used and lovingly shared with the world if it is to live up to its potential.

Prayer: This Day I pray that my faith helps me live up to the potential that God would have it be. May its voice sweetly and boldly proclaim God's goodness. May it grow more harmonious each day.

On her deathbed, Susan B. Anthony is reported to have said:
Oh yes, I'd do it all over again. The spirit is willing and I feel the same
desire to do the work, but the flesh is weak.
It's too bad that our bodies wear out while our
interests are just as strong as ever.

It is hard to find fault with Ms. Anthony's reasoning. It sounds like her passion to live a life of significance was intact to the very end. It can also be guessed that she wore out instead of rusting out. The woman, who labored in the trenches of reform for nearly six decades to bring about women's right to vote, still was filled with passion as her life ebbed. She would not give up.

Samuel May, who was a fiery abolitionist, once castigated Susan B. Anthony for her views on marriage. Mr. May said, "Since you are not married, you have no right to speak about marriage."

Ms. Anthony retorted, "In all due respect, Mr. May, if I follow your logic, since you are not a slave, I would have to presume that you have no right to speak out against slavery."

A life of significance lived to its very end is a life of hope.

Prayer: This Day I pray for persistence and perseverance. May my significance always be grounded in hope and a passion to fully live each day until I die.

The wolf will live with the lamb, the leopard will lie down with the goat,
the calf and the lion and the yearling together;
and a little child will lead them.

—Isaiah 11:6

A director of a large metropolitan zoo wanted to dazzle people with a unique exhibit. He put a lamb and a lion together in the same cage. This unusual pairing brought visitors by the thousands from near and far.

A news reporter was quite taken by this display and asked the zoo director if having such diversity in the same cage presented any unusual problems.

"Not really" the director replied. "Of course, we have to put a new lamb in every couple of days."

The director must have been a literalist. He must have read Isaiah's account of the Peaceable Kingdom and thought it meant that a perfect harmony of all creation was possible. The director must have thought that in such a Peaceable Kingdom, the lion would lose its taste for lamb chops. There is nothing wrong with a literal understanding. Isaiah is talking about a time of perfect harmony and tranquility among all creation.

But, Isaiah is talking about more than just the eating habits of carnivores. He is talking about a future time when tranquility and harmony will come because God has sent His Chosen One—the Messiah. Seven hundred years before the fact, Isaiah was talking about the coming of Christ. And, what is to be the hallmark of Christ's coming? Peace, justice and harmony. The Peaceable Kingdom is the centerpiece of Christ's entry into the world. Those epic words of the angel to the shepherds some seven centuries later ring that same peaceable theme: **"Glory to God in the highest and on earth peace and goodwill to all."**

Peace, justice, and harmony are more than noble ideas. They are the living Christ among us.

Prayer: This Day I will work for peace in my tiny part of the world, for as a peacemaker I am modeling Christ.

> *If it were not for the changeability of the weather,*
> *most people could not start a conversation.*
>
> —Mark Twain

If the weather is unseasonably mild during the winter months, some one will surely say, "Well, you can bet we will pay for this come summer." If the weather is colder than an Artic pump handle, it is certain that someone will predict a hotter than usual summer. Whatever we get—be it good or bad—is seen as the harbinger of things to come. More often that not, the thing to come is bad news weather.

It is as if God has a huge chalkboard and an enormous piece of chalk with which He keeps score. Can't you just picture God mumbling to himself, "Well, let's see, around the middle of February I gave them a couple of warm days, so I'll just plan on making mid-July hotter then usual. That will fix 'em!"

That is a theology of retribution. Such a warped theology always demands that grace and suffering come in equal portions. Have a nice winter day, and then pay for it with summer sweat. Enjoy a pleasant autumn afternoon, and endure a blizzard in January.

My guess is that weather prognosticators who demand equal grace and suffering have the same view of God's presence in other areas of life. Whatever grace is shed in someone's life is somehow balanced by an equal helping of suffering, sorrow, and brokenness. They believe that if you have some joy, you must have an equal quantity of sorrow. Such a theology forgets that God indeed does have a big chalkboard. But that chalkboard has been wiped clean with the life, death, and resurrection of Jesus Christ.

So, if we have an unseasonably mild winter day, why not enjoy it instead of worrying about how hot it might be next July?

Prayer: This Day I will bask in the certain knowing that grace is not earned and never balanced by sorrow. Today, I will especially thank God for his big eraser that refuses to keep score.

> *Even though I walk through the valley of the shadow*
> *of death, I will fear no evil, for you are with me;*
> *your rod and your staff, they comfort me.*
>
> —Psalm 23:4

The evening news nearly always carries a section that fits into the category that I call, "Beware of things that will harm us!" Here is an incomplete list of things that will harm us:

tobacco in any form	coffee	vicious dogs	spider bites
West Nile virus	high winds	blizzards	alcohol
not wearing a seat belt	air bags	snake bites	tap water
plane crashes	hail	red meat	bee stings
eating too much	firearms	heights	fast driving
sugar substitutes	drugs	too much rain	radiation
unwashed hands	tornados	earthquakes	terrorists
undercooked meat	flu	too little rain	pollution
not locking your doors	germs	anthrax	bombs
things that fall from the sky		not eating enough vegetables	
nations with nuclear capabilities			

Although this list is not complete, you get the idea. It is a dangerous world out there, and there are many things that will harm us. It seems to be the mission of our media to keep us informed about how dangerous our world is. However, it is a bit sad that we are not reminded on a daily basis that God's hope for each of us is to navigate through this world unharmed. Indeed, the world is a dangerous place, but God is there to keep us safe. Apparently that does not make news.

Prayer: This Day I will balance the world's dangers with absolute confidence in God's hope for my safety. Today, I will ask God to take my hand and lead me through all the dangers.

Acts of creation are ordinarily reserved for God and poets, but humbler folk may circumvent this restriction if they know how. Plant a pine, for example, one need be neither God nor poet; one need only own a shovel.

—From *A Sand County Almanac*
by Aldo Leopold

Aldo Leopold's classic, *A Sand County Almanac,* is considered by many to be the primer of the environmentalist movement. My first impression with Leopold was that he was a meddlesome advocate who was out of touch with reality. I have come to understand Leopold as a common-sense thinker who saw harmony between all living organisms as imperative for our survival.

Interestingly, Leopold believed that all creation is a living organism. A mountain is living and breathing in the same manner that the eagle that soars over its peaks and through its valleys is endowed with life. If we are to be the caretakers of creation, we must embrace the land, streams, mountains, and forests with the same dignity, reverence, and compassion that we have for the creatures that live within these environs.

To think of the soil, air, and water as living companions of our own existence was born with Aldo Leopold. By today's standards, Leopold's writing seems a bit elementary. That is the lot of a pioneer. We know that water quality matters to more than just the fish that call it home. We know that erosion tears apart the seams of the land and leaves it with wounds that may never heal. In the land's woundedness, we also feel hurt. We know that a species lost is gone forever.

We need more Aldo Leopolds. Not just to preserve our resources, but also to teach us to value them as a parent would his or her child. For it is only when we begin to see all creation as God's living canvas, that we can assume our role as companion and not as conqueror.

Prayer: This Day brings me to a new understanding of my place in creation, for I am but a part of the whole. Today, I take greater ownership of my role as caretaker, because I know that the whole of creation is far bigger than I have ever understood before.

He causes the sun to rise on the evil and the good, and sends rain on the righteous and the unrighteous.
—The words of Jesus as recorded
in Matthew 5:45b

Make no mistake about it, life is not fair. We have all seen bad things happen to good people. Perhaps, even more unsettling is the fact that seemingly good things happen to bad people. Everyone of us knows someone who has cheated, walked on the shadowy side of life, or has deliberately and wantonly oppressed and brutalized others, yet they somehow prospered. Or, we have seen the indignity and injustice of the suffering of a saint. Indeed, life is not fair!

Life is unfair because we think we do not get what we deserve. A bad thing happens to us and we cry, "Foul! I do not deserve this." A good thing happens to us and we silently smile to ourselves and say, "There, that is more like it." I do not believe we get what we deserve.

We do not get what we deserve, and that is good news. I am grateful that God's justice differs from my sense of justice and that I do not get what I really deserve. I do not get slam-dunked by God for the times when I think I can do it all by myself. I do not get squashed when I try to be godlike. God does not ignore me when I get too busy with life and I forget to invite him along on the journey. No, we do not get what we deserve. Instead of what we deserve, we get God's grace. We get God's unmerited favor, unearned regard, and unyielding love.

Am I ever glad I do not get what I deserve!

Prayer: This Day I will rejoice in the unfairness of it all! Today, I will give particular thanks for my measure of grace and for God's unwillingness to give me what I really deserve.

In the beginning was the Word, and the Word was with God, and the Word was God.

—John 1:1

John's words draw us deeper into the unfathomable mystery of God. The great mystery of creation is how could the creator preexist creation? Now, the mystery gets even deeper. John tells us that the Word of God, or the mind of God that we encounter in Jesus Christ, was present before time began. My puny mind cannot wrap itself around such an enormous idea. The best I can do is say to myself, "Oh well, perhaps one day I'll understand, but for now I am content to put all this in a box and mark it 'Paradox.'"

There is some comfort in not understanding the fullness of God. Suppose I did comprehend the fullness of God. Then I would have reduced the omnipotence of God to a human mind. God would then be no bigger than my mind. That would be a scrawny and frail God! Moreover, if I could somehow manage to grasp the totality of God, then I would have the mind of God and therefore have no further need of God.

No, God is bigger than my mind, and I am grateful for that. I can live with the mystery, but I cannot put my faith into and abandon my life to a God who can be contained in the frailty and the puniness of my mind. Thus, I welcome the paradox, for the mystery is where the omnipotence dwells.

Prayer: This Day I will gladly let God be God. Today, I will delight in the mystery and abandon myself to God's omnipotence.

> *Begin at the beginning . . . and go until you come to the end: then stop.*
> *—Alice's Adventures in Wonderland,*
> Lewis Carroll

A plaque reportedly hangs near the birthplace of Abraham Lincoln. The plaque records a brief conversation that took place in 1809. It reads:

"Any news down at the village, Ezzy?"

"Well, Squire McLain's gone to Washington to see Madison swore in, and ol' Spellman tells me this Bonaparte fella has captured most of Spain. What's new out here neighbor?"

"Nuthin, nuthin at all, 'cept fer a new baby born to Tom Lincoln's. Nuthin' ever happens out here of any importance."

Some of history's greatest events go unnoticed until much later. A birth in Hodgenville, Kentucky, was called "nuthin." The most important birth in all of human history drew the interest of only a tiny handful of shepherds and a few dignitaries from a far eastern country.

Beginnings are not the big thing. It is what grows out of a beginning that really counts. Christian life is not a test—score poorly and be a failure forever. The good news within the Good News is not about how it began, but how well was it lived out. Be it a stable in Bethlehem, a log cabin in Kentucky, or a new life in Christ, the beginning is not the event of vital importance.

We are works in progress much like a book. The opening line does not tell the whole of the story. To what a life ultimately ascends cannot be guessed in its beginning. Like brushing off the thirteenth president's birth as nuthin,' what awaits a life newly committed to Christ can never be estimated. In Christ, you are a work in progress.

Prayer: This Day I will press on in my faith journey. Today, I will grow in faith, hope, and love.

But because of his great love for us, God, who is rich in mercy, made us
alive in Christ even when we were dead in transgressions
—it is by grace you have been saved.

—Ephesians 2:4–5

I once was a guest preacher in a rather conservative church. I suspect that laughter was not a part of their regular worship experience. For these serious Christians, mirth and worship were polar opposites. Salvation was important business, and it certainly was no laughing matter.

I preached on the theme of God's rich mercy that we call grace. Together we explored the mystery of why God chose to shine His unfathomable love on us. Grace is not earned, merited, or handed out as a reward. Grace is simply freely given without merit, explanation, or condition. That is the mystery of grace.

The free nature of grace makes it our most precious of all gifts. We are wholly dependent upon the gift of grace both in this life and in the next. All of this made good sense to that conservative congregation. They nodded and smiled in agreement as I preached. However, I might have pushed the point a bit too far when I said, "I am so dependent upon grace that I told my wife, Marilyn, that if we were to have another child, I think we would name her Grace."

Marilyn's reply was quick, simple, and fully captured the spirit of grace. She said, "You have it all wrong. It is because of God's grace that we will not have another child at our age!"

I was not invited back as guest preacher the next week.

Prayer: This Day I will embrace God's grace for the precious gift it truly is. Grace belongs in that realm of unexplainable, yet certain. It is free, yet precious. It is real, yet unseen.

> *There is a time for everything, and a season for every activity under heaven.*
>
> —Ecclesiastes 3:1

It was a crisp February morning on the Clam River. No, crisp is not the word. It was cold—minus two degrees cold! It was cold enough that the fringes of the fast running water wore the jagged edges of ice. Yet, six mallard ducks swam happily in the river's quick current. They paddled vigorously against the current just to keep from a rapid ride down the Clam. The six mallards were as content in this frigid bath as a Minnesota tourist in January on the white sands of a beach in Honolulu. I watched from the comfort of the living room as the six ducks frolicked in the river. I could not help noting that these were not just six ducks. It was three pairs of mallards. A courtship of sorts was unfolding before me on that nearly frozen stretch of river.

Some historians claim that Valentine's Day has its origin in the fact that mid February is the time of waterfowl courtship. I suppose it would be hard to prove, and probably its exact origin is clouded by legend, but this annual ritual of pairing is the first harbinger of spring. As incredulous as it might seem, what I saw on the river this near-zero morning was the beginning of spring. Nature has a precise clock that varies little from year to year. The ducks' eggs have to be nested early enough to give the ducklings the full advantage of summer and autumn in which to grow. Yet, it has to be late enough in the spring to avoid frozen eggs or frostbitten ducklings. Every moment matters— too soon and the year's crop is lost cold. On the other hand, too late in the spring, the young cannot thrive through next year's winter. Given this tight schedule, a February swim is a vital part of the ritual.

I never tire of the wonder of the ongoing harmony of creation. God thought of everything. The cycle of life that unfolds in mysterious precision is just one tiny piece of God's handiwork. Try as we might, we cannot improve upon it without impacting the harmony in some other way. I can appreciate that harmony as divine, even though I understand so little of it. More than that, I can be forever grateful on a cold February day that I was not born a mallard duck!

Prayer: This Day I will pause to marvel in the harmony of creation. Today, I will see the Spirit of God's love lived out in its harmony.

Come to me, all you who are weary and burdened,
and I will give you rest.
—The words of Jesus as recorded
in Matthew 11:28

It is a poor day when we do not receive at least two catalogs in the mail. These home-shopping catalogs cover an amazing array of specialty items. These are unsolicited catalogs that offer everything from golf equipment to hunting and fishing supplies, from clothing that only an emperor could afford to vegetable seeds, from hard-to-find gadgets to lingerie. We have had catalogs that sell only cigars or wine. Of course we get the usual assortment like L.L. Bean, Sears, and J.C. Penney, but these specialty catalogs far outnumber the usual.

I have been told that the mail order industry uses our zip codes to determine if we are likely buyers. It makes sense when you think about it. If you live in Florida, you are probably not too interested in dog-sledding supplies. If you live in Kansas, a salt-water fishing catalog may not capture your interest. Our zip codes have something to say about our income, tastes, needs, interests, life styles, and culture. Some broad assumptions can raise the odds for a sale by the mail order company.

It is good that Jesus did not make such sweeping assumptions about who needs to be comforted and healed. He just said, "All of you." I am grateful that God's zip code is more inclusive than it is exclusive.

Prayer: This Day I celebrate that I qualify for the "ALL" group. Today, I want God to know how grateful I am to be included in his needy group.

But Ruth replied, "Don't urge me to leave you or to turn back from you.
Where you go I will go, and where you
stay I will stay. Your people will be my people and
your God my God."

—Ruth 1:16

There are all too many unflattering mother-in-law jokes. The mother of our spouse is often the brunt of ridicule and the model of a meddling relative. The story of Ruth and Naomi sets a new standard and shows us a refreshingly new model for mother-in-law and daughter-in-law relationships.

In the toughest of times, Ruth was a woman of unyielding commitment to her mother-in-law, Naomi. She did not let anything dissuade her from total commitment to Naomi. Common sense, Naomi's urging, and the miserable trek that stretched out before them would not discourage her from following her husband's mother. She was committed to her relationship with such tenacity that she was willing to give her life if need be. Ruth chose to leave her home, her relatives, her culture, and even her gods to follow this woman who was her late husband's mother.

Why is all this important to us? What difference would it make to us if Naomi and Ruth had parted company? Other than a story about commitment, why ought we care about these two widows? Sixteen generations after these two women made their journey out of the foreboding deserts of Moab, a child was born who was Ruth's descendant. His name was Jesus. Once again, God chose well when he chose Ruth. God uses ordinary people to accomplish His plans. He also relies on us to live in relationships if these plans are to take root and grow. Here is the story of commitment to relationship growing the extraordinary from the ordinary.

Prayer: This Day I will take a personal inventory of my closest relationships to see if they are in good repair. If they are not, I will do whatever it takes to renew my life's most basic commitments.

Before I formed you in the womb I knew you,
Before you were born I set you apart.

—Jeremiah 1:5

How would you like to begin this day with a thought that is bigger than your mind can begin to comprehend? Scary thought, huh?

Imagine this: before you were anybody, you were somebody to God. Or, to say it another way, you existed in the mind of God before you had a physical presence. That is hard to wrap our minds around. It is a bit like those tough questions like what preexisted God? Or, what is beyond the outer limits of space? Or, what time was it before time?

Perhaps we can put this into simpler terms that are not so difficult to grasp. Let's just say that God is your oldest and dearest friend. The fact that God knew you before you were known to anyone is still a metaphysical enigma. But, none-the-less it is a comforting thought to know that you and God go way, way, way back. It is comforting to know that after all these years, it is still you and God.

Prayer: This Day I will be content to live alongside the great mysteries of life. I will still my passion to fully understand the ones that dwarf my imagination, stifle my wisdom, and always remain paradoxical. Today, I will simply take heart in knowing that God is God and I am his.

God said to Moses, "I AM WHO I AM. This is what you are to say to the Israelites: 'I AM has sent me to you.'"
—Exodus 3:14

A sheep pasture is not a place where you would expect to find one who is a candidate to be voted "most likely to succeed." Shepherding is smelly business that features loneliness, poor pay, low reward, and crummy hours. It is not often that a shepherd is chosen to have a conversation with God.

But, that is exactly what happened to Moses. He was going about his business watching the flock of his father-in-law, Jethro, when he had an encounter with God. There he was, trudging along with a bunch of blatting lambs behind him when a voice came out of a burning bush. The voice identified himself as the God of Abraham, Isaac, and Jacob. Moses must have been dumbstruck!

Moses asked "Who will I tell the people if they ask who sent me?"

God said, "Just tell them the I AM WHO I AM."

I'll bet that helped clear things up in Moses' mind. Sometimes God places things on our hearts that are not easy to do and even harder to explain to others. My guess is that Moses swallowed hard and said to himself, "This ain't gonna be easy!"

Of course, we know that God chose well when God chose Moses. Easy or not, Moses was a man with an unquenchable thirst for faith. God has a way of knowing us better than we know ourselves, and He seeks us in the ordinary places of life. And, sometimes God asks the extraordinary of us.

Prayer: This Day I will ask: How would you have me serve today, God? Today, I will wait a moment for the answer before I launch into the day

Jesus said, "This, then is how you should pray:
'Our Father in heaven,
hallowed be your name,
your kingdom come,
your will be done,
on earth as it is in heaven.
Give us today our daily bread.
Forgive us our debts,
as we forgive our debtors.
And lead us not into temptation,
but deliver us from the evil one,
for yours is the kingdom and the power,
and the glory forever.'"

—The words of Jesus as recorded
in Matthew 6:9–13

Of this I am certain: *It pays to pray.* I have not the slightest idea how prayer works. Perhaps it is a pipeline that goes directly to God. Perhaps it shapes our inner being and brings us into harmony with God. Maybe prayer is an oneness that cannot be attained in any other way. It could be that prayer draws from some source of truth and life that is in a dimension that we cannot comprehend. I really do not know how prayer works.

But, not knowing how a thing works does not mean it does not have value. Neither does our ignorance of the way something works mean that we ought not use it. Just because I am totally clueless about how this computer works, does not mean that I must write in long-hand. Because I do not understand electricity, does not mean that I am destined to live in darkness. And, although I cannot explain how gravity works, I am not obliged to live in fear of falling off the planet.

No, there is much truth to blessed ignorance. It is simply enough to say that *it pays to pray*.

Prayer: This Day God will hear my voice in prayer. Hopefully the meditations of my heart will never be an unfamiliar sound to God's ears.

Jesus said, "One thing you lack. Go, sell everything you
have and give it to the poor, and you will have
treasure in heaven. Then come, follow me."

At this the man's face fell. He went away
very sad, because he had great wealth.
—The words of Jesus as recorded
in Mark 10:21–22.

Karl Barth said, "The purpose of the gospel is to comfort us in our affliction and to afflict us in our comfort." Hard image to grasp, isn't it? How can the gospel be both comforting and afflicting?

Mark records this story about a man who came to Jesus who was troubled about his eternal life. He was tormented and he was seeking comfort. Jesus assured the man that there was a way to eternal life. That way was to simply give up his worldliness and become one of his followers. It does not sound like discipleship was the problem here. It was the man's love of wealth. The man could not bear the thought of giving up his wealth, so he slowly walked away with his head hung low.

It is interesting that Jesus did not run after the man saying, "Wait! Wait! There may be another way. Let's talk this over and see if we cannot find a softer, easier way that is more palatable for you." Jesus let him walk. It must have taken a great deal of restraint on Jesus' part. Mark tells us that the man was sad, but I think Jesus was even sadder. What made Jesus sad was to watch a man give up his hope for eternal life. The wealth, power and prestige that slipped through Jesus' hands that day meant nothing to him. It was the loss of the man's soul that saddened Jesus.

The man sought comfort in his affliction; what he found was affliction in his comfortable lifestyle.

Prayer: This Day I will pray for a heart that mourns for those who seek only comfort. Today, I will redouble my efforts to comfort the afflicted.

*Unless the LORD builds the house, its builders labor in vain.
Unless the LORD watches over the city, the
watchmen stand guard in vain.*

—Psalm 127:1

There is nothing we can accomplish on our own accord. We like to think we are in complete charge. We like to believe we are the sole masters of our own destiny. Yet, any undertaking we attempt is destined for ultimate failure unless it is in concert with God's will.

That is a rather humbling thought. It is not one we like to admit. It does not mean that God is against our best efforts or is somehow opposed to our vision, hopes, and hard labor. It simply means that the best and most noble of plans may not always be part of God's overall plan for His children and His creation. That can be sobering.

Before you begin to think this is all futile, consider this: suppose some evil person or ideology was to gain total world control. Suppose some oppressor or tyrant dominated the world. Then it would seem that God's plan had failed and evil had won the final victory. This is what makes the ultimate sovereignty of God so precious.

It is a great assurance to know that God is God and only God has the overall scheme of things well in hand. The power that keeps us safe is the same power that keeps us from having to be God.

Prayer: This Day I will seek a sense of harmony in how my plan and God's plan can work together. Today I will gladly let God be God, and I'll be me.

*A man who has riches without understanding is
like the beasts that perish.*

—Psalm 49:20

Understanding is not an easy process. It is unlikely that any of us will ever come close to complete understanding. Our individual interests, experiences, education, and perhaps to some degree, our genetic makeup all impact our understanding. Mark Twain once said that the best way to get rid of prejudice and misunderstanding was to visit another culture. Suddenly, another culture makes more sense when shared rather than observed from a book or another's opinion.

Understanding is a process that evolves over time. It has a tendency to never be static. As soon as we come to one new understanding, we have to rethink all others. It is like a child building a tower of wooden blocks. When it topples, all have to be reset.

The psalmist reminds us that God is the sole source of all understanding. It is a matter of perspective that begins in the understanding that God, and God alone, is the epicenter of all blessings. To lose sight of the fact that God is the source of all goodness is to deny his existence and to understand ourselves as fully empowered to shape our own destinies. Such an understanding leaves us no more enlightened than, as the psalmist says, the beasts of the pastures. What sets us apart from all creation is that we can comprehend the omnipotence of God. Or sort of understand it, that is, because that, too, is beyond understanding.

Prayer: This Day I will pray for understanding. Today, I will work diligently to set aside opinion, toss away prejudice, and see others in a new light.

Know that the LORD is God. It is he who made us, and we are his; we are his people, the sheep of his pasture.

—Psalm 100:3

Thinking of myself in sheep terms is not especially comforting. Having tended a flock of sheep, I can attest that these woolly creatures are generally weak-willed and far from intelligent. Sheep are masters of the blank gaze. For them it is not an act, because there is not much going on behind that stare of nothingness. Admittedly, lambs are cute and cuddly, but brilliant they are not. They lack problem-solving abilities and are quite content to rely upon following a leader who may lead an entire flock into harm's way. Sheep are **dumb!** So, to be called a "sheep in his pasture" causes me to flinch a bit.

Although I cringe at being called a sheep, I am delighted to be called a "sheep in his pasture." That certainly eases matters considerably. Why? Because it speaks to whose I am and not who I am.

Who am I?

Hopefully, I am one of God's willing followers. And if that means being a sheep, then so be it.

Prayer: This Day I will practice sheephood. If that means being one of God's humble followers, I will be content. If it means to simply love and follow God's call, I can do that, too.

*Jesus said, "Come unto me all you who are weary and burdened, and I
will give you rest. Take my yoke upon you and learn from me, for I am
gentle and humble in heart,
and you will find rest for your souls. For my
yoke is easy and my burden is light."*
—The words of Jesus as recorded in
Matthew 11:28–30

Jesus is intensely interested in our physical comfort. Many of the
Gospel stories take place around a table or at a feast. One story
takes place at a wedding reception. It is clear that Jesus came down
on the side of having a good time. He wanted his followers to have a
zest for life. Those who paint a picture of Jesus as a dour and suffering
servant miss the fact that he lived with gusto. He lived large.

For a man with a taste for conviviality, it is natural that he would
assure us that he did not want us to live weary lives. He is invested in
our burdens. His mission was not to add to our misery, but to lighten
our loads.

Take a moment to rethink your image of Jesus. How do you see
him? Is he smiling and gladly offering you a hand? Or, is he frowning
at you with his hands on his waist in total disgust? Is Jesus a joy to be
with, or someone you want to avoid? Is he adding to your load, or is
he saying, "Can I carry that for you?"

Prayer: This Day I will delight in sharing my load with Christ. Today, I will rethink my image of Christ. I expect to find him
more likable than ever.

Then they (the crowd) asked him, "What must we do to do the works
God requires?" Jesus answered,
"The work of God is this: to believe in the one he has sent."
—The words of Jesus as recorded
in John 6:28–29

If you drop a pebble in a still pool, it will send out ripples in all
directions. The tiny waves radiate in a nearly perfect circle that set
up a disturbance that can last for some time. If you drop the same
pebble in a swift stream, it will hardly be noticed. The rushing waters
will swallow the pebble, and its disappearance will go unnoticed.

The busyness of our lives is like a body of water. If we live placid
lives, we are like the still waters, and thus more attentive to the Holy
Spirit. If we are rushing here and there at a hectic pace, we are like the
babbling brook that is oblivious to God's call.

Does that mean that God would have us live a quiet, monastic
existence? No. The real trick is to somehow manage to strike a harmony between busyness and serenity, work and play, thought and
action.

The crowd asked Jesus, "What work really matters?"

Jesus answered, "Believe in me."

Therein is the pathway to harmonious living: be busy and believe
in Christ. That is how we can simultaneously be a rushing brook that
is filled with life and a placid pool that is open to God's call in our
lives.

Prayer:　This Day I will pray that my busyness is calmed so that I will
have time for God. I will also pray that my quietness is stirred
with a passion to serve Christ.

Never be lacking in zeal, but keep your spiritual fervor,
serving the Lord. Be joyful in hope, patient in affliction,
faithful in prayer. Share with God's people
who are in need. Practice hospitality.
—Romans 12:11–13

Paul instructs the fledgling community of faith in Rome to live and serve with a sense of zeal. He urges them to be prayerful and willing to share. These are attributes that set a Christian community apart from the rest of the world. We ought to be recognized by our service, hope, and prayerful attitude. Who could argue with Paul's' words to the Romans? It is sound advice for today's church.

Paul adds two words to his list of good works—practice hospitality. It comes almost as an afterthought. It is as if he is saying to them, "Oh, by the way, it would be a good idea to practice hospitality, also."

The practice of hospitality is far from an afterthought. The good works we do are of little worth if we are inhospitable people. The mission checks we give to the poor, a Sunday school that is bursting at the seams, a church calendar that is filled to capacity, or a sanctuary that cannot hold another worshiper is nothing if we are inhospitable to one another. The real test of the Christian heart is not measured in stewardship dollars or biblical knowledge. *The Christian heart is measured in how we treat one another.*

That is what Jesus meant when he said, "Love the Lord your God with all your heart and with all your soul and with all your mind. This is the first and greatest commandment. And the second is like it: love your neighbor as yourself" (Matthew 22:37–39).

Jesus is saying, "Be hospitable!"

Prayer: This Day I will especially practice hospitality. Today, I pray that the measure of my heart, as seen in how I treat others, boldly tells the world that Christ dwells therein.

*Do not sacrifice to the LORD your God an ox or a
sheep that has any defect or flaw in it, for that
would be detestable to him.*

—Deuteronomy 17:1

One day a twenty-dollar bill and a one-dollar bill were lying side by side in a cash register. The two became close friends. But alas, they both knew their lot in life was never to be together. Tomorrow morning would bring a new business day, and they would be separated and have to go their separate ways. So the two bills agreed that if their paths ever crossed again they would waste no time getting to know one another. Theirs was to be a lasting friendship.

The next morning the twenty-dollar bill and the one-dollar bill were passed out as change. They went their separate ways. But they never forgot one another. A year or so passed, and one day the two old friends were united once more.

"How has it been for you?" asked the one-dollar bill.

"Oh life has been great! I have been used in some of the finest restaurants, the grandest malls, and the biggest theaters. I have been to Disney Land, the World Series, and the Super Bowl. I have been to Europe twice in the last year. But enough about me. What about you?"

The one-dollar bill said in a quiet voice, "Oh, you know how it is for a one-dollar bill. It is just go to church, go to church, and go to church."

Prayer: This Day I will be sure that God gets my first and best fruits. Today, I will be sure that He gets a generous portion of my best.

Do everything without complaining or arguing.
—Philippians 2:14

Have you ever had a stone in your shoe? Sure you have. The tiniest pebble can irritate your foot and make you miserable. When you think about it, the mass of the pebble when compared to the whole of you is remarkably insignificant. Yet, the tiny pebble makes you miserable. Every step you take, there it is. It becomes a constant reminder, an uninterrupted discontent, and a constant annoyance.

There is only one solution: sit down, take off your shoe, dump out the stone, and put your shoe back on again. This is not too difficult.

So, why do we walk around so long with a stone in our shoe? Do we like the misery? It could be that we are embarrassed to remove our shoe because there might be a hole in our sock. But, the fact is we walk around a lot with minor annoyances that have easy solutions. To be sure, there are a few who rather enjoy the complaining or desire the attention that a limp can bring. However, the vast majority of us just put off the simple solution.

Complaining does have its value. Complaining can right an obvious problem or set straight an injustice. But complaining for attention or pity is no more than walking around with a stone in your shoe. Sit down, take off . . . .

Prayer: This Day I will listen to myself. What do I hear? Does the shoe I wear need to be dumped? Or, is my complaining moving toward an improvement? Today, I will listen.

*There is a time for everything, and a season
for every activity under heaven.*

—Ecclesiastes 3:1

A wise pundit once suggested that winter could be shortened and summer could gain a few days if we simply changed the calendar. The idea that February does quite nicely most of the time with just twenty-eight days is the basis for his plan. This twenty-eight day month could be expanded. We could shorten January and March from thirty-one days to twenty-eight days each. The plan would yield up to a six-day savings in winter days. We could add these six days (two each) to June, July, and August. Thus, we would have to endure nearly one less week of winter and gain nearly another glorious week of summer.

Before you scoff at the idea, consider daylight savings time. Doesn't this make about as much sense as turning your clocks back an hour every fall and ahead an hour every spring?

It just might work!

Prayer: This Day help me see that my time is a gift from God. I cannot hoard it. I cannot give it away. I cannot sell or trade it to another. All I can do is live it to its fullest and share it in ways that are pleasing to God.

It is only by risking . . . that we live at all.
—William James

It was a yearly tradition for my grandfather and me to build a kite. It was a way to use up a winter day and prepare for spring. When the spring breezes began to blow, grandfather and I were always ready with a new and bigger kite than we had launched the year before. Grandfather knew all about kites. His kites were not just a collection of paper, wood, and string. His kites were pieces of art that were designed to fly high. One winter we turned out a huge box kite that was bigger and better than any of our previous models. We called it the "Big Boy." It was red and blue with a long yellow tail. Big Boy was our pride and joy.

The big day came. It was a perfect March day. There was a gentle, warm breeze—not too strong and not too light—just right! We put an extra ball of string on Big Boy. Today we had grand expectations. This was going to be the best kite flight ever.

The kite was launched. Up, up, up it rose. As it soared, the blue and red kite became a smaller and smaller dot against the sharp blue spring sky. With the excitement of a child my grandfather said, "Give it more string, Jerry! More string! More string!" We ran across the cow pasture letting out more and more string. Up and up Big Boy flew.

"More string! More string! Give it all you have got!" shouted Grandfather. Then a sudden wind current caught the kite and it went out of control. The string snapped. The kite that had been a small dot in the sky now made a sickening, twisting descent to earth. There was nothing we could do but stand there with a hollow, empty feeling in our stomachs as our winter's work came crashing down.

I ran to the heap of balsa and red and blue tissue paper that had once been the pride of our work and dreams. I knelt down and tried as best as I could to choke back my tears. Grandfather came up behind me and put his gentle hand on my shoulder and said, "Jerry, sometimes in life you just have to let out all the string. Sometimes you just have to risk it all."

Prayer: This Day I will ease away from the comfortable and be a risk taker. Today, I will let out all the string!

Let not your heart be troubled. Believe in God and believe also in me.
—The words of Jesus as recorded
in John 14:1

Our calico cat, Callie, is a warehouse of curiosity that is tempered with a healthy sense of fear. She explores with interest, yet her curiosity is always kept in check by a bit of wise caution.

A large siding door that looks out into the backyard is one of her favorite vantage points from which to view the world. Here she can observe squirrels, rabbits, and the change of seasons in relative comfort. Here, too, she can keep check of an occasional dog or cat that might happen to cross her domain. Whenever one of these intruders crosses the yard, the fur on Callie's neck and shoulders stands at attention. She lets out a low, guttural growl that sounds as threatening as an alligator clearing its throat. Of course, all this brave, bold, and bellicose posturing is done behind the safety of the kitchen window.

One evening, Callie saw her own reflection in the sliding glass door. She immediately thought it was an intruder who had entered her realm. She let out one of her growls. Much to her surprise, the image growled back. This was a frightening experience that sorely tested the depth of her resolve. This usually easy border patrol had turned into risky business. Her calico hair stood on end. She paced around the kitchen and went back to the glass door and growled again at her own image. The cat in the glass door growled back, so she paced some more. Finally, Callie did about the only thing she could do—she went to her bowl. After having steeled her fears on a tuna treat, she rolled up in a furry ball and went to sleep!

As I watched this show of foolish bravery, I thought about the times I have had to confront fears of the unfounded and imagined variety. Such fears waste energy, add to our anxiety, and leave us ill prepared to deal with what really matters in life. As intimidating as it may seem, growling at our reflection is useless work. God knew we would encounter unfounded fears. God knew there would be times when we need more than a tuna treat and a nap. God knew just how much we need Jesus' assurance.

Prayer: This Day I will reconnect with the One who banishes all fear. Today, I will use caution and respect, but never fear.

He has filled the hungry with good things . . .
—Luke 1:53

There are those who study church growth. They survey what makes a church vital and alive and what are the markers of a dying church or one that has become stagnant. Their observations are helpful, though sometimes a bit painful.

Dr. Roger Ray has observed an unexpected phenomenon from these studies that may surprise you. *Churches that are really booming are the ones that ask most of their members.*

Ray writes, "While I hear a lot about making the church more accessible and making worship a 'low threshold' experience, what we are seeing is that some people are catching on to the fact that symbolic religion is about as nutritious as a caffeine-free, diet soft drink. It's cold, it's carbonated, and it's sweet, but there is nothing nutritious there. On a steady diet of it, you will die of starvation."

Dr. Ray's observations make a good case for Mutual Ministry. In a market that packages everything as "lite," "diet," or "caffeine free," our hunger for faith is best satisfied by serving Christ. The shortcomings of "Christianity Lite" is far from a new idea—just a new way of understanding the joy of discipleship.

Prayer: This Day I will nourish my spirit on a hearty faith. No "Christianity Lite" will satisfy my hunger.

*Consequently, you are no longer foreigners and aliens, but fellow citizens
with God's people and members of God's
household . . . with Christ Jesus himself as the chief
cornerstone. In him the whole building is joined
together and rises to become a holy temple in the Lord.*
—Ephesians 2:19–21

What are the markers of a faith community that is filled with life? An alive faith community might have a parking problem on Sunday mornings. Better still, an alive community has parking problems on days other than Sunday. You might be inconvenienced by the noise, dust, and the interrupted traffic flow that is caused by construction.

Alive faith communities have noisy children, a buzz at coffee hour, and laughter in its halls. Here, there is an understanding of the difference between stewardship and dues, as well as the difference between committed giving and tipping.

An alive community takes risks, boldly ventures into the unknown, and sees challenges as opportunities rather than as dangerous problems. It puts the needs of its people first and puts the institution in a distant second place.

Alive communities are willing to try new ventures, and if they should fail, they have the courage to get up and try again. It meets all people where they are and lovingly helps them to where God hopes for them to be. You will notice that alive churches honor their past, live in the present, and embrace the future. In these you will not find worship of the past, complaint about the present, or fear the future.

Prayer: This Day we lift a prayer of renewal for all faith communities. The kingdom of God is here and now if we have the vision, the faith, the support, and the courage to make it happen. The living Christ is here and now.

This is to my Father's glory, that you bear much fruit . . .
—The words of Jesus as recorded
in John 15:8

It is not a bad idea to see what the experts think before you invest. So *Consumers' Report* is a good place to consult before making any major purchase. There is a tongue-in-cheek *Consumers' Report* website for religion. It looks official, but it is just a spoof. The website is only a whimsical comparison of several major religions. It gives the appearance of serious inquiry and in depth research. However, it is much to do about nothing.

The report's final conclusion states: "If you are looking for a good over all religion, you can't go wrong with Christianity."

Now, that's a relief! Can you imagine embracing a religion that did not rank at or near the top of the *Consumers' Report*? But, would you trade your faith in for a new faith if it did not meet the expectations of a product comparison panel? Would you have to have the latest if a newer, glitzier faith came along? Would you trade your relationship with Jesus Christ for a scientifically proven faith if some laboratory-test results proved that another faith was superior?

I doubt if any of us would rely on another's evaluation for a matter as important as our faith. How one entrusts and shapes one's faith journey is a personal matter. Yet, each of us has to some degree been led to our faith by another's confession, persuasion, and encouragement. Not a single one of us discovered Christ wholly on our own. We have been led, shown, and convinced. Like a *Consumers' Report*, another tried first and then shared with us the worth of a life in Christ.

So, how does your faith rank? Is it worth sharing with another?

Prayer: This Day I will quietly, but convincingly share Christ with another. If done well, I might not have to use words.

> *Each new American*
> *To be taken as a golden grain*
> *And lifted, as the wheat of our bodies,*
> *To matter superbly human.*
>
> —Jean Toomer

You matter!

Now that is a cheery thought. If you think you do not matter, just remember the 2000 presidential election. When the counting, the re-counting, and the recounting the recounting finally came to a close, less than 300 votes separated the two candidates.

Although I am not a mathematician, I am intrigued with the minuscule percentage of less than three hundred votes in a total of nearly one hundred million. It is about the same as counting one hair on a grizzly bear's coat. What are the odds? What an amazing historical happening! The 2000 election was as close as any we have seen in recent history.

This is not a first in history. In fact, many important elections have come down to just one vote. Oliver Cromwell was elected Protector of all England by just one vote. Cromwell's nemesis, Charles I, was sent to the executioner by just one vote. You matter. What you think, what you say, and how you vote matters.

We have come face-to-face with the undeniable fact that every vote matters. Each individual voice in this chorus of 100,000,000 has significance. Never again can anyone say, "What do I matter?" You do matter. You do have significance. You are a difference-maker. One vote is a king-maker (or in our case a President-maker). That makes you matter!

Prayer: This Day I will humbly consider my significance. Today, I will take ownership of what I have always known—I matter.

I have come that they may have life, and have it to the full.
—The words of Jesus as recorded
in John 10:10

Upon discovering that she had cancer, Erma Bombeck wrote a column that explored how she would have lived her life if she had it to do over. In part, Erma wrote:

I would have gone to bed for the day when I was sick instead of pretending that the earth would go into a holding pattern if I weren't there for the day.

I would have talked less and listened more.

I would have invited friends over to dinner even if the carpet were stained and the sofa faded.

I would have taken time to listen to my grandfather ramble about his youth.

I would have never insisted that the car windows be rolled up on a summer day because my hair had just been teased and sprayed.

There would have been more "I love you's."

. . . But mostly, given another shot at life, I would seize every minute . . . look at it and see it . . . live it . . . and never give it back.

In a few words, Mrs. Bombeck has said to us, "Don't sweat the small stuff. Life is to be lived by the living. Therefore, while you have life, live it well!"

Jesus said, "I came so that you would have life and have it in full." (John 10:10)

Be it Bombeck or Christ, the message is the same: Learn to live fully and abundantly. The greatest sorrow of all is not in dying, but in dying before you have lived.

Prayer: This Day I will strive for abundance. Today, abundance does not merely mean more stuff, it means more life.

Whoever serves me must follow me; and where I am, my servant also will be. My Father will honor the one who serves me.
—The words of Jesus as recorded
in John 12:26

I borrowed the following story from my South Dakota rancher friend, Denny Pressler, who regularly clips and sends a grand variety of trivia. It is anybody's guess where Denny might have found it.

This is the story of four people named Everybody, Somebody, Anybody, and Nobody.

There was an important job to be done and Everybody was sure that Somebody would do it, but Nobody did it.

Somebody got angry about it because it was Everybody's job. Everybody thought Anybody could do it, but Nobody realized that Everybody wouldn't do it. It ended up that Everybody blamed Somebody when Nobody did what Anybody could have done.

I might add that Everybody was delighted when Somebody did what Nobody thought Anybody would ever get around to doing.

Whew! I'm confused!

Prayer: This Day I will practice servanthood. Serving others is too precious to relegate to Anybody, Somebody, Everybody, or Nobody.

Live among others as if God beheld you;
speak to God as if the whole
world was listening.

—Seneca, paraphrased

CAN YOU SAY?—

Can you say in parting with the day that's slipping fast,
That you helped a single person of the many you have passed?
Is a single life rejoicing over what you did or said?
Does some one whose hopes were fading now with courage look ahead?
Did you waste the day or lose it, was it well or poorly spent?
Did you leave a trend of kindness or a scar of discontent?
As you close your eyes in slumber, do you think that God would say—
You have made the world much better for the life you've lived today?

—Author unknown

No question about it. This day is a gift from God. What we make of it is our gift to God.

Prayer: This Day is a precious gift. It will not come my way again, so I will use it to the best of my ability. And just perhaps, if I use it wisely, I might ease another's walk through life.

There is no loss without some measure of gain.

—Unknown

The events of September 11, 2001, grounded every plane in the sky. Delta Flight 15 was one of the flights that was forced out of the air on that fateful morning. Not one of the 200+ passengers expected to spend four days in Gander, New Foundland. But, a four-day stay on this lunar-like landscape turned out to be the new itinerary that was forced upon them.

Gander, Newfoundland, is a stark, treeless, and uninviting place. It is populated by a few thousand hardy souls and a few hundred thousand sea gulls. It is not a place that will ever receive a four-star rating in any tour guide. So, as the Delta Flight 15 passengers joined the 6,600 other passengers from 39 similarly grounded planes, the hopes of a grand holiday were dashed. This was no picnic. Schedules were trashed, plans were changed, and lives were interrupted. Who would want to spend four days on the gull-splattered rocks of this sub-arctic wasteland? You would think that the spirit would have been mutinous at worst and cranky at best.

The people of Gander rallied. They opened their homes and kitchens to this uninvited hoard. They prepared home-cooked meals, offered their cars, lent their phones, and even made fresh towels and warm showers available to the weary travelers. The townsfolk redefined genuine hospitality.

How could they ever repay the hospitality they had received? An impromptu town meeting was held on Delta Flight 15 as it proceeded from Gander to Atlanta. They addressed the question: what could they do to show their appreciation? A passenger who was a surgeon spoke up and reminded his fellow passengers that the children of Gander had virtually no opportunity to go to college. He suggested they establish the Delta Flight 15 Scholarship. An offering was taken to seed that scholarship. Slightly more than fifteen thousand dollars were raised in flight from Gander to Atlanta.

In the midst of this horror, confusion, and interruption of life, the best came out in these travelers. Indeed, there is no loss without some measure of gain!

Prayer: This Day I will try to take whatever comes my way and lovingly squeeze it until it yields a bit of worth. I will not allow it to slip away as a total loss.

> *Few things are harder to put up with than the*
> *annoyance of a good example.*
>
> —Mark Twain

Probably Harley Warrick is not an artist with whom you are familiar, but you have seen plenty of his work. Harley painted more than 4,000 barns across America with the big Mail Pouch Tobacco ads.

Harley began his career as a barn painter in 1945. He worked for the Mail Pouch Tobacco Company for fifty-five years. He slapped thousands of gallons of paint on weathered barn siding for a mere $32 a week. After the Mail Pouch Company discontinued their barn-painting campaign in 1969, Harley kept on touching up his work at his own expense. When a barn's big sign began to fade, Harley would show up with buckets of black, white, and yellow paint to retouch his handiwork. He continued working until a month before his death at age 76.

Harley's gift was a labor of love that some would argue had great artistic worth. Some claim that these barns were a bold stroke of Americana and free enterprise at its finest. Others saw the chewing tobacco ads as an ugly pox mark on the countryside. Some didn't care one way or another.

What is interesting about Harley Warrick is the fact he touched the lives—arguable in a positive, negative, or neutral way—of every American in the last half of the twentieth century. His work moved us to smile, to look away in disgust, or to simply ignore. Presumably a few were moved to go buy his employer's product. Harley Warrick touched us, but he always remained anonymous.

Harley's work has much to say about quiet service, anonymity, plugging along doing your job, and doing it the best you possibly can. It has much to say about making a difference. I doubt if Harley Warrick's name will make it into many sermons or art exhibits. But, he surely was man of quiet resolve who used his particular giftedness. He may have moved some to go out and buy a package of Mail Pouch. What is most inspiring about him is that he fully used his giftedness and made a lasting difference.

Prayer: This Day I will be a difference maker in someone's life. Perhaps it will be by bold example, or maybe by just quietly caring for another.

---

*On reaching Jerusalem, Jesus entered the temple area and began driving
out those who were buying and selling there. He
overturned the tables of the moneychangers and the
benches of those selling doves, and would not allow
anyone to carry merchandise through the temple
courts. And as he taught them he said, "My house
will be called a house of prayer for all nations,
but you have made it a den of robbers."*

—The words of Jesus recorded
in Mark 11:15–17

There is a great urge to make Jesus a soft, gentle soul. The image of
an enraged Jesus who is tearing up a temple is hard to swallow.
How do we reconcile the pleasant, quiet Good Shepherd image with
an enraged zealot?

One way is to rename it. Some call this outbreak of anger "righteous indignation." Some call it a fury with a cause. Call it what you
will, but the fact is that Jesus was cranked!

Anger does have its place. It can be a great motivator. A contemporary example was the outrage this nation endured in the freedom
marches that changed our understanding of civil rights. Anger at injustice can bring about justice. And that is a good thing. Yet, anger
can also be the catalyst that brings about abuse.

Rage and anger can also be like fire. It cooks our meals, warms
our homes, and builds our cars. Fire also destroys our homes and
takes lives. It is all a matter of when and how it is used.

Someone once described justifiable anger in this way: Suppose
you see someone abusing a puppy. You ought to be angry. If you are
still angry about it six weeks later, you have an anger problem.

The message is a simple one. Be vigilant about anger. Use it sparingly and wisely. Never linger with it as a friend. And when it has done
its work, put it away.

Prayer: This Day I will carefully dispense my anger. Today, I will
work toward indignation rather than wrath.

*When Jesus saw him lying there and learned that he had been in this
condition for a long time, he asked him,
"Do you want to get well?"*

*"Sir," the invalid replied, "I have no one to help me into the pool when the
water is stirred. While I am trying to get in,
someone else goes down ahead of me."*

*Then Jesus said to him, "Get up! Pick up your mat and walk."
At once the man was cured; he picked up his mat
and walked.*
—The words of Jesus as recorded
in John 5:6

Picture this if you will: an invalid has been lying on a mat beside a pool of healing waters for thirty-eight years. All that time, presumably, no one had ever asked him, "Can I help you into the pool?" All those years, the man just laid there.

Jesus changed all that in an instant. He asked, "Do you want to get well?" I think Jesus was asking the man if he had the courage, the desire, and the guts to make a life-changing decision. Or, was he content to live on the sympathy of others? Had he grown to see himself as a victim?

I think Jesus saw right through the man's physical malady and recognized it was a spiritual and emotional problem.

The man put up a faint argument with Jesus. He said, "Well, try as I will, I can never get into the pool. There is always a crowd on the steps and no one seems to want to help me."

Picture this: thirty-eight years waiting in line to get into the pool. Jesus was not moved by his feeble excuses. He simply said, "Pick up your mat and walk." The man did just that! Jesus was not harsh. He did not blame the man. But, he was not sympathetic to his whining and sorry excuses.

There are many healings. They can be physical, emotional, spiritual, or relational. Some healings need surgery, medicine, or counseling. Some just need a careful look at self.

Prayer: This Day I will strive for total wellness. I will need God's help to know when to comfort, when to confront, and when to counsel.

For we do not preach ourselves, but Jesus Christ as Lord, and ourselves as your servants for Jesus' sake. For God, who said, "Let light shine out of darkness," made his light shine in our hearts to give us the light of the knowledge of the glory of God in the face of Christ.
—2 Corinthians 4:5–6

After a miraculous conversion, John Newton had a long and distinguished career as a hymn composer and preacher. The 18th-century hymnist is best remembered for what is perhaps the world's most beloved and recognized hymn, *Amazing Grace.*

Newton preached in London and in a tiny village church called Olney. He had a passion for writing and brought a refreshing voice to Protestant theology. Toward the end of his life he was asked to preach at a large church in London. The aging Newton had some reservations about accepting the invitation. His eyesight had dimmed and his memory was fading. However, he felt called to once more proclaim the Good News.

The eighty-three-year-old John Newton stepped to the pulpit and said that day:

My memory fades, but I can remember two things.

First, I am a great sinner. And second, Christ is a great savior.

Having said that, the old man said, "Amen," and sat down. No more needed to be said.

Prayer: This Day I will try to simplify my faith. All I really need to know is that God is and I am not God.

> *God is our refuge and strength, an*
> *ever-present help in trouble.*
>
> —Psalm 46:1

George Barna and Associates study church management and church growth. Barna and his group recently placed phone calls to more than 3,700 American Protestant churches and discovered that your odds of someone answering the church phone were about 4 in 10. He surmised from this dismal record that a community of faith that says it is there to serve people in distress and brokenness ought to be more available than 40% of the time.

What if God operated at that level? Imagine what you would think if you prayed and heard a kindly voice respond:

"Greetings my child. You have reached God. I am sorry, but I am unable to take your call at this time. However, I want to help.

If you are seeking hope and affirmation, press 1.

If you need forgiveness and pardon, press 2.

If you seek divine guidance, press 3.

If you are in need of physical, emotional, or spiritual wellness, press 4.

If you wish to review your heavenly transcript, press 5.

If you want to ask a theological or biblical question, press 6.

If you have financial concerns, press 7.

If you want supernatural help for your Monday night football team, press 8.

To review this menu, press 9.

If this prayer is an emergency, or if you still want to speak to someone, stay on the line and the first available operator will transfer your call.

Have a real good day! And remember, I love you!"

What if God put you on hold or just failed to be present to you in your time of need? If the Church of Jesus Christ is to be a presence in the lives of all who seek God, then the least we can do is be present. Since we expect God to respond to us, then, as the Church of Jesus Christ, we must be available to all who seek hope, affirmation, and wholeness.

Prayer: This Day I will take ownership of my role as the hands and arms of Christ. Today, I will do whatever it takes to be available to another in need.

"So I say to you: Ask and it will be given to you; seek and you will find;
knock and the door will be opened to you.
For everyone who asks receives; he who seeks finds;
and to him who knocks, the door will be opened.
—The words of Jesus as recorded
in Luke 11:9–10

A Prayer for This Day

L oving God, your Holy Word says that if we ask, we will receive. So, we ask for peace and tranquility to begin in our homes and move throughout the community. We pray that that peace would prevail in our schools, our church, our nation, and in every village and capital in the world. We ask for good health—physical, emotional, and spiritual—to be part of every life. We ask that old hurts and worn out grudges would be forgotten. We ask that words like hunger, abuse, rage, and poverty would seldom be backed up by evidence.

Your holy Word says that if we seek, we will surely find. So, we seek wisdom to know how you would have us live. We seek solidarity to know how you would have us live together. We seek community so that together our living matters to every citizen. We seek solace, peace, equality, and, above all else, hope.

Your holy Word says that if we knock, the door will be opened to us. So, we knock on the door of opportunity that we might serve in ways yet unseen. We knock to be welcomed into your eternal household. We knock on the door of justice, longing for equal justice in our realm and expecting you to be the final judge in your realm.

We ask, we seek, and we knock. We willingly give to you the very essence of our being, knowing that fullness in life comes from the abandoning of self; that full lives grow from tiny seeds of faith that are well cultivated; that wholeness is the mending of brokenness that only you can give.

This Day we ask, we seek, and we knock, not only for ourselves, but also for all—the just and the unjust, the strong and the weak, the youthful and the seasoned, the present and the forgotten.

Those who are really in earnest must be willing to be anything or nothing in the world's estimation.
—Susan B. Anthony

Significance is perhaps one of life's most valued words. To come to the conclusion that your life has significance is one of our richest rewards. To know you have found your niche is among life's greatest joys. To discover and live your bliss is a life well lived. Ms. Anthony sounds like one who lived with a good measure of significance because she found her niche and lived with a sense of bliss.

You have likely known someone who has lived a life that he or she feels is void of significance. As their earthly clock winds down, they apologetically try to explain how they spent their gift of life. Perhaps a twinge of blaming others seep into their explanation. Maybe it was hard luck. Or, it could be the person always felt misunderstood. Whatever the reason, the most pitiful of all lives is one lived void of significance.

How do you measure significance? Are there viable markers that denote significance? I think so.

To have lived in such a manner that a tiny portion of the world notes that you have passed this way, is a life of significance. Your significance might be the unreserved respect of a harsh critic. It could be a bit of beauty you leave behind. Your significance might be a bit of your wisdom passed from your children to their children. As you travel the road of life, your best marker of significance is having faithfully used your God-given gifts in a manner that helps another.

A life of significance is a life that makes a lasting difference.

Prayer: This Day I will strive for significance rather than greatness. Today, I will put my passion into doing for another. For it is in unselfishly doing for another, I will best know significance.

The wolf will live with the lamb, The leopard will lie down with the goat,
the calf and the lion and the yearling together;
and a little child will lead them.

—Isaiah 11:6

Isaiah describes the Peaceable Kingdom. Our efforts have been mixed and feeble in the realm of Peaceable Kingdom building. There have been moments in which it looks promising, and there are times—such as this very time—in which the realization of the Peaceable Kingdom looks mighty dim.

Albert Einstein once said, "You cannot simultaneously prepare for war and peace." He was saying in essence that stockpiling billions of dollars worth of nuclear arms was not the road to the Peaceable Kingdom. You cannot pound peace out of an enemy. You cannot bomb evil into oblivion. You cannot nuke evil. Bigger bombs, bigger armies, greater alliances, and more frightening weapons of enormous destruction will never lay the foundation for the Peaceable Kingdom.

Mutual respect and faith in God's power to bring peace and justice to all are the keys to the Peaceable Kingdom. Sword rattling, threatening, and ultimatums have failed miserably.

Now is the time to give peace a chance and become citizens in God's Peaceable Kingdom. If that sounds too simplistic, then consider the alternative.

Prayer: This Day the world sorely needs peace. Help us to balance our ability to grow peace with our brilliance in bomb building.

> *There is a time for everything . . .*
>
> —Ecclesiastes 3:1

I once met a woman who was a nun in the Marynoll order. The Marynolls primarily work as missionaries. They travel to far-off and dangerous places to bring the gospel to some of the poorest of the poor. The nun had worked in computer engineering before entering the convent. She became fed up with the fast-paced business world and felt a calling to serve Christ.

Her first assignment was in Zimbabwe, Africa. She was sent deep into the bush to a primitive village to become the headmaster of a Christian school. Her first act was to call a staff meeting. So, she sent out a memo to the principal for a meeting to take place at 8:00 AM on Monday morning. Eight o'clock Monday morning came and no one showed up. She sent another memo for a meeting on Tuesday. Tuesday came and still no meeting. She sent a third memo for a meeting on Wednesday with the same result. Finally, on Thursday morning, at about 9:00 AM, the Principal strolled into her office wearing a big smile and graciously introduced himself.

"Where have you been?" she asked. "I called a meeting for every day this week and you show up on Thursday as if all is well! What is the deal?" she roared.

"Well, I started out early on Monday morning. But, on my way I met my friend George. He had been ill for some time and his vegetable garden needed weeding. So, I weeded George's garden. On my way here on Tuesday, I met a friend whose mother was very ill. I sat with her and comforted her in her final hours. On Wednesday morning my son had a fever. He needed some medicine from the next village. So, I attended to his fever. But, today I am here!"

The good nun suddenly realized that her world was no longer measured at the speed of computer science. In Zimbabwe, Thursday morning at 9:00 AM was about the same as Monday morning at 8:00 AM. Time was not in itself sacred. Time among the people in Zimbabwe had to be balanced with responsibility. A friend's weedy garden, a dying woman, or an ill child were more important than time.

Prayer: This Day I pray that I will use my time wisely and for the good of another.

Jesus loves me—this I know, For the Bible tells me so.
—Lyrics by Anna Bartlett Warner

Author Fred Craddock writes:

"The women from Central Avenue Christian Church that came to our house and brought a pair of Buster Brown shoes that fit me, and enabled me to start *Sunday School—those women didn't just bring me* a pair of shoes. You know what else they brought?
They brought me a picture book of stories about Jesus.
I needed those shoes. I really needed those stories."

Who brought Christ to your door? Was it a parent? Was it a grand parent? Was it a friend, a teacher, a chaplain, or a jailhouse preacher? Was it a recovered alcoholic, a dying man, or a televangelist?
Who brought you the shoes and the stories you needed?
One more question—have you ever thanked them?

Prayer: This Day I will thank the lady who gave me the stories I needed. How will I thank her? By telling someone else who needs to hear the story.

> *"Twixt the optimist and the pessimist*
> *The difference is droll:*
> *The optimist sees the doughnut*
> *But the pessimist sees the hole.*
> —McLandburgh Wilson

Spring brings baseball season. It is as if the sun has crossed a particular latitude that triggers school children to rummage through their closets to find baseball gloves. It is the smell of neat's-foot oil rubbed into dry leather to loosen it up. It is the clatter of spikes on the sidewalk. Spring means baseball regardless of temperature.

A Little League father stopped at the park one afternoon to watch his son's team play. The two teams were already on the field. As the father sat down in the bleachers behind home plate, he asked one of the boys if there was any score?

"Yeah," said the lad, "we are behind fourteen to nothing."

"Really," said the father. "I have to say you don't look very discouraged by the score."

"Discouraged?" the boy asked with a puzzled look on his face. "Why should we be discouraged? We haven't been up to bat yet!"

Prayer: This Day is a good day to embrace the beauty of spring. Today is no day to allow discouragement to sap its joy.

Fear not that your life shall come to an end, but rather that it shall not have had a beginning.

—Anonymous

It would be interesting to meet the anonymous author of the above thought. Was it someone whose life had nearly run its course and the author felt an overwhelming sense of lack of accomplishment? Or, was it one who had achieved much and wanted to encourage others to accomplish more? Was it someone who had lived life to its fullest, or one who had lived miserably and miserly? There is no way for us to guess if this anonymous one is sharing his or her wisdom as a caution or as an inspiration for others.

Have you ever considered what Jesus thought about his own life? Was he content with his mission, or did he see it as a failure? Certainly Jesus had a sense of destiny, for he went to the cross willingly. There is that moment of resolution in the Garden of Gethsemane (Luke 22:39–43). And there are Jesus' words from the cross declaring, "It is finished." There does seem to be some measure of satisfaction in his having accomplished his mission. Yet, Jesus preached about the coming kingdom of God. Did he see it? Or, did he feel a sense of disappointment?

There is an ingredient in the life of Christ that is radically different from all others. *Jesus' life is not finished.* Since the church is the ongoing body of the living Christ, there is still the opportunity for a new beginning every day.

In these days before Easter, we can reflect on how we can make certain that Jesus' mission has fulfillment. There is much unfinished work yet to be done. We still have the opportunity for assuring its final victory. Perhaps the best news within the Good News is that Jesus' mission is not really finished. Rather, it is coming into a new beginning with each new believer. For the kingdom of God, when perfect harmony and tranquility reign, is not yet a finished mission.

This Easter season, consider the unfinished work we have to do in the name of Christ.

Prayer: This Day I will be a willing worker in God's kingdom. Hand me a shovel, a pen, or a hammer and I will gladly labor for Christ.

The Power of Positive Thinking
> —Title of a book
> by Norman Vincent Peale

Jim wore the scars of another time. The most notable was a tattoo in his right forearm. It was a homemade tattoo that lacked either artistic quality or symmetry. The letters were rounded, simple, and a bit askew. It said: BORN TO LOSE. Ironically, Jim was anything but a loser. Those three words, etched in blue ink below his skin, were a poignant reminder of another time. They spoke to the Jim of long ago. The "Before Jim." The "Tragic Jim." The "Negative Jim." The "After Jim" was a positive, helpful, and filled-with-life man who was born to win. Yet, Jim's once-upon-a-time negativity was still there for the world to see.

I once saw an expensive S.U.V. that had a license plate that read: NO HOPE. I was drawn into the message of negativity with more than passing interest. Was the driver saying, "There is no hope of ever paying for this $55,000 truck?" Was he saying, "There is no hope of ever convincing my wife that I need this truck?" Or, was he merely stating his negative philosophy of life itself? I'll never know.

The vast majority of us go through life with neither a *born to lose* tattoo nor a *no hope* license plate. At least my friend Jim and the S.U.V. driver were unafraid to make a bold statement of their negativity. Most of us are both far more positive and much less vocal. Yet, that does not mean we are always totally silent about the matter of hope and positive thinking.

Jim and the S.U.V. driver cause me to wonder: What silent message of positive hope do I proclaim to the world? And, what would it take to say it even more boldly?

Prayer: This Day my prayer is to live in a positive manner. There will be no "*born to lose*" tattoos or "*no hope*" license plates in my life today. For such negativity would push Christ out of my life.

*We know that in all things God works for the good of
those who love him, who have been called according to his purpose.*
—Romans 8:28

In the 1870s, my great grandfather was a homesteader in Kansas. He and another young man left their parents' farms in Winnameg, Ohio, and struck out to seek their fortunes. They found the land a hostile place. It was a tree-less prairie that hosted an unforgiving climate. When the Kansas sun shines, it shines with brutal vengeance. When the winter winds blow across this forest-less land, it blows with the same measure of unkindness.

Since there were no trees, lumber yards, or brick kilns, the two young homesteaders were obliged to use the only building material they could find. They built a hut of sod. The sod hut did a marginal job of keeping out the snow and the wind, but when it rained, it poured inside. This house of soil was altogether inadequate and no doubt added to the two men's discomfort.

Their trek into the great heartland and their experiment with Kansas farming only lasted a couple of years. It was too much for the two lads, so their bold venture ended and they returned to Winnameg. My great grandfather's Kansas adventure ended as many did. Only one in three who homesteaded in the late 19th century stayed for more than five years. As the two young men made their way back to Winnameg, my guess is that they felt a certain measure of defeat. Probably, they also felt a certain measure of relief when they left the earthen burrow for a house with siding, windows, and a floor. Kansas life was not to be for the two men. They both went ahead and had successful lives back in Ohio.

Was it failure or success? Who knows? One thing is for certain: all things work together for good for those who love God (Romans 8:28). Their experience also clearly shows that one failure does not define a life.

Prayer: This Day is a good day to celebrate the pioneer spirit that grew the church of Christ, brought freedom to this land, and binds us as hopeful people.

Wait for the LORD; be strong and take heart
and wait for the LORD.

—Pslam 27:14

What ten words top your list of least-liked words? Might they be among these?:

1. Cancer
2. Fired
3. War
4. Hate
5. Poverty

6. Abuse
7. Racism
8. Nuclear weapons
9. Gossip
10. Wait

Does #10 surprise you? Think about it—does anyone like to wait? Do you suppose that is why a waiting room is called a reception area?

We are an impatient lot. A cartoon in the New Yorker Magazine showed a couple of American tourists running into the Louvre saying, "Where is the Mona Lisa? We are double parked!"

My brother once had a plaque that hung in his office that said: "God grant me patience, but please hurry!"

We wait a lot in life. A couple waits for a child to be born. The sick wait for tests; wait for medicine to work; wait for health to return; and then, they may wait for death. Employees wait for a raise. Coaches wait for results. Farmers wait for spring to come, seeds to sprout, rain to come, crops to mature, and harvest to beat the snow. Then he waits for the markets to improve.

Wives wait for husbands to get home. Husbands wait for wives to get ready to go someplace. Parents wait for their children's maturity. Children wait for a driver's license. Police wait for a suspect to return to the scene of the crime. Criminals wait for the police to move on to another suspect. Churches wait for a ministry to attract the needy. The unchurched wait for a church to meet their needs.

We wait, and wait, and wait, and then we wait some more. Waiting is a given; being strong and taking heart is a matter of choice.

Prayer: This Day I will use my waiting time wisely. It will be filled with God's strength and hope.

*"If you hold to my teaching, you are really my disciples. Then you will
know the truth, and the truth will set you free."*
—The words of Jesus as recorded
in John 8:31–32

Have you ever wanted to make a major change in your life? Have
you ever wanted to get rid of a troublesome habit? Or is there
some toxic behavior that threatens your well-being and happiness that
you would like to change? Change is not easy, but it surely is not
impossible. If you want to tackle a major life change, you might consider H.O.W.

Several of the recovery support groups have coined the acronym
H.O.W. as the wisdom at the heart of recovery. The acronym stands
for Honesty, Open-mindedness, and Willingness.

Let us consider honesty.

The brand of honesty we are talking about here is not the simple
variety that is commonly called "cash-register" honesty. Cash-register
honesty means you would not steal from an open cash drawer. A person with cash-register honesty might even make a spectacle out of
being undercharged or given too much change. Cash-register honesty
is the minimum expected degree of truthfulness. It is inherent honesty.

The honesty of H.O.W. is brutal honesty. It is breaking down the
hardest of all barriers—lying to self. Brutal honesty quits making excuses. It does not thrive on blame. It refuses to find fault. In the wake
of brutal honesty, excuses, placing guilt, lying to look good, and heaping blame all shrivel and die. The idea is that as long as one does not
have to take personal responsibility for one's actions, change is impossible. Honesty breaks the shackles of denial. It is the beginning of
any life-changing adventure.

Jesus knew all about honesty. He said, "By knowing the truth, you
will know freedom."

Prayer: This Day I will practice a new brand of honesty. Knowing
that true honesty begins within me, I will need God's help.
Because being honest with myself may involve the toughest person I have to convince.

> "... I am sending you to them to open their eyes and turn them from
> darkness to light, and from the power of Satan to God,
> so that they may receive forgiveness of sins and a place
> among those who are sanctified by me."
> —The words of Jesus as recorded
> in Acts 26:17–18

The second bit of wisdom in the H.O.W. of major life changing is open-mindedness.

Once the barrier of dishonesty is removed, the locked safe that holds open-mindedness is weakened. When you think about it, an open mind could not cohabit with a dishonest mind. Once the walls of dishonesty are cracked, an open mind has a much better chance of breaking through. One follows the other in that order.

An open mind is a mind that does not harbor prejudice. There is no room for resentments, self-pity, or blame. An open mind invites change. It refuses to say, "Never!" Rather an open mind will say, "What if?" It has a hunger to learn, a passion to grow, and an excitement about new discoveries that are made on almost a daily basis. Open-mindedness does not wallow in the past. It will not engage in self-blame and personal deprecation. An open mind is less prone to criticizing others. It shows a passion for possibilities. One that used to live with a negativity that saw no hope is gone, while a new positive outlook takes the place of crippling negativity. An open mind rejects shame and blame with the same vigor.

An open mind welcomes the new and rejects the old way of thinking. It sees in others many possibilities that might apply to one's life. An open mind is a vacuum that draws in new hope, new ideas, and new potential.

It has been said that a mind is a terrible thing to waste. A closed mind is a terribly wasted thing.

Prayer: This Day I will unlock the mind God has given me. To what new horizons that might take me will be an exciting journey. I will need some help in this, because the baggage of shame, resentment, and negativity are old familiar companions.

For if the willingness is there, the gift is acceptable according to what one has, not according to what he does not have.
—2 Corinthians 8:12

Willingness rounds out the H.O.W. of major life change. The willingness of change is unreserved. It comes without reservations or restrictions. There are no conditions. It cannot be withdrawn, compromised, or edited. The brand of willingness we are talking about is akin to total abandonment. It is an all-out, throttle-pulled-back, and bent-over kind of willingness.

Willingness flows nicely from open-mindedness. The mind first conceives or accepts. But putting a new idea into action takes a high degree of willingness. Willingness has an elastic quality about it. It is willing to stretch. If failure is the first result, there must be a willingness to try again. Willingness is slow to accept defeat. It has a tenacious quality about it that can stumble and fall, yet remain intact. Willingness is seen in a sense of optimism that will not allow compromise.

The three—honesty, open-mindedness, and willingness—are a bit harsh. Moreover, *complete* honesty, open-mindedness, and willingness is the brand that is demanded of you. Partial helpings of any of the three will never bring results. What is asked of you in the face of change is brutal honesty, absolute open-mindedness, and uncompromising willingness.

Tall order you say? Yes, but has anything of real worth in your life ever come easily? Now that you know H.O.W., what will it be?

Prayer:　This Day I will dig deeply to uncover all the willingness I can muster. Today, half measures will not be my choice.

*There is a time for everything and a season for
every activity under the heaven . . .*

—Ecclesiastes 3:1

Some things in life are so predictable. Sets of questions go with each of the seasons. They are asked with such frequency that they have become clichés. For example, in mid-December someone will surely ask, "Got your Christmas shopping done?" Later in January, someone will ask, "Cold enough for you?" As March rolls around surely there will be those who say it looks like an early spring while others will say that spring is late this year. Of course, summer brings the inverse of January when someone says, "Hot enough for you?" As summer ebbs and shopping for school clothes begins, the most-oft-asked question has to be: "Where did summer go?"

We live in a world of predictability.

Perhaps the sorrow of March is that no one ever says, "Where has March gone?" Nobody seems to care. March is a blasé month. We wear a bit of green and eat cabbage in mid-March. We celebrate the first day of spring in late March (often having more to do with celestial happenings than thermometer readings). Yet, March does not seem to matter to most of us.

March is winding down, and who cares? Surely there must be some redeeming quality. Maybe March is an important time of gestation. March is when the bulbs begin to quietly stir below the soil's crust. It is when that splendid annual happening that is beyond mystery begins. The once-frozen earth breaks forth with new life. Where gray snow and honeycombed frost held life in limbo, new stirrings have begun. Soon, greenery and flowers will blanket the land. The weariness of winter will be put away for another season. Or at least until someone says, "Looks like it might frost tonight."

Poor March. It is so despised and so overlooked. Before it leaves us, ought we not say just once about this noble month, "Where has March gone?"

Prayer: This Day I will take time to drink in the mystery that surrounds me. Today, I will celebrate the ongoing creation of new life. And if I do it well, I will see new life both around me and within me.

*When we look closely at those around us, another surprising picture
emerges. The least attractive, least interesting, and
least credible people turn out to be those who have suffered
little. Those who are deep, believable, and wise have been
through a lot. So, while we do not want suffering,
we can salvage it, recycle it, and turn it into
the very best stuff. In fact, we cannot acquire
the very best stuff of life in any other way.*
—James R. Kok

It seems there has been a rash of natural disasters lately—earthquakes, tornados, hurricanes, floods, and droughts of epic, biblical proportions. It seems that no continent, no political boundary, and no region has been spared horrendous suffering. Millions have been plunged into suffering. We are witnessing global hurt.

James Kok, in his book, *Waiting for Morning: Seeking God in Our Suffering,* explores the mortar that binds us all together—the world of human suffering. He puts the subject of inevitable and unavoidable tragedy into as positive terms as possible. Though no one welcomes suffering, Kok points out that there is some value in loss.

Another author, Robert Hestene, says that some suffering has purpose. He says that purposeful suffering is like interrupted wealth, sleep, and health. None of them can be fully appreciated until they have been interrupted.

Our lives have been, and probably will continue to be, interrupted by natural disasters. There is not much that can be done to avoid such harsh interruptions or the companion suffering that accompanies them. However, we can use that suffering to redefine hope, to measure our resolve, and as Kok says, "to find our very best stuff." Beyond that, the suffering of others tests our compassion and generosity. Our response to another's suffering is the tangible evidence of our loving others. The natural disasters that another is obliged to endure can bring out the very best stuff in us.

Prayer: This Day I will weigh the words of my compassion with the acts of my life. Hopefully, they are a good match. In suffering (mine or another's) I will have to reach deeply into my inner self for the very best stuff.

In all of God's creation, people are the only creatures that have the ability to blush (or the need to do so).

—Mark Twain

Mirth matters. It is not pushing it too far to say that laughter is part of what defines us as human. We are the only members of creation who truly laugh. Sure, a dog wags his tail to show affection or delight. A cat purrs, and birds sing. But, genuine and deep-within-your-soul laughter is human. Laughter is what sets us apart. And, it is not just meant for merriment. Research has shown that people who laugh heartily and on a daily basis live longer and have fewer serious illnesses. Laughter has been called "the spirit of God dancing within."

Consider you ability to laugh and how you use it. Now, take a step further and consider your ability to laugh at yourself. Of course, not everyone has mastered that ability. Some are a bit reluctant to enjoy self-inflicted humor.

Laughter in general, and the ability to laugh at ourselves in particular, has a spiritual dimension. When we are incapable of laughing at ourselves, we are taking ourselves far too seriously. We have elevated self above others. We have set ourselves apart as too sacred to be a bit flawed. Laughing at our foibles, our mistakes, and our idiocy takes a good measure of self-confidence.

Writer Ralph Milton points out that dictators and tyrants do not allow humor. Dictators find their being the brunt of a joke as completely repulsive. They see political satire as threatening. Milton says you can judge a nation's dedication to freedom and liberty by the ability of its leaders to take a joke. My guess is that in Iraq Little Billy stories might work, but Little Saddam stories are off limits. Given the level of political satire in this country, we must be either the freest people to ever live or have the most tolerant leaders.

The next time you feel a bit of mirth, think of it as your spirit dancing. Then thank God, who is the choreographer who made it possible.

Prayer: This Day I will laugh at me! Today, I will let my spirit dance a lively jig.

*Strange when you think of it . . . not one is known in history or in legend
as having died of laughter.*

—Marcel Proust

David Green is the owner and editor of a small town newspaper with fewer than 2,500 subscribers. His one-person publication makes up for quantity with quality journalism and reporting that keeps his community well informed. His newspaper has won a number of national journalism awards for publications of its size. David Green is a consummate April Fool's Day prankster. He delights in taking foolery to a higher plain. Given that he has full control of his newspaper and a splendid imagination, David's April Fool's pranks are akin to Orson Wells' radio Halloween hoax.

A few years ago, the paper's front page told of an Admiral A. Pearle Phool (think about it) having made plans for Navy submarine races to be held in the tiny Bean Creek that winds its way through David's little town. On another April Fool's Day edition, David had the same A. Pearle Phool declaring that much of southern Michigan was about to be annexed by the State of Ohio because of a legal technicality that defined the border between the two states.

You can be sure that a few of David's readers are indignant about having fallen for such nonsense. Some are insulted and feel offended. A few even cancel their subscription. For a small readership, every subscriber matters.

So, why would David Green deliberately fabricate and publish an article that might cost his paper a precious subscription or two?

It is simply because David Green refuses to take life too seriously. Life is too short to always be serious. A bit of mirth, a touch of joy, and a generous helping of laughter are the ingredients of spiritual wellness.

David's pranks are never intended to offend. That is not his style. He simply urges those whom he loves to lighten up and begin April with a good laugh. After winter's doldrums, most of us need a good laugh!

Prayer: This Day I will try to offend no one. At the same time, I will try just as hard to not take myself too seriously. When this day is done, I will thank God for the laughter that lightens my load.

*For God has rescued us from the dominion of darkness and brought us
into the kingdom of the Son he loves,
in whom we have redemption and forgiveness.*
—Colossians 1:13–14

When the homesteaders pressed westward in the late 19ᵗʰ century, they found little building material on the prairie. Chunks of sod that baked in the sun to form crude bricks were about all they had for housing material. So, many became known as "soddies."

A diary kept by a family of sod-hut dwellers tells of having lived a mole-like existence for five years. Then a bit of prosperity came their way. They had saved enough money to buy a small pane of glass to put into the earthen wall. The small pane of glass let in enough light to bathe the darkness of the room with a mellow light. Imagine having a shaft of light as a luxury! It is interesting that the family chose a windowpane as the first luxury they allowed themselves. It shows that living in darkness has to be a lonely existence. Within each of us is a longing for light.

Perhaps it was the darkness that sapped many of the homesteaders' resolve. One has to wonder, was it the bitter wind, the long winter, and the brutal heat, or was it perpetual darkness that wore them down? Could the elements have been endured if they had just a bit of light?

Paul says that light means everything in our lives.

Light does mean everything. If Christ had not illumined our lives, we would all still be living in miserable darkness.

Prayer: This Day I will relish the blessing of light. For the Light of Life has shown into our lives and no darkness will ever overcome it.

> *I lift up my eyes to the hills—*
> *where does my help come from?*
> *My help comes from the LORD,*
> *the Maker of heaven and earth.*
>
> —Psalm 121:1–2

For those of us who love college basketball, we have just gone through our finest hour. The National Collegiate Athletic Association (N.C.A.A.) basketball tournaments have named a new national champion. Sixty-four of the nation's best teams played a single elimination tournament. Only one is left standing. A new national champion has been crowned. One team has played its way through a grueling schedule and can now hoist the banner to its rafters that tells the world it is college basketball's best. We affectionately call this process "March Madness."

In a recent game, the commentator mentioned that there are only three college basketball players who have made more than one thousand career assists. What is an assist? It is setting up a teammate so that player can score. An assist is giving up the ball so that another might excel.

Basketball, like life, presents its times of selfless sharing. It is good to know that a few gladly and willingly help another do well. Assists do not draw the same fame that baskets do, but no one can deny that assists win games.

Could it be that Jesus was thinking about our being assist leaders when he said, "Love your neighbor as you love yourself"? Maybe he was saying, "In my book, assists count more than baskets. Now go lead the league in assists!"

Prayer: This Day my goal will be to quietly, anonymously, and unselfishly help another excel. Today, I will be an assist-maker.

So do not worry, saying, 'What shall we eat?' or `What shall we drink?'
or 'What shall we wear?' Do not worry about
tomorrow, for tomorrow will worry about itself.
—Matthew 6:31,34

Someone once said that if you want to make God laugh, tell him your plans.

However, planning is surely not to be understood as an opposition to God. Planning is not offensive to God. Maybe a better way of saying it is to make plans, but not in indelible ink.

Plans need to have the quality of interruptibility. I am not sure if interruptibility is a real word, but you have probably already guessed that it means the quality of welcoming an interruption. Interruptibility is when we allow our agendas to come in second behind another's needs.

Interruptibility is when a friend needs a bit of encouragement, our time is less important than the friend's need. It is when a child needs a hurt kissed away, the ironing will wait. Or when a spouse needs to be told, "I love you," "I'm sorry," or "I forgive you," all else is hugely unimportant. It is when a son or daughter needs a ride to the library, the lawn mowing can be done tomorrow. When a dying friend needs to hear our voice, work will keep. When an aged aunt needs a visit at that nursing home you so despise entering, personal comfort will have to wait. When a friend or coworker questions if life is really worth living, a hug, a smile, a prayer is what really matters at that moment.

Make plans, but be willing to drop everything when another is in need. That is interruptibility. That is taking time to love another regardless of our agenda.

Sure, God laughs when we tell him our plans. But, God smiles when we show him that our plans can be interrupted!

Prayer: This Day nothing will be so important that I cannot be interrupted. Today, I will practice and try to perfect my interruptibility.

> *"I am a bear of very little brain, and long words bother me."*
> —Winnie-the-Pooh,
> by Alan Milne

I love words. My favorite regular feature in *Reader's Digest* is "Testing Your Word Power." Though I seldom score particularly high, I still love the challenge. Words are the crayons on our canvas of communication. They inform. They can delight. They surely convey.

There are words that we use that do not exist, yet are real to us because they convey meaning. For example, everyone knows that "pertnear" means close, a short distance, or having nearly happened. I suppose that "tain't" is a conjunction of 'tis not and ain't. And who could ague that "slurripy" means anything other than patronizingly sweet? None of these are real words, yet they do convey meaning.

Consider "entrustedness." Now there is a word! It is the quality of owning another's trust. To display entrustedness is to quietly live with a sense of reliance. It is to be a confident, a faithful resource, or a person in whom trust can be placed with confidence.

Maybe another word for entrustedness is friend. Yes. I like that! As Winnie-the-Pooh says, "Long words bother me."

Prayer: This Day's most sacred undertaking and most important task is to be a friend. If I do that one thing well, I will have made much of this day.

But he said to me, "My grace is sufficient for you, for my power is made perfect in weakness."
—2 Corinthians 12:9

I am far from a computer expert. In fact, it is a stretch to say I am computer literate. My relationship with my computer is a love/hate relationship on its best day. There are few keystrokes that I have mastered upon which I have become reliant. My computer has a "Find" function that searches all the stored files for a phrase or a particular word. When found, the file or files can be retrieved. This can be hugely helpful at times and can save many hours of looking for a topic in the cyber bowels of this machine I call my friend and loathsome adversary.

Recently I used the "Find" function to try to retrieve a file that had a Little Billy story in it. I discovered I had filed twenty-seven Little Billy stories in the last twenty-four months. The "Find" function was not especially helpful in this case because it did not narrow the search. I still had twenty-seven documents to look through to find what I originally sought.

It occurred to me that Little Billy stories are good examples of a bad example. Now that is a strange genre. There is a bit of Little Billy in all of us. He is the time when we wished we had remained silent. He is our brashness when shyness would be better. He is our brutal honesty when diplomacy would be more helpful. Little Billy is precocious, outspoken, and far too anxious to find fault. He is self-centered, at times indifferent, and yet, always loveable. We like Little Billy simply because we understand him so intimately. Little Billy is not perfect, but he is surely loved.

It causes me to wonder: Does God have a "Find" function for Little every one of us?

Prayer: This Day I will give thanks for the delicate balance of imperfect me and God's perfect grace. Today, I will tell him so.

Among all the diseases of the mind there is not one more epidemical or more pernicious than the love of flattery.
—Sir Richard Steele

Gene Cwalinski is one of my oldest and dearest friends. Gene is a quiet, thoughtful man who is a master of one-line philosophy. I know that Gene would be surprised to hear this, but his one-liners have been the seeds of wisdom from which more than a few sermons have sprouted. I call Gene's minute philosophies "Gene-isms."

One of my favorite "Gene-isms" was addressed to a young man who was prone to whining and complaining about how badly he was being treated by his employer. The whiner droned on relentlessly about how he had been slighted, overlooked, and treated with mock indifference by his boss. The poor fellow moaned and groaned in self-pity for what seemed like an hour. Finally, Gene had had enough. He said to the young man, "Maybe you ought to try the Flattery Prayer."

"What's that?" sobbed the whiner.

"Oh, it is just a short prayer that I use whenever life has unjustly taken me for granted," said my friend.

"How does it go? asked the young man.

"It goes like this," said Gene. "Dear Lord, would that I always be as easily flattered as I am offended."

No more was said. The discussion was over, and, mercifully, so, too, was the whining!

Prayer: This Day, O Lord, may I be as easily flattered as I am offended. Amen.

The significance of man is that he is that part of the universe that asks the question, What is the significance of Man?

—Carl Becker

My brother, Curtis, is an interesting man. He has many and varied interests and can speak with a good measure of understanding on many topics. Perhaps his greatest gift is his ability to see what others might easily miss. He is a keen observer of the human condition.

Curtis also has a wonderful wit. He has an uncanny ability to make marvelous observations and then comment on them in a most disarming way. He is a mix of Art Buckwald, Andy Rooney, and Paul Harvey all rolled into one. Often he comes up with one of those zingers that causes me to say to myself, "I wish I had thought of that!"

One day Curt and I were traveling on an interstate highway. We stopped at a rest area and started walking toward the plaza building. Curt paused in front of the plaque on the corner of the building and read it with great interest. It said:

The Arthur W. Tweedy Memorial Rest Area

Curt dryly said, "Won't that be great? To be a man of such stature that they name a public restroom after you!"

The fact is that probably none of us will ever have a college library, a highway, or for that matter, even a rest area named for us. Remarkable significance that spans perpetuity probably is out of reach for most of us. However, that does not mean that our lives lack significance. We do matter. What we do matters. And, how others see us matters.

More than all this, we matter to God.

Prayer: This Day I want to live in such a manner that I matter. Knowing fully well that the work I do or the things I own are not the stuff of significance, I will honor my Creator by making my day matter to another.

*And the peace of God, which transcends all understanding, will guard
your hearts and your minds in Christ Jesus.*
—Philippians 4:7

On an April day in 2002, the morning news showed two starkly
different pictures of churches. One was live coverage of the Queen
Mum's funeral from Westminster Cathedral in London. The other was
also live coverage of the siege at the Church of the Nativity in Bethlehem,
Israel.

Each of these holy places informs and shapes our Christian journey—one as a touchstone of Protestantism, and the other the place of
our Savior's birth. Each is unique, honored, and rich in history. Each
is holy. For the believer to stand in either of these churches, there is
not a shred of doubt that this is holy ground. Though no building has
a monopoly on the presence of God, it is here in these sacred places
that we feel God's intersection with our earthly walk.

On that April day one of these sacred places was being harshly
and brutally profaned and misused. Tanks surrounded the place of
Jesus' birth while two hundred armed terrorists occupied its hallowed
halls. The sacred was profaned. The holy was tragically abused. In another sacred place, a people lifted thanksgiving to God, rejoiced in eternal hope, and honored one who had lived long and well. Here, the holy
shined, brought hope, and celebrated our shared faith.

Tanks and thanks. How bewildering all this must be to God? It
must bring sadness to God's heart when He sees this wretched dichotomy. Likely we will not figure it all out and probably will never
fully comprehend God's sorrow. Ours is to know with certainty that
the church of Jesus Christ will prevail, and along with it will come
eventual peace.

Given this stark contrast and confusion, pray that the holy would
be restored, sacred revered, and peace would forever be ours.

Prayer: On This Day, I pray for peace. Today, I pray that the holy will
be forever holy, global peace be eternal, and the justice of
God's kingdom will begin on this day.

*Someone's sitting in the shade today because someone
planted a tree a long time ago.*
—Warren Buffet

Every one of us is an heir to the generosity of another generation. We were born into a world that had all the necessary resources with which to pursue life. We were born into a family, a church, a community, and a nation that had been expecting us. All the resources were in place to meet our every need.

We were born into a world where there were hospitals and a health care system to attend our physical needs. There were schools, colleges, universities, and libraries to pass on the collected wisdom of the centuries that came before us. There were roads and bridges to carry us from place to place. We were born into an ordered world in which laws and a sense of human decency were well established. The church was a living and vital presence within the world when we arrived here. And, as Warren Buffet reminds us, there were even shade trees to provide comfort from the blistering sun. We are the privileged heirs and the consumers of another generation's kindness and vision.

Now it is our turn. Our generation's time has come to get out the shovel and plant a tree so the next generation can find solace from the summer sun. The tree we plant is one of faith. It is a shade tree that will provide for the future and attend the needs of those who are yet to know Christ.

The world is in process. The completeness of creation is a yet-to-be-finished event. The spiritual needs that those future seekers will bring may differ from those our generation brought. Some will bring the same spiritual hunger and sense of purpose we sought. The exact shape of the future is still in process. As a people of faith, who see beyond our personal comfort and desires, we need to think of ourselves as planters. We are planters who are poised to plant for the future. We are about to plant shade trees for those whom we will likely never meet. It is the right thing to do, simply because we have sat in the shade of another's generosity.

Prayer: This Day I will gladly pick up the shovel and plant for the future's sake. Today, I will cultivate Christ's church that it may offer shade to a future traveler.

> *The perfect marriage is not the result of finding the*
> *perfect mate. It is the art of being a perfected mate.*
> —Seen on a church sign in Ohio

There is a world of truth in that anonymous statement. That truth goes far beyond a formula for marital bliss. It speaks of self-understanding of who is in charge of our lives and how we live in any relationship with another.

First, it draws the boundary lines around our tiny sphere of influence. I am the only person I can change. I alone am in charge of me. No one else can change me, and I cannot change another. As much as I would like to change others so that they could see things my way, it is beyond my ability.

Second, I am in charge of my own happiness. My well-being and fulfillment is not dependant upon another. Each of us has our own physical, emotional, and spiritual needs. Others can help in the process through their encouragement, good example, and shared experience. But, in the final analysis, I am an autonomous being who is in charge of my own destiny. My soul is mine, and mine alone, to attend, to nurture, and to keep well fed. As much as I would like to blame another for my moments of unhappiness, the fact is that my bliss is my business.

Third, successful relationships thrive on compromise and caring for another. Successful relationships are built on the foundation of mutual appreciation for the other's uniqueness. You are not exactly like me and I am not exactly like you, but that is what makes each of us unique. Successful relationships understand that the other makes you a better person, and, hopefully, you add to the other's life also.

Finally, the situation is far from hopeless. I am not expected to be perfect. I can change. And although I will never be perfect or without fault, I can continue to progress toward betterment. A perfect marriage (or any relationship) is grounded in knowing that each member's journey toward perfectedness begins with the other.

Prayer: This Day I will work on the biggest endeavor, the most important assignment, and the most difficult undertaking of all—me. Today, I will be content to make the betterment of self my vocation. Perhaps in so doing, I will improve the lot of another.

When I say . . . "I am a Christian"

When I say . . . "I am a Christian"
I'm not shouting, "I am saved."
I'm whispering, "I am lost."
That is why I chose this way.

When I say . . . "I am a Christian"
I don't speak of this with pride.
I'm confessing that I stumble
And need someone to be my guide.

When I say . . . "I am a Christian"
I'm not trying to be strong.
I'm professing that I'm weak and pray for
Strength to carry on.

When I say . . . "I am a Christian"
I'm not bragging of success.
I'm admitting I have failed and cannot
Ever repay the debt.

When I say . . . "I am a Christian"
I'm not claiming to be perfect.
My flaws are too visible, but God believes
I'm worth it.

When I say . . . "I am a Christian"
I still feel the sting of pain.
I have my share of heartaches
Which is why I seek His name.

When I say . . . "I am a Christian"
I do not wish to judge.
I have no authority
I only know that I am loved.

—Author unknown, copied
from EOCC Orrington, Maine

Great deeds are usually wrought at great risks.

—Herodotus

A shipload of weary travelers came to the shores of New England. They built their homes in New England and set about the business of building a community. They carved out a tiny village, cleared some land on which to plant, established a set of rules and order, and built a meetinghouse in which to worship God and to conduct the affairs of the community.

The second year, they elected a town government. The third year, that elected government made plans to build a new road that was to extend westward five miles into the wilderness. Not everyone was in favor of this plan. In the fifth year of the community's wilderness experience, they voted to impeach their elected officials because they thought that building a road into the wilderness was a waste of public funds. Who needed to see what was five miles deeper into the forest? What was there? Why go?

Strange is it not? A people who were willing to risk everything and to travel 3,000 miles across the Atlantic on a small ship were now stifled in their tracks. A people who had risked it all and braved unspeakable hardships had lost their pioneer spirit. These same adventurers who had crossed an ocean were now unable to press another five miles into the unknown. Their vision had become atrophied by complacency. Their sense of destiny had withered and died.

A clear vision that comes only from a personal relationship with Jesus Christ is the road into the wilderness. Without that relationship our world becomes that pitifully tiny village of faith in which we find comfort. Without a Christ-centered vision for the future we, too, can be stuck in our little clearing. We, too, can be like those colonists whose atrophied vision kept them blind to the glorious vastness that lay beyond their boundaries. A life that is void of faith is one that is obliged to live on the fringes of possibilities.

Prayer: This Day I will press on with boldness. Today, I will gather my faith, my shovel, and my axe and begin to blaze that road into the uncharted wilderness that God calls me to trudge.

In this world there are only two tragedies. One is not getting what one wants, and the other is getting it.

—Oscar Wilde

Do you have a pioneer spirit? Can you imagine yourself as a pioneer? What must it have been like to gather in the spring of the year along with a hundred or so others waiting to embark on a grand journey? How could you decide what to take and what to leave behind?

Loading one of those tiny Conestoga wagons with all you would need to start a new life must have been an agonizing time of decision-making. There would be no room for frivolities or luxuries. The quiet pleasures of life and that which adds beauty would find no corner in a pioneer's trunk. Bare essentials were all that could accompany the settlers. Here, you would have to separate your needs from your wants.

As the pioneers pressed westward from St. Louis and other gathering towns, their needs and wants began to redefine themselves. As the mountain ranges grew steeper, the trails more treacherous, and the oxen's strength waned, what seemed like a need back in St. Louis was now a want. And so the day would come when the team was so exhausted and weak, and the load still too much to bear, that a decision had to be made. To lighten the wagon, do you throw the trunk that holds your grandmother's wedding dress to the side of the road, or do you toss the iron plow over the edge? That is painful decision-making.

Life comes to that on our faith journey. What really matters? What do I think I must have and what can I live without? What can I leave behind as I travel forward?

Prayer: This Day I will inventory what really matters in life. The debris I leave behind only adds to the challenges of my journey. Today, I will travel light with only a generous bundle of faith.

---

*There are two days of the week about which and upon which I never
worry. Two carefree days, kept sacredly free from fear and apprehension.
One of these days is Yesterday . . .
And the other day I do not worry about is Tomorrow.*
—Robert Jones Burdette

Do you remember when you were a child and you thought there
were monsters under your bed? Do you remember how you did
not dare let your hand dangle over the edge of the bed just in case the
monster grabbed it? What did you fear? Were you really afraid of the
dark? Were you afraid you might be pulled under the bed? Might a
monster devour you?

The more you let the monsters under the bed occupy your mind,
the more real they became. A shadow that the hall night light cast on
the wall looked like a monster's hunched back. The wind outside your
window sounded like its fiery breath. The snoring that came from the
room down the hall was really the monster's guttural purr. The more
you let it seep into your mind, the more real it became. Finally, you
just had to pray a prayer of strength—"I am not going to let this monster get me." About then you fell asleep and awakened the next morning in a monster-free world.

It has been some time since monsters under the bed have plagued
me. But, the ability to give life and power to unfounded fears never
leaves us. The monsters change. They no longer have fangs, fiery breath,
or fearsome growls. The monsters we face in adult life are of a different sort. They are just as imagined, just as fictional, and no more life
threatening than the ones that lurked under our beds as children. And
the strategy of escape is also just the same: just pray past the monsters
and you will awaken into a monster-free world.

The next time the monsters try to plague your well-being, capture
your peace, and devour your solace, do what has always worked. Pray
past the monsters!

Prayer: This Day I will be stingy with the power I allow negative
thoughts and fears to have in my life. I will pray past that
which threatens to devour me.

All the animals and all the creatures that move along the ground and all the birds—everything that moves on earth—came out of the ark, one kind after another.

—Genesis 8:19

Some years ago, I came across a Noah's ark print in an antique shop. It was not especially old. The frame was mostly unremarkable. The print had faded a bit. But, there was something that set this apart from every other artist's interpretation of Noah's ark. The animals were coming down the gangplank!

The sky was sunny and bright instead of threatening and gloomy. The land was green and lush instead of soggy and filled with mud holes. One of Noah's sons was plowing the soil, while another planted seeds. Clean clothes flapped in the breeze from a clothesline that was strung between two trees. The animals looked glad to be free from the stench of the ark. This was a time of repopulating the land. It is a picture of restoration. It is resurrection.

Every Noah's print I have ever seen depicts the hurried rush to get the animals on board the ark. A looming storm is brewing. The whole scene is gripped in danger, fear, and the unknown. It is a time of impending doom and destruction. As the belly of the ark fills, you cannot deny that death is imminent.

How the two prints differ. One portrays death, while the other focuses on life. One shows misery, while the other holds forth hope. One features fear, while the other centers on promise. It all has to do with which way the animals are headed–up out of harm's way, or down into restoration.

Which way are the animals headed on your gangplank?

Prayer: This Day I will herd my flock of life into restoration, life, and resurrection. I will gladly leave the smelly old life behind as I live in the midst of God's promise.

The LORD is my strength and my shield;
My heart trusts in him, and I am helped.

—Psalm 28:7

You cannot give to another that which you do not have yourself. This is the one basic and universal truth about caring for another. This truth stands above all others. Self-care is imperative for the caregiver.

If you hope to encourage another, you must first have a sense of encouragement. If your wish is to give another a sense of peace, you must first have a sense of serenity. If you want to love another, you must first be a loving person. If you want to share Christ with another, you must first have a relationship with Christ.

It all sounds a bit selfish. Putting self first seems to be dichotomous to Christian teachings. But, think about it. You cannot give to another that which you do not have yourself. We have all seen caregivers who give and give and then give some more. One day the well is empty. There is no more to give. They have failed to replenish their spirits.

If we are to drink first from that well, how do we keep the well flowing?

It begins with self-respect. Knowing you are worthy is the beginning. You matter to God. Your well-being is important to God. And, God has provided all you need to refurbish and recharge your giving spirit.

Having your priorities in order is the next step. Are you a caregiver to be recognized at some annual banquet, or to be asked to stand in a service of worship some Sunday morning to receive a round of applause? Is your goal a long list of service projects in your obituary? Or, is your expectation nothing in return? What are your intentions and your priorities?

Finally, once you have cared for self and assessed your priorities, you need to thank God for positioning you as the giver. Then your heart is in the right place, and you now have all it takes to give to another.

Prayer: This Day I will unashamedly take care of me first. Then, after having carefully looked at my intentions, I will thank God. I expect then to be a difference-maker in another's life.

> *But for the grace of God, there go I.*
>
> —Unknown

As often as "But for the grace of God, there go I" has been quoted, it seems unusual that the original author is lost to the ages.

Those nine words are universal to every human life. Every one of us can point to some near calamity that has happened to us and say, "but for the grace of God." We can admit to some risky behavior when we somehow avoided huge consequence, and say, "but for the grace of God." We can remember some occasion when we were pulled from the chasm of oblivion by some inexplicable force and say once more, "but for the grace of God." Or, we can look upon another's brokenness and say, "but for the grace of God." There is nothing other than God's grace that has sheltered us from certain disaster.

One of our pilgrim forebears, John Bradford, said it this way:

> The familiar story, that, on seeing evildoers taken to the place of execution, he was wont to exclaim: "But for the grace of God there goes John Bradford," is a universal tradition, which has overcome the lapse of time.

These are nine words that cannot be attributed to any one mind. Nine words that every human life can point to and with solemn honesty say, "Right on!" And, as Bradford points out, these are not just universal and explicable; they span all time.

Thus, when God created the world, he must have spent the second week fashioning grace. For grace, like the sun, the moon, the seas, the land, and all creation has been with us from the beginning.

Prayer: This Day I will not take God's grace for granted. I will help myself to a generous portion and give thanks.

You-all means a race or section, Family, party, tribe, or clan;
You-all means the whole connection of the individual man.
—Anonymous, Taken for You-All,
the Richmond Times Dispatch

Some clever wit once wrote:

Xvxn though my typxwritxr is an old modxl, it works wxll xxcxpt for onx of thx kxys. I'vx wishxd many timxs that it workxd pxrfxctly. Trux, thxrx arx forty-two kxys that function, but onx kxy not working makxs thx diffxrxncx. What if our church pxrformxd likx my typxwritxr—not all thx pxoplx working togxthxr propxrly. You might say, Wxll, I'm only onx pxrson. It won't makx much diffxrxncx." But you sxx, a church, to bx xfficixnt, nxxds thx xfforts of xvxry pxrson. Thx nxxt timx you think your xfforts arx not nxxdxd, rxmxmbxr my typwritxr, and say to yousxlf, "I'm a kxy pxrson and thxy nxxd
mx vxry much."

It is easy to say, "I am but one person. What can I do?" You can be a difference maker. The entire gospel is written for the perspective of community. No one person or group of people has all the blessing, all the power and authority, or has a sole monopoly on God's truth. We are a community bound together in the body of Christ. A missing partner in this community is like the typewriter with a missing "E."

In the same manner that one person cannot do it all, neither can a community become all God intended with any piece missing. The wonder of the Good News is not, "Hey, look at what I have done!" The wonder of Christ's church is, "Look at the amazing things God is doing through all of us!"

Prayer: This Day is a day of community-building. Today, as one in Christ, we can be kingdom-builders.

*Unfortunately many Americans live on the outskirts of hope—some
because of their poverty, some because of their color,
and all too many because of both. Our task is to help
replace their despair with opportunity.*
—Lyndon B. Johnson

The story has been told of the major shoe company that sent two salesmen to interior Africa to open new sales territories. A few days after they arrived, one of the salesmen telegraphed a message back to the home office. "I will be returning home on the first available ship. The situation here is hopeless. Everyone here goes barefoot all the time."

It was several days before the second salesman wired the home office. His telegraph was accompanied by an order for fifty pairs of shoes. It read: "Send more shoes at once. Prospects are unlimited. No one here has shoes!"

Poverty is a matter of perspective. So, too, is opportunity. One salesman saw no opportunity; the other saw unlimited opportunity. I once knew a man who said that wealth was largely between your ears. Life does present challenges. And, we can see them as obstacles or as opportunities.

Holding fast to God's will in a world that would prefer to answer to a lesser deity can be understood as opportunity or as insurmountable challenge. Living out one's ministry when your life is already too busy is another. Being of generous heart when the budget is tight is one more example. It is all a matter of perspective. Taking full ownership of what God calls you to do can be understood as too overwhelming, or as one of life's greatest opportunities. It is as my friend says—largely between your ears.

Prayer: This Day I will be cautious about what I label as challenge and what I call opportunity. Today, I will be slow in giving up when the job seems a bit tough.

THE BRIDGE BUILDER

An old man, going a lone highway,
Came at the evening, cold and gray,
To chasm, vast and deep, and wide,
Through which was flowing a sullen tide.
The old man crossed in the twilight dim;
The sullen stream had no fears for him;
But he turned when safe on the other side
And built a bridge to span the tide.

"Old man," said a fellow pilgrim near,
"You are wasting strength with building here;
Your journey will end with the ending day;
You never again must pass this way;
You have crossed the chasm, deep and wide—
Why build you the bridge at the eventide?"

The builder lifted his old gray head;
"Good friend, in the path I have come," he said,
"There followeth after me today
A youth whose feet must pass this way.
This chasm that has been naught to me
To that fair-haired youth may a pitfall be,
He, too, must cross in the twilight dim;
Good friend, I am building the bridge for him."
—Will Allen Dromgoole

T he *Bridge Builder* is a simple reminder that a life well-lived is one
that leaves good evidence of having passed through this world.
Why not build a bridge to ease another traveler's journey today?

Prayer: This Day I will give much thought to whose journey I might
ease. Today, I will not settle for just thinking about it. I
will pick up the tools and begin building.

> *"But I tell you: Love your enemies and pray for those who persecute you, that you may be sons of your Father in heaven."*
> —The words of Jesus as recorded in Matthew 5:44–45

How do you deal with prickly people? Do you avoid them? Do you try to straighten them out? Do you give them a dose of prickly back?

Prickly people cannot be avoided. There are some who seem to delight in bringing a twinge of misery to others. Perhaps their lives are so wretched and laden with misery that they feel some measure of relief in sharing their wretchedness with others (at best a perverse idea). Maybe they do not know any better. They were born into sorrow, brokenness, and hurt and have been losing ground ever since. Maybe prickly people suffer from some profound psychosis. Maybe they are just jerks!

The fact is that we do encounter prickly people along life's way. Having some strategy to cope with prickly people is a must.

Here is what *not* to do:

- Do not try to out-prickly a prickly person. They will only turn up the prickliness.
- Do not try to run away. There is no place to go.
- Do not try converting them. It is a useless cause that will take all your energy.
- Do not preach to them. They have already heard it all.
- Do not sink to their level. They have then won the game.
- Do not try to psychoanalyze. Leave that for the experts.
- Do not try to purchase their affection. You do not have enough money.

So, what is left to do? Pray for them.

Prayer: This Day I will be content to change one person—me. Today, I will lovingly lift my voice for those who annoy me most. I will also pray that I am no one's prickly person.

> *It is a consolation to the wretched to have*
> *companions in misery.*
>
> —Publilius Syrus

John Ray said, "Misery loves company." To have someone who is willing to commiserate with you is a relief. It has a way of validating your sorrow, disagreeing with the injustice, and healing the hurt you bear. To console someone is a noble endeavor. To show sympathy or to genuinely care for another is one's love for another put into action.

Yet, sharing another's misery can be poisonous. Surely you have met someone who says, "I know just how you feel. Let me tell you about the time . . . ." Commiseration may be just a permission slip for someone to parade his or her unresolved hurt. The affection of a fellow pilgrim in pain may be no more than toxic validation.

It is like pigs wallowing together in the same mud hole. When the day is done, both are unrecognizable because they are equally covered in mud. The mud hole has gotten deeper and smells a bit stronger. And tomorrow it will likely invite the same two pigs back to the same hog wallow. Commiseration solves little.

Do we ignore another's hurt? Are we to avoid the downtrodden? Is life's safest strategy one of keeping a safe distance between your healthy self and the forlorn?

Of course not! We are called to be caring people. Our mandate is to engage the world's suffering and do whatever it takes to bring about solace, healing, and hope. We are to love one another. To walk along life's way holding the hand of one who hurts is never easy. The first question is not "Will I walk with one who hurts?" The first question is, "Whose needs are being met in this walk?"

Prayer: This Day I will try to understand the difference between caring and commiserating. Today, I will care for another because I truly care.

*The fool doth think he is wise, but the wise man
knows himself to be a fool.*
—William Shakespeare

A sense of resolve is a virtue. We admire determination. One who sets his or her mind to a task and remains unbent, even when it would make sense to cave in, is our hero. We celebrate those who never sway.

So, what about unyielding resolve when the cause is lost? What do you do when new evidence shows that your cause is not the best choice? What about those times when you feel compelled to change your mind?

Someone once said, "Only a fool never changes his mind."

Here is the conundrum: We applaud resolve, yet we know that stubbornness is no virtue. Perhaps the way through this maze is to be able to separate stubbornness from determination. Stubbornness refuses to look at other possibilities. It becomes a personal matter in which the individual is defined by the issue. Stubbornness is a closed mind. It is a fear-filled agenda that ponders, "What will they think of me if I change my mind?"

Determination weighs the evidence. It is willing to be in constant flux and open to minor tuning if need be. Determination keeps principles and personalities apart. Healthy resolve is brave and does not fear change. It holds truth above popular opinion.

Go ahead. If changing your mind liberates you from looking foolish, then be a fool. Such foolishness lasts only for a moment. Ignorance is forever.

Prayer: This Day I may need a big helping of courage. For today I will make a sincere effort to use my resolve in the best way possible.

*It is only by risking our persons from one hour to another
that we live at all. And often enough our faith . . .
is the only thing that makes the result come true.*

—William James

As winter's sterile beauty gives way to spring's flowers, Patty Hansen's wonderful story about two seeds is a poignant reminder of the price one pays for failing to be a risk-taker.

There were two seeds that lay side by side in the warm, fertile spring soil.

The first seed said, "I want to grow! I want to send my roots deep into the earth and to drink in all that life has to offer. I want to thrust my sprouts through the earth's crust and to reach toward the sky. I want to unfurl my tender buds like banners that announce the arrival of spring. I want to feel the warmth of the sun on my face and the cool of the evening's dew on my petals."

And so, the seed grew.

The second seed said, "I am afraid. If I send my roots into the dark unknown, there is no telling what I might encounter. If I push through the hard soil, I might well find that the world is hostile and dangerous. And, what if a cutworm devours my tender shoots? What then? Perhaps the sun will be scorching rather than inviting. No, it is much better that I remain here where it is safe."

A hen was scratching around the yard one day and saw the tiny seed that chose not to grow. The chicken promptly ate the seed.

Those who refuse to risk and to grow get swallowed up in life.

God calls each of us into the unknown. Make no mistake about it—that can be scary. But, unlike the reluctant seed, we have the unconditional assurance of God's presence and the unyielding support of one another. Fear not, for we are so loved and supported we will never be swallowed up by life.

Prayer: This Day I will take what I might have thought was a risk. However, I know that with God's presence and the support of others, there are no real risks.

*I thank my God every time I remember you. In all my prayers for all of
you, I always pray with joy because of your partnership in the gospel
from the first day until now, being confident of this, that he who began a
good work in you will carry it
on to completion until the day of Christ Jesus*
—Philippians 1:3–6

Gail Mann, Joann Hosetettler, and Morris Meeker are three names
you have likely never heard. History will not record their names.
School children will never have to remember their contribution to
society. There will never be a plaque dedicated to their labors. No
park will be named in their memory. No library will have these three
names over its entrance. Canonization will surely not be their lot.
However, Gail, Joann, and Morris changed the world for me.

"How did they change your world?" you ask.

These two women and one man were my Sunday school teachers.
They opened a new world to me. They told me about God's love, his
mercy, his grace, and his hope for me. They told me how God wanted
me to behave. They gave me a set of life's instructions. They showed
me where to find Deuteronomy and John 3:16. They prayed for me
when I was sick. They sent a postcard when I missed Sunday school.
They put a gold star beside my name when I made an effort to get out
of bed on Sunday morning. They noticed my new shoes. They did not
mention my ragged haircut. They called me by name. They baked
brownies because they were my favorite.

The three did something beyond all that. They told me about Jesus.
And, that changed the world for me—both today and forever.

Take time today to thank the Gails, the Joanns, and the Morrises
who told you about Jesus. It is never too late to tell them that they
changed your world.

Prayer: This Day brings a new sense of gratitude for those who nurtured my spiritual growth. Today, I will say, "Thank you for
telling me about God's love."

For where two or three come together in my name, there am I with them.
—The words of Jesus as recorded
in Matthew 18:20

A story is told about a man who fell away from his faith. He had endured much sorrow. Life had shown its unfairness to him. His wife had died in childbirth. The infant joined her mother in heaven a few days later. The man's crops suffered from drought. Bills piled up. Life had become a long parade of one misery after another. The man's faith began to ebb. "Why me, Lord?" he railed, "What have I done to deserve all of this?"

The man grew bitter. He shook his angry fist at God every waking moment. He became a spiritual recluse. He quit attending worship.

"Who cares about me?" he said. "Surely God does not care, and neither do those who claim to be Christians."

The local pastor visited the man's small cottage one day. He sat in silence as the man heaped ridicule upon him, his God, and his church. The pastor quietly endured the man's wrath, his insults, and his obtuse logic that neither God nor neighbor cared. He wanted the pastor to know he did not need anything the church had to offer and they would not be seeing him this Sunday or any Sunday again.

It was a winter day, and a fire roared in the fireplace as the two men sat at the kitchen table. The pastor stood up, went over to the hearth, and taking a pair of tongs, lifted a bright red ember from the fire and placed it on the hearth. He then sat down at the table in silence.

"So, what is that supposed to mean?" the man asked.

"Oh, I just thought you might like to see how long an ember can glow when it is alone on the hearth and apart from the fire."

The man understood and began his journey back to faith through a caring community.

Prayer: This Day brings me solace because others care. For today I understand that that which is singularly impossible is doable through community.

Ninety Percent of Caring is Just Showing Up
—Title of a book by James R. Kok

Apathy, sympathy, and empathy—the siblings "Pathy." The three "Pathy brothers" sometimes get a bit confusing. They seem to merge with one another. What looks like empathy really is sympathy. When we grow weary of giving sympathy, it can become disingenuous and the result is apathy.

Apathy says, "I don't care." Sympathy says, "I feel sorry for you." Empathy says, "I am with you."

Apathy is never the response of a caring person. Since we are commanded to love one another, apathy is incongruous with caring.

Sympathy is the easiest of the three. Yet strangely, sympathy can be the least productive. Just sobbing with another solves nothing. Where one was hurting, now two are bereaved. How is that helpful? Sympathy also has the curious ability to drain another rather than to restore another's hope and solace. Sympathy may be our first response, but not one that will ever bring healing and restoration.

The tough one of the "Pathy" brothers is empathy. Empathy demands of us to be present, yet apart. It calls for separation, yet togetherness. It invites us into another's brokenness, yet keeps us as a bystander. Empathy is caring without judging. It is support, encouragement, and presence. In the face of crisis, most of us want to say something profound. Empathy asks us to be present and to be still. Empathy says, "I am with you. Lean on me. Together we can move through this." Above all else, empathy takes practice.

Prayer: This Day I pray that my journey will allow me to take another by the hand, to really care, and do it with no expectation of anything in return. Today, I will practice empathy.

> *For we are taking pains to do what is right, not only in*
> *the eyes of the Lord but also in the eyes of men.*
> —2 Corinthians 8:21

The mechanic said, "Ah, what da heck! I'll charge them for a new oil filter and leave in the old one. Who'll ever know?"

The butcher turned the well-aged pork chop over in the meat case and said, "Ah, what da heck! This side still looks okay."

The farmer put a dozen big spuds on the top of the sack at the roadside stand and said, "Ah, what da heck! They'll think they are all that size."

The police officer tore up the ticket and put the $20 bill in his pocket and said, "Ah, what da heck! Who'll ever know?"

The eighth grade algebra test was a doozy. The boy in the third seat of the second row said, "Ah, what da heck! Everybody cheats sometime."

The punch-press operator turned in a phony time card and said, "Ah, what da heck! This company is big enough; they will never notice."

The CEO juggled the books and said, "Ah, what da heck! The bottom line is what counts."

Citizenship matters. How we treat one another makes a huge difference. Ethical behavior is everyone's responsibility. Because a community is the sum total of its individual parts, every individual matters.

Each of us is a community-builder and a difference-maker. We do that one "Ah, what da heck!" at a time.

Prayer: This Day I am wholly responsible, because the tiny part I control makes up the whole. Therefore, I will take my role seriously and carefully consider how my actions shape others.

He got up, rebuked the wind and said, "Quiet! Be still!"
Then the wind died down and it was completely calm.
He said to his disciples, "Why are you so afraid?
Do you still have no faith?"
—The words of Jesus as recorded
in Mark 4:39–40

Does the word "Millennium Force" mean anything to you? It sounds like a video game, an activist group, an action toy like Superman, or the name for a new vitamin that restores hair, memory, and virility. But, if you guessed video game, militant group, action toy, or vitamin, you are wrong—not even close. "Millennium Force" is the name of a new roller coaster that has been installed at Cedar Point. It is the highest (310 feet), fastest (100mph), the longest (1.3 miles), and the steepest (80-degrees) of any roller coaster in the world.

I do not see the point in paying perfectly good money to get scared and sick. Once, my son and I spent half a day deep-sea fishing off the coast of Bar Harbor, Maine. The charter boat captain was delighted and said, "What a day to be fishing!" For myself, I thought that the seas were choppy and rough. The sun beat down on us, there was the stench of old bait, and before the day was over, things got a lot worse! I began to say to myself, "This is almost having too much fun." I learned that day that seasickness is "the gift that keeps on giving!"

When I think about riding something like the "Millennium Force" or a deep-sea charter boat on rough seas, I think about the wisdom of deliberately invoking fear and sickness. Life has plenty of scary moments and rough rides without paying perfectly good money to gain the experience.

It is good to know that faith still calms life's storms—those we choose and those that choose us.

Prayer: This Day may toss me about on the rough seas of life. It may be one of calm and tranquility. Either way, I know my faith is my rudder, my topsail, my compass, and my life jacket.

The true man sings gladly in the bright
day, sings loudly of May—
fair-aspected season.
—John Matthews, "From the
Isles of Dreams"

Today is May Day! The tradition of May Day goes back into the dark recesses of our forgotten past. Many cultures and dozens of religions have honored the coming of summer that is marked by the first day of May. Exactly who first founded this celebration of greenery, new life, and the warming sun is unknown. In many places around the world dancing, feasting, and singing are the only business of this day.

In a number of modern cultures, dowdy cranks have tried to put an end to the celebration of May Day. They label it as pagan and profane. Those somber reformers have not had their way. Youthful exuberance and the sheer delight of this new season will not be silenced. In many cultures, May Day is here to stay.

Have you ever wondered how "Mayday!" became the universal distress signal? A plane is off course and losing altitude and the pilot yells into the headset, "Mayday! Mayday! Mayday!" A ship is lost at sea and the radio operator puts out the universal distress signal: Mayday!

How has the glad celebration of new life become the universal cry for help? Is it easy to type on a telegraph key? Is it because it is linguistically comfortable for many tongues? Is it because is so easy to spell? Why May Day?

How do you see May Day? Is it a disgusting pagan ritual? Is it a cry for help? Or, do you understand it as: Summer at last! Praise be unto God!

Prayer: This Day I will try on the outdoors and celebrate this season of renewal and life. Today, I will bask in the sun, put aside busyness, and try to rediscover my youthful exuberance.

> *. . . it is the wretched taste to be grateful with*
> *mediocrity when the excellent lies before us.*
> —Isaac D'Israeli

It will happen to every one of us some day. In some manner, in some distant time, and in some voice, each of us will be asked, "So, what did you do with the giftedness that I gave you?"

How will you answer that? Will you say:

> "I played it safe. Mediocrity was my motto. I went for the popular. I refused to take risks. I always avoided any conversations that might cause controversy—especially in matters of religion and politics. I did not rob, murder, or lie. I was mostly faithful and dependable. But, all in all, I played it safe. I gladly settled for mediocrity."

How do you think that will play? Do you think mediocrity is what God had in mind when he breathed life into you?

Settling for the norm and the ordinary will be a huge disappointment to our Creator. God has entrusted each of us with particular gifts that he expects will be used. That is why God gave them to you in the first place. God's expectation is for that giftedness to be used lavishly and not stingily. Mediocrity may keep you from failure and disappointment, but it just as surely bars you from the potential God has breathed into you.

Be a bold risk-taker! After all, God sure took a risk on every one of us.

Prayer: This Day is a good day to take a risk for God. When it comes to kingdom building, playing it safe, living to avoid losing, and settling for the ordinary will not do.

Blessed are the peacemakers . . .
> —The words of Jesus as recorded
> in Matthew 5:9

Have you ever noticed a predictable pattern in the words that accompany war? It matters little if the commentator is speaking of Nazi Germany, Cuba, Iraq, Iran, or some terrorist group.

First, an evil leader is at the root of the dilemma. Then there are words like genocide and ethnic cleansing. These are followed by the fact that the oppressor is brutalizing his own people. Women and children are being abused, people are homeless, and hunger and disease reap innocent victims. People are displaced. Hope is a forgotten comfort.

Evil has a pattern. It always begins with an ideology that one, or a few, power-crazed individuals proclaim. It feeds on the smoldering hatred from the past. It gains momentum through old grievances that are either real or imagined. Then it escalates into rage that knows no boundaries. The end result is that nothing is left that is sacred. Human life, dignity, property, and hope no longer have value.

Of all that forfeits value in the time of war, none is greater than the loss of hope. If there is to be hope for the absence of future wars, it does not begin with a prayer that all the Hitlers and the Husseins would instantly vanish from this earth. Evil men and women will come and go. That is out of our control. What is within our control is what we do about the smoldering heap of hatred that nourishes and gives life to evil's insanity. Without hatred, the rhetoric of such evil is no more threatening than a gnat is to an elephant. Although it is easier to point to the world's evil than to take ownership of it, the world will only know peace when the garbage dump of hatred is buried for good. In the vacuum of a world void of hate, evil will shrivel and die, as it should.

So, guess where lasting peace will ultimately begin? It does not begin when the world knows no more despots. It begins with each of us.

Prayer: This Day I will see my role as peacemaker as my most important work. Today, I will do my part in starving my world of hatred.

It is doubted whether a man ever brings his faculties to bear with full force on a subject until he writes upon it.

—Cicero

Old Cicero has it right. Writing does draw one deeper into a subject. When we merely talk about an idea, we can always retract what we said, or we can add to it. Or, we can say, "What I really meant was . . . ." When you write on a subject, it must be exactly what you want to convey to another.

Writing does present some limitations that the spoken word easily conveys. Writing lacks gesture and voice inflection. When you are speaking, you have the added advantage of seeing how your words are being perceived. When you write, you are left to only guess how your thoughts are being heard. You have no sense of audience interaction or reception. For some of us (myself included) spelling is another limitation. Sometimes we have to settle for a $2.00 word when the $10.00 one is phonetically out of reach. Yes, writing does have its limitations.

What about communications in our present time? The proliferation of e-mail and phone conversations, that convey a thought and then vanish into space, clearly changes how we think and communicate. Gone are those wonderfully eloquent letters written by a Civil War soldier in the glow of a wax candle from a rain soaked tent in Gettysburg. There are written words that ooze from the soul and preserve a moment in history for posterity's sake. Today, we just tap out a few words on a computer, and click on "send," and off into space flashes our thoughts—never to be savored again.

If Cicero is right, then we are denying future generations a glimpse of our souls and our deepest yearnings. It keeps silent that which defines our time and celebrates our humanity. The fullness of our thoughts will never be realized. What a tragedy!

Look at what you are depriving yourself of by not writing to a friend and telling him or her how much their friendship has added to your life. Not only will they know how much they mean to you, but by having written on the subject, so too will you.

Prayer: This Day I will write to a friend. I will tell my friend how much their friendship has added to my life. Who knows? Maybe they will write back.

God is my Copilot.
—Author unknown, seen on
a bumper sticker

If God is your Copilot, then you need to change seats! That is how at least one critic sees it. Placing God in a subordinate position or second in command is no place for God. Asking for directions only when needed puts God in the wrong place also. And to press the analogy a bit further, God as your copilot puts him on a lower pay scale than you. God belongs in the Pilot's seat. He is the chief navigator. God is the Captain of the ship. One does have to ask, is copilot any place for God?

The poor soul who coined this zippy bit of wisdom probably never dreamed that he or she was putting God in second place. The intent was to portray God as a companion on your faith journey. It was an innocent way of saying, "God rides with me."

Borrowing from the bumper sticker genre, perhaps one of those signs that say "Baby on Board" could be refitted to say "God on Board." Another possibility is a high performance car that says, "Powered by God." Maybe a "My God is an Honor Student at . . . School." You could even try the political election rhetoric on your bumper, "God in 2004!"

It is always dangerous to push an analogy too far. And it may appear to the reader that the well-intentioned "God is my Copilot" author is getting unnecessary criticism. It is still better that God has a seat in your plane's cabin than left behind.

Prayer: This Day God is pilot, navigator, ground control, and radar beam on my faith journey. Today, I will turn over the controls to God.

*When tempted, no one should say, "God is tempting me." For God cannot
be tempted by evil, nor does he tempt anyone;
but each one is tempted when, by his own evil desire,
he is dragged away and enticed.*

—James 1:13–14

Tom Sawyer stood before Aunt Polly and said, "I don't know why I
done it? I guess the devil made me do it." A century later, comedian Flip Wilson's characterization of Geraldine used the same flawed
theology when she fell to temptation. Neither Tom Sawyer nor
Geraldine had convincing arguments that they were powerless over
Satan's charm.

It is flawed enough to say that Satan draws us into temptation like
reluctant lambs at the slaughterhouse, but to imply that God tempts is
outrageous. God is not in the business of temptation. There is no reason to ever believe that God wants to test your resolve. Never, never,
never would God want to see just how much you could take. There is
no divine reward or medal given for high resolve in the face of temptation.

Consider the husband who loves his wife. Would it make sense for
his wife to suggest that he begin dating another woman just to test his
love for his wife? Of course not! What about a recovering alcoholic?
Would it add quality to his sobriety if he worked as a sober bartender?
Never! Or, what about a cancer survivor? Would a few cigarettes be a
good test to see if his lung cancer was really in remission? Again, it
would be absurd! Yet, none of these is any more absurd than thinking
that God tests us with temptation.

Whoever dreamed up the notion that God delights in testing us
with temptation surely has a puny view of God's goodness and grace!

Prayer: This Day I will take full responsibility of my choices. Today,
I understand that God and I are on the same team.

> *Remember that you ought to behave in life as*
> *you would at a banquet.*
>
> —Epictetus

How do you behave when you are absolutely sure no one is looking?

Is there any part of your conduct that you keep privately tucked away from public scrutiny? Are your anonymous ethics the same as those the world sees?

These are tough and searching questions. They may make you flinch just a bit. However tough they might be, they are nonetheless worth examining.

A young lad took up rough talking on the school playground. He knew exactly how loudly he could utter his obscenities so his peers heard him, but the playground teacher did not. He grew casual with his ugly talk. Words that would never be heard in his home began to lace his playground vocabulary. Soon, three words out of every ten were R-rated, but always said in a voice that was inaudible to the playground supervisor. He left his vulgarity on the playground, and at home he spoke like a perfect little gentleman.

Of course, you can guess that one day the young boy got his language and his place confused and blurted out a mouthful of trash at the supper table. He had lived two lives too long.

The same is true for those who look good in public, but act differently when they are sure that no one is looking. Sooner or later, two lives will be too much. The curious part in all this is that the ugly comes out when least wanted. It is never the good when least needed. Remember the cursing schoolboy? It was not that he had nice things to say on the schoolyard; it was that the ugly within him poured out at the supper table.

Double lives are just too confusing!

Prayer: This Day I will live as if I am on public display. After all, before the One who matters most, I really am never alone.

Nothing true or beautiful or good makes complete sense . . .
—Reinhold Niebuhr

One of America's great growth industries is elective cosmetic surgery. It has become a $9-billon-a-year industry. Now, add to that total the number of people who cannot afford cosmetic surgery. And to that number, add those who may or may not be able to afford it, but fear surgery. There must be a staggering number of people who are unhappy with their appearance.

This is not some new phenomenon, and it surely is not a commentary on the growth of vanity. **We have never liked how we look!**

Think about it. It is not a gender specific idea. Both men and women try to change their looks. We use lipstick, makeup, and shoulder pads. We pierce our bodies in all manner of ways and in all locations with jewelry. We add tattoos, eye shadow, and grow beards. We cultivate a mustache and then we shave it off. Balding men take a thin wisp of hair, let it grow a couple of feet in length, and then swirl it around to make it appear like a full head of hair. We curl, straighten, shave off, color, braid, and spike our hair.

Every culture tries to improve what God has given us. Necks are lengthened. Lips are distorted. Ears are elongated. Heads are shaved, and some are even tattooed. Other body parts are distorted, removed, or enhanced.

We just do not like how we look! The raw self seems to leave something to be desired. It crosses all of human history, every culture, both genders, and all religions.

None of this is serious business. Within the bounds of good taste and the limits of pain, it is really unimportant what we do to add beauty to our physical beings. Much of it washes off, wears off, or grows back, so no permanent damage is done.

Here is what keeps me from experimenting: What if I stand before God and he says, "Who are you? You look vaguely familiar, but . . . ?"

Prayer: This Day I will be me. Today, I will put my self aside and be glad that I am.

May 9

Look to the LORD and his strength; seek his face always.
Remember the wonders he has done . . .

—Psalm 105:4–5

Some wise pundit coined the acronym F.R.O.G. It stands for:

FULLY RELIANT ON GOD

Not to be outdone, another wit added E.D. to F.R.O.G. and now has—

FULLY RELIANT ON GOD EVERY DAY

Probably F.R.O.G. or F.R.O.G.E.D. will never work its way into any mainstream liturgy or denominational worship book. No biblical survey test in any seminary will ever ask for an essay on the Gospel writer John's interpretation of F.R.O.G.E.D. in the postmillennial world. It is not likely that it will show up as one of America's favorite hymns. In fact, most people of faith would be stunned if you asked them if they were F.R.O.G.E.D. On a bad day, such a question might even insult them!

The stuffy opinions of liturgies, seminaries, and hymnists aside, F.R.O.G.E.D. is worth consideration. How about it? Are you fully reliant on God every day? Have you learned the delicate skill of abandoning every aspect of your life to God on a daily basis? Or, is God a T.O.A.D. in your life?

What is a T.O.A.D.?

THERE ONLY AT DISASTER

Which is it for you? Total abandonment every day, or just when times get tough?

Now let's see? S.A.L.A.M.A.N.D.E.R. Wonder what theological nugget we can fashion from that?

Prayer: This Day I will begin honing the daily skill of total abandonment to God. No more of this "just when I need God" will do.

My command is this: Love each other as I have loved you.
—The words of Jesus as recorded
in John 15:12

Our Puritan forebears were a dour lot. Commenting on Puritanism's grim view of life, the Reverend Steven Ware Bailey put it this way:

> The sad genius of Puritanism was living in the constant grip of fear that somewhere, someone might be having fun.

Much of the puritanical moral view was based on an understanding that God was filled with wrath and more than delighted to bring a world of hurt on unrighteous people. These were the people who grew up on the epic sermon Sinners in the Hands of an Angry God! Someone once said that the heart of 18th-century theology could be summed up as, "I am bad and God is mad!"

Tragically, the notion of a God of retribution who is focused on getting even with a world filled with surly brats is still very much alive. The doctrine of human depravity still has its followers. To be honest, when you survey the evil, the crime, and the outrageous behavior that makes the six o'clock news every evening, human depravity is hard to argue against. We are capable of doing bad. But, is God mad?

No. I think God is more sad than mad. God must weep when He sees war. The heart of God must just break when He watches a pristine stream used for a garbage dump. He must feel deep sorrow when a spouse is beaten, a child is ignored, and an elderly person is stuffed away out of sight. God must be sadly perplexed when his sons and daughters are called inferior because of their skin color. God must look at the world's nuclear arsenal, and millions without food and say, "What is going on with my people?" God's heart surely must ache for the man or woman who lives rejected and sick with AIDS. God is sad.

The Puritans thought God was mad and their self-denial would bring about reconciliation. God is not mad. God is sad, and no amount of our drabness is going to cheer him up. What will bring reconciliation? Jesus answered that question—a kinder, gentler, and more loving people.

Prayer: This Day is a good day to begin making the world a gentler and kinder place. I will begin in my little corner.

Praise the LORD.
Give thanks to the LORD, for he is good;
his love endures forever.
Who can proclaim the mighty
acts of the LORD or fully declare his praise?

—Psalm 106:1–2

How do you develop an "Attitude of Gratitude"? Is just "Thanks, God" enough? Or, is there more to an "Attitude of Gratitude" than thanks?

A retired professional football coach was being inducted into the Hall of Fame. He was asked to make a few remarks at a press meeting. The coach said that he was born into a poor family in a tough neighborhood. In order to survive, he had to learn how to out-tough the toughest. He worked hard. He never lost sight of his dream to someday play professional football. His dream came true. He made it to the big leagues! Though his playing career was cut short by injuries, he still wanted to be part of the game. He got that chance as a coach. Again, hard work, determination, never losing sight of his dream, and sheer guts took him to the Super Bowl—not once, but twice. The coach, now retired, summed it all up when he said, "Before you is a self-made man!"

Really?

Mark Twain once said that the person who thinks he is self-made worships a creator who is a fool.

Celebrating our self-made selves leaves no margin for an "Attitude of Gratitude." Living with a profound sense of appreciation demands that our indebtedness is focused outside self. Whom you thank is whom you worship.

Living with an "Attitude of Gratitude" begins by understanding the difference between gratitude and grandeur.

Prayer: This Day will be lived in an "Attitude of Gratitude." I will take time to survey both who I am and *whose* I am.

Adam was but human—this explains it all. He did not want the apple for the apple's sake, he wanted it only because it was forbidden.
—Mark Twain

Temptation is a terrible thing! Forbiddenness adds a degree of mystery. It fuels our wants. It heaps desire on that which is off limits. It is the broth that evil laps up and nourishes its strength within us. The heart of temptation would cease to beat if it were not for forbiddenness.

Twain had it right. It was not the apple for the apple's sake that drew Adam's interest. After all, Adam and Eve lived in a grand orchard. They could have all the pears, oranges, bananas, and pineapples they wanted. But, that big, red, bright, shiny apple was off limits. The fact that it was forbidden is what sent Adam and Eve to the center of the orchard to have their fill of apples.

Adam and Eve's problem was not that they were tempted. Temptation, in and of itself, is not a sin. Giving in to temptation was their downfall. Brokenness and separation are not about temptation. It is when we give life to our off-limit desires through action that temptation becomes real.

Had Adam and Eve just said, "No. We have all we need and more. Heck, we even have fruit we haven't named yet! Thanks, but no thanks. Keep your apples, Satan." If they had just counted the rich blessings God had so graciously given them instead of drooling over the apple.

That was a long time ago. Surely we have learned from their mistake. Haven't we?

Prayer: This Day I will weigh my blessings, and when I still hunger for the stuff that is off limits, I will ask God to make my hunger go away. I think He will understand.

"Watch out that no one deceives you."
—The words of Jesus as recorded
in Matthew 24:4

The following was a whimsical filler published in a newspaper as an attempt to poke fun at the world of scientific research.

WARNING! CARROTS CAN KILL YOU!

Some tongue-in-cheek food safety facts from the Miner Institute in Chazy, New York:

- Nearly all sick people have eaten carrots. Obviously, the effects are cumulative.
- An estimated 99.9% of all people who die from cancer have eaten carrots.
- Another 99.9% of people involved in auto accidents ate carrots within 60 days before the accident.
- Some 93.1% of juvenile delinquents come from homes where carrots are served frequently.
- Among people born in 1839 who later ate carrots, there has been a 100% mortality.
- All carrot eaters born between 1879 and 1899 have wrinkled skin, have lost most of their teeth, have brittle bones, and failing eyesight, if the ills of carrots have not already caused their death.
- Even more convincing is this report from a noted team of medical researchers: Rats force-fed twenty pounds of carrots for thirty days developed bulging abdomens. Their appetites for wholesome foods were destroyed.

It has been some time since I first discovered this research. I am not certain if it still stands or if another well-funded study has shown that broccoli has the same detrimental effects on wellness.

Prayer: This Day I will pay attention to what I call truth. Today, I will feast on God's truth.

The more things change, the more they remain the same.
—Alphonse Karr

Every one of us has an example of something that seems to be new that is really old. The inverse is just as true when we uncover an old truth that is now understood as surprisingly new.

Churches seldom throw anything away. Their archives are often bulging with treasured scraps from the past. Browsing through a large package of dusty old papers of the First Congregational Church, I came across a bulletin for the order of worship for the Sunday school class in 1898.

The bulletin caught my interest in the remarkable change in worship that the last century has produced. Not surprisingly, the language was strictly the King James Version with lots of thees and thys. The order included strict and rigid instructions that clearly meant business. One clause read: "When the bell rings, instant silence and face the piano." The service closes with instructions to "Disperse quietly without signal and be present next Sunday and bring a new scholar." Reading this, I had the sense that woe be unto the worshiper who was only casually committed!

What really intrigued me in this yellowed and brittle bulletin was under the heading entitled "The watchword for 1898." It posed the question: "What Would Jesus Do?" The newest rage in Christendom is the What Would Jesus Do? or W.W.J.D? bracelets. They are seen on believers' wrists from young to old. Just think, we had the W.W.J.D. idea a full century before it swept the nation. I am not sure if this is an old idea that is new again, or a new idea that is very old.

My friend, the late Jack McCoy, said, "We had the idea a hundred years ago. We were just waiting for someone to invent Velcro!"

Prayer: This Day is one more day lived in the lasting truth of God. For in God's truth is the unchanging in an ever-changing world—my rock and my salvation, indeed!

> *Wait for the LORD; be strong and take heart*
> *and wait for the LORD.*
>
> —Psalm 27:14

There are two majestic oak trees that stand in our back yard. They are mature trees that are perhaps three feet across at the stump and maybe fifty feet tall. The two are altogether impressive trees of great worth. Like many of their species, the two oaks keep their leaves until mid winter. When all the other trees have lost their leaves in the fall, it is only then that they begin to drop leaves. When winter reaches its full furry, the two oaks lose their last leaves. It is as if these two gigantic oaks are out of step with nature. While all the other trees rush to autumn nakedness, these two oaks hang on to their leaves.

Then the same out-of-step-with-nature phenomenon takes place again in the spring. When the ash trees, maples, and flowering shrubs have all set their summer foliage, the two oaks still stand in complete starkness. While life breaks out all around them, they stubbornly stand with barren branches that reveal no sign of life.

Then one day in late May, the two trees will begin to come to life. It takes no more than three or four days for them to burst froth with full plumage. It is almost an overnight transformation that takes them from barren branches to full foliage.

I suppose there is a reason for this. Probably some time way back when the world was young, the oak family learned it was not wise to put out leaves when there was still danger of frost. So the great-great-ever-so-great grandmother oak taught her offspring to be patient. The impulsive oaks that paid no heed to patience did not survive. Those who were willing to quietly stand in their winter coats, while the rest of the forest bloomed, found that a lethal frost was no problem. The impetuous lost out to frost, while the quiet and patient lived on and thrived.

In Christ we have that same gentle transformation. The psalmist says, "Be patient and wait for the LORD."

Prayer: This Day I will patiently wait on that great transformation that God is working in my life.

Be still and know that I am God.

—Psalm 46:10

My brother, Curtis, is an interesting man. He may well be the best self-educated person I have ever known. He can speak with some degree of intelligence on nearly any subject one might suggest. An electrical engineer by trade, he is a skilled cabinetmaker, a fine wood carver, and a glasscutter. He has a rich knowledge of baseball trivia and Sherlock Holmes minutiae. His particular interest is history. He can name the Confederate generals who fought at Shiloh (he can even tell you what Shiloh means in Hebrew). Curt has an inquisitive mind that is always exploring some new and likely unusual subject. For Curt, the more oblique and obscure a thing might be, the better it is to explore.

Quite to my surprise, Curt's new passion is the Dead Sea scrolls. He reads every archeological abstract and article he can find on the subject. Some of his Dead Sea scroll research has become surprisingly technical and scholarly.

However, Curt's pursuit of knowledge is not always too scholarly. He is an avid reader of those tabloid magazines you find at the checkout counter at the grocery store. I once asked him why it was that a man who could quote from Homer's *Iliad* would sully his mind with checkout counter pulp trash?

His answer was swift, direct, and disarming. He said, "Sometimes you just need some chewing gum for your mind!"

Maybe we are all in need of some chewing gum for our minds. Perhaps we need a lighter fare that asks fewer questions and listens with deeper intensity. Perhaps that is what the psalmist had in mind when he wrote: "Be still and know that I am God."

Prayer: This Day I will practice stillness before God. Today, I will deliberately separate myself from the noise, the questioning, and the bewildering pursuit for answers. Today, I will be still.

Be still before the LORD and wait patiently for him.

—Psalm 37:7

Karl Marx once said that religion is an opiate for the masses. That is both insulting and wholly untrue. The sole function of an opiate is to act as a mind-numbing drug to temporarily lift one out of the ugliness of life. Opiates feed escapism. One's love for God is not a trivial matter that merely lifts the believer into the numbness of perfect bliss. An opiate may induce ecstasy, but unlike faith, it never calls to action, empowers, gives hope, affirms, or heals a broken spirit.

Opiates lead to destruction. Faith leads to wholeness. Opiates lead to the gutter or the grave. Faith guides one on a path that goes in a different direction. Marx may have understood the importance of how a society organizes its wealth and economy, but he was sorely misinformed about religion.

However, it is not to say that every opiate has a pharmaceutical foundation. Any overindulgence that numbs the mind is an opiate. Work can be an opiate. So too can sex, gambling, food, and alcohol. And, carried to an extreme, even religion can be added to the list of overindulgences.

Some opiates are not destructive. A diversion that quiets one's spirit like a vacation, a morning walk, a good novel, a day spent at an art museum, or an afternoon at the ballpark brings quiet to the soul. There are countless ways that a sense of serenity and calm lift us out of the drudgery of life. Call these respites opiates if you will.

Of course, the dilemma is that serenity needs continued maintenance. The vacation will end. The morning walk will not last for the day. The novel will be passed on to a friend or put back on the shelf. The art museum will lock its doors at six o'clock. And, the last out in the ninth inning will empty the stands. The inherent weakness of opiates is that they never last.

That is the main difference between faith in God and any other place to seek solace—it is without end.

Prayer: This Day I seek solace, hope, peace, and tranquility. Today, O Lord, my soul turns to you for respite.

*Show me your ways, O LORD, . . . guide me in your
truth and teach me, for you are God my Savior,
and my hope is in you all day long.*

—Psalm 25:4

An old prospector packed his saddlebags and set off for the far west with his donkey. They trudged over the vast stretches of prairie land as days turned into weeks, and weeks turned into months. Finally, one day the prospector approached the Grand Canyon. He stopped and tiptoed up to the edge of the great canyon and stood in awe. There before him, a mile wide, eighteen miles long, and hundreds of feet deep was one of the most spectacular geological formations on earth.

The prospector turned to his donkey and said, "Whoa! Somethun' must'a happed here!"

If years from now a future traveler were to pass through your community, would there be evidence that something must have happened here? Has God's hope and truth taken root through you?

Prayer: This Day God's truth and hope will guide my path. Today, his lasting goodness is my compass.

*If there is anything that we wish to change in the child, we should first
examine it a see whether it is not something
that could better be changed in ourselves.*

—Carl Jung

Leo was an angry man. He began life as a complainer, nurtured his complaining into paranoia, and then became just angry. He was sullen, bitter, and prone to fits of rage. Leo kept his sharp tongue well honed. He was thoroughly disliked. Leo's neighbors avoided him as much as possible. He had accused almost every one of them of some imagined grievance. He ridiculed, belittled, and alienated his entire community. All in all, Leo was one of God's lesser victories.

One spring day, Leo was the victim of a serious farming accident. He would live, but there would be snow on the ground before Leo could expect to be out of his body cast. The situation only exacerbated Leo's bad humor.

On a Saturday morning in May, two dozen of Leo's neighbors formed a work bee. The very ones Leo had ridiculed, the ones he had insulted, and the men he had accused of all manner of grievances were there. They brought their tractors and implements to Leo's farm and in less than twelve hours fallow ground was turned into freshly planted cornfields. For that one day, the farmers forgot Leo's bad nature. One of their number needed help, and as despicable as Leo had been, the farmers put it all aside on that day in May.

Leo's wife rolled his cot onto the front porch. He lay there silently, wrapped in a woolen blanket, and watched the dust roll off the army of tractors as they went back and forth across his fields. Finally, the last furrow was turned, the last seed fell, and the dust settled. The last tractor drove past the old farmhouse porch where Leo's cot had been placed. The last farmer waved to Leo and drove on.

Leo wept that day. Leo changed that day. In fact, the whole neighborhood became a better place that day.

Prayer: This Day may bring a chance to live beyond the ordinary. Maybe today will be the day God can work through me to give another a glimpse of his goodness. I will gladly and quietly be ready to be an agent of his change.

We are therefore Christ's ambassadors, as though God were making his appeal through us.

—2 Corinthians 5:20

Working one summer as a hospital chaplain trainee, I met many people who were in the midst of crisis. Every evening when I came to work, there would be a list of those who were to have surgery the next day. My job was to visit each of them the night before surgery. Their concerns, their fears, their unresolved commitment, and their sense of hope and confidence were the object of my visit. I would always ask them for permission to pray with them. Some were delighted. Some were lukewarm. A few—a very few—flatly refused to allow me to pray. They just said, "No!" I learned to take no personal offense at those who said, "No!"

One man who said, "No!" stands out in my memory. He was to have a leg amputated the next morning. He was lying in the bed with a blank, frozen stare. I introduced myself, "Good evening Mr. . . . , I'm Chaplain Jones from Pastoral Care. I understand you are having surgery in the morning. Can I help in any way?"

Without taking his eyes off the ceiling, the man said, "Get the "H" out of here. And take your Christian hypocrisy with you. Here I am with my right leg rotting off and you want to tell me how nice Jesus is. Well, take your Bible and get your blankety-blank self out of here! I have seen enough religion in my life, and I sure as "H" don't need any now." I left. The next morning I learned that the man had died in surgery. Even though he had ripped me apart, I was deeply saddened.

What had made the man so bitter? I'll never know. I can only guess that somewhere, sometime, he had seen, or believed he had seen, the church of Christ say one thing and act in another manner. He believed the words and actions of the church were a mismatch. I can only assume that the man died hating Christ. For that I am truly saddened.

We are ambassadors of Christ. Be aware that it is an awesome responsibility.

Prayer: This Day I pray that my example of living for Christ leads another to have some of the inexplicable peace that he gives. Today, I will take my ambassadorship seriously.

> *But his delight is in the law of the LORD and*
> *on his law he meditates day and night.*
>
> —Psalm 1:2

As a young man, one of my favorite ways to spend a Saturday afternoon was to visit Ray Gallup's wood shop. Ray was a cabinetmaker who did not like to be bothered when he was working. But, on Saturday afternoon, he shut off the lathe, the planer, and the saw and swept up the shop. It was a time and place for the men of the neighborhood to gather for a cup of coffee.

The men would sit around the wood stove and talk about weather, crops, the markets, and politics. Ray had a big pot-bellied-wood stove that he kept well stoked with scraps from his shop. A coffee pot had simmered on that stove all day long. I do not think that anyone ever made a fresh pot of coffee in that old graniteware coffee pot. When it got weak, Ray just added more coffee grounds. When it was too strong, he added some more water. When you drank a cup of that coffee you knew you had had a cup of coffee!

Though few of these men had much formal education beyond high school, they were well read and had years of experience as quiet observers of life.

I like to think that some of my most cherished informal education took place in Ray's wood shop. He, and others like him, taught me the wonder of story. These men were master storytellers who knew how to pick the right words and how to use them sparingly. They could paint the canvas of your mind with word images. Their well-crafted tales danced across the theater of the mind with grace, beauty, humor, and truth. These men had a wondrous storehouse of stories.

There was a bit of wisdom, as succinctly said as I have ever heard, at one of those gatherings in Ray's shop. It is one I have never forgotten. Old Ray sat by the fire on a nail keg as he took a long pull on his pipe and thoughtfully said, "You know, I've been thinking. Congress has labored for two centuries making laws. They have written more laws than any library in the world could hold. All that ink just to sum up what the Ten Commandments said 3,000 years ago. Why don't they send all the politicians home and all of us just agree to live by the Ten Commandments?"

Prayer: This Day will have meaning if I live simply and faithfully. I can complicate it or I can live in simple truth. Today, I will choose simple.

> *Those who cannot remember the past are*
> *condemned to repeat it.*
> —James Robinson

You and I were born into a world that had an enormous pool of collected wisdom. We are the heirs of centuries of laws, manners, art, culture, and literature. Each generation has added to the collective body of wisdom—some more than others.

What must it have been like in the beginning? Do you suppose Adam said to Eve, "Look Eve, I have this funny, white, roundish thing. I think I will call it an egg. Maybe we can eat it."

"Where did it come from, Adam?"

"I got it out of a bird's nest."

"No, I mean where did it come from before it was in the bird's nest?"

"Well, Eve, maybe you don't want to know where it really came from."

Or, what about the first person who tasted rhubarb? Can you imagine biting down on a big stalk of rhubarb and saying, "Wow! That will make great pie!"

We are all the beneficiaries of collective wisdom. Each one of us is responsible for keeping a piece of it alive and hopefully adding a minor contribution to the pool. A familiar cliché says, "You do not have to reinvent the wheel." But, we do run the risk of being wheel inventors if we are not good keepers of wisdom.

What could you tell your child or grandchild today that would keep him or her from having to re-invent, re-discover, or in learning, might feel a twinge of pain? What wise treasure do you have to pass on to another? What will really matter to them in their life's journey?

Prayer: This Day I will use to pass on a bit of wisdom. Knowing fully well that each generation has to make its discoveries and its mistakes, I will not legislate or demand. I'll just gently encourage.

Live Simply so that Others May Simply Live
—Seen on a bumper sticker

What price do you extract from creation? What does it cost to keep you?

Those are tough questions that none of us could ever calculate. Trying to discern our share of the world's resources that belongs on our tab is incalculable. The true cost of water, highways, steel, rubber, wood, petroleum, and thousands of other resources are not within our grasp. Compounding the dilemma is the fact that many of these resources are not replaceable. So, trying to reckon what each of us extracts from creation is unfathomable.

This is for certain: We Americans use a disproportionate amount of the world's resources. It stands to reason that we would eat the biggest piece of the pie, because we have more roads, more automobiles, and more of everything else than the rest of the world. That is nothing that should cause shame. Beating ourselves up about our rich blessing is a useless bruise to bear.

Do you remember when you were a child and your father or mother told you to eat your cauliflower because there was a starving child somewhere in the world who would be delighted to have that much cauliflower? Of course, by the time the U.P.S. deliveryman got the cauliflower to Afghanistan or to the Congo, it would no longer be palatable (as if cauliflower ever were palatable to a child).

Though the cauliflower example is a weak argument for world hunger, it still holds a nugget of truth. Every one of us could use less. It will not necessarily feed the starving. Our self-sacrifice may only stretch the world's oil supply by a few years. And, our feeble efforts may only be a token in a world with more than six billion gluttonous appetites for affluence. True, our singular conscientious efforts to use less may make little difference. The easy response is, "Who cares?"

God does, and so, too, do the unborn!

Prayer: This Day I will gratefully use my portion, but not more than what is due me.

*Consistency, Perseverance, and Questioning are
the three requisites of spiritual life.*
—Caitlin Matthews

You have likely met a "spiritual shopper" along life's way. A spiritual shopper is one who is always in search of a new and more satisfying spiritual journey. They long for the path to real truth. They have read all the books in Barnes and Noble's self-help department. They follow every new guru who claims to have found the well of human bliss. Spiritual shoppers have attended every church in the community, they have tried the diets, done the meditations, chanted the chants, and read the tracts. Still, their spiritual quest goes unsatisfied.

Consistency matters, because consistency fosters growth. Suppose you had a serious operation—maybe a heart bypass. During the early post-surgery days, you would be fed clear liquids and Jell-o. Then, some soft foods would be slowly introduced over a few days. Finally, you are back on a regular diet. Spiritual shoppers want the full course and want it now. No wonder they choke, get confused, or fail to grow. Spiritual growth begins in the beginning and sticks to it. Spiritual growth demands consistency.

That is what Jesus was teaching when he said, "If anyone says to you, `Look, here is the Christ!' or, 'There he is!' do not believe it. For false Christs and false prophets will appear and perform great signs and miracles to deceive even the elect—if that were possible. See, I have told you ahead of time" (Matthew 24:23–25).

If you are waiting for a better prophet, a more capable Savior, or a wiser teacher of truth than Christ, you will wait until eternity. Consistency matters.

Prayer: This Day will be lived in consistency, not because I fear change or think there is a better and softer way. It is simply because a steady diet of consistency nourishes my soul best.

*Be joyful always; pray continually; give thanks in all circumstances, for
this is God's will for you in Christ Jesus.*

—1 Thessalonians 5:16–18

Perseverance matters. The spiritual quest demands perseverance in prayer, meditation, and study. It asks us to stay connected when life is at its finest. It asks the same connectedness when life is like camping at a garbage dump. Perseverance means that we stick to our faith in two important times—when we want to, and when we do not want to.

Perseverance on our spiritual quest may mean to keep doing what is working. It may also mean to keep searching when what we are doing is not working. It asks us to press on when our soul is exhausted. It moves us to acknowledge the author of our solace in life's sweet moments. It nudges us to pray when we are too tired, to be cheerful when we are weary, and to be grateful for companionship when life goes awry.

Paul says to pray continually. He was well aware that this means praying on our good days and on not-so-good days. The world's spiritual giants have one attribute in common—they learned how to keep on keeping on. Perseverance matters.

Prayer: This Day I will press on. No matter what it brings, be it one of life's sweet moments or smelly times, I will keep on keeping on.

The life which is unexamined is not worth living.

—Plato

Alongside constancy and perseverance, our faith journey demands that we learn how to question.

Questioning is not of the rhetorical sort or the doubting type. Rather, spiritual questioning is like taking an inventory. It asks, "Am I on the right track?" "Are my motives pure?" And, "Are my prayers prayed and my life lived a good match?"

Questioning is not easy. It is not for the timid or the lukewarm. Ruthless and honest questioning takes courage. The safest and easiest way through life is to never do a self-analysis. Avoiding a critical and searching look at self may be the most comfortable track, but surely not one designed for growth.

If questioning is like taking an inventory, the results can never be completely negative. When a merchant inventories his stock, he has both assets and debits. Too often we opt for the harshly critical in our self-examination and only see our faults. Such is not true questioning.

So, how about it? How does your faith journey go? Is it on track? Are your words and your actions congruent? Have you chosen this path for the right reasons?

One other dilemma with an introspective self-examination—only the asker can answer.

Prayer: This Day brings an uncomfortable task. For today I am taking a fearless and searching inventory of my faith journey. I will need a good measure of courage and honesty that only God can give.

Delight yourself in the LORD; and he will give you the desires of your heart. Commit your way to the LORD; trust in him and he will do this.

—Psalm 37:4–5

There is a huge difference between commitment and contribution. The next time you sit down to a breakfast of ham and eggs, remember that the chicken made a contribution, while the hog made a commitment.

Commitment has a permanent aspect about it that contribution lacks. The chicken gets another chance the next day to make a contribution, but it is a one-shot deal for the hog. Commitment requires selflessness. The hog held back nothing, but the chicken has lots more eggs to give on another day.

Commitment reaches deeply into the core of our being and brings forth the best in us, because selflessness is at its heart. It cannot be written off on our taxes. It cannot easily be withdrawn. It asks more of us than easy, comfortable, and painless support.

I once was a visitor on two consecutive Sundays at different churches of the same denomination. One was in a rather depressed neighborhood. They asked for volunteers to help at the homeless-shelter kitchen. They needed dish washers, servers, clean-up help, and people who were willing to peel potatoes. Many hands were raised when asked for help. The next Sunday we attended a church in a more affluent neighborhood. Under the announcement section in the church's bulletin was a request for help for the local homeless shelter. It said, "Please make your tax-deductible checks payable to . . . ."

One asked for commitment and one begged for a contribution.

Prayer: This Day I will make my contribution, and hopefully it will be solidly grounded in commitment. Today, I will try to set aside self. Knowing that this is not going to be easy, I will need lots of God's help.

He will endure as long as the sun, as long as the moon,
through all generations.

—Psalm 72:5

Have you ever stretched out on the grass on a summer evening and looked at the stars? On a clear night there is a staggering number of celestial dots. If you squint real hard, even the tiniest specks seem to gather light. You cannot help noticing that some stars form a pattern. Every school child can recognize Orion's Belt or the Big and Little Dippers. The North Star is easy enough to find. But, for the casual observer, most of the heaven's constellations are just pinholes in the night's sky. They dazzle us. They draw us into an almost hypnotic spell, and yet always remain a mystery.

Humankind has long been interested in stargazing. Our great-great-ever-so-great-grandparents spent countless hours studying the stars, the planets, and the moon. They knew about tides and seasons and when it was best to hunt, fish, or plant seeds just by looking at the heavens. One generation told the next what to look for in the sky. That generation passed it on to the next, and to the next. They drank in the mystery of the great celestial dance across the evening spans above them.

Today, we can predict within seconds the exact time a comet will streak across the sky. We know about eclipses, meteors, and cosmic orbits. We have named a thousand—maybe tens of thousands—of stars. We have tide tables that are specific to every port. We have it all down.

Right?

Not really. We can accurately predict, but we are still in our infancy as we ponder the mystery. Knowing when the next lunar eclipse will come is not the same as knowing who put the moon in the sky. We still stretch out in the grass on a summer's night and wonder. In part, that is what it means to be human.

Prayer: This Day I will ponder. Knowing fully well that I do not have to solve the mystery in order to believe, I will delight in believing, and continue to find joy in wondering.

For you have been my hope, O Sovereign LORD, my confidence since my
youth. From birth I have relied on you;
you brought me forth from my mother's womb.
I will ever praise you.

—Psalm 71:5–6

Shelly and Mark were young, ambitious and very much in love. They shared a passion and a dream. Mark's father had died and left his son a run-down and much-neglected dairy farm. Shelly and Mark struggled with the idea of quitting their jobs and rebuilding that dairy. It would not be easy. There would be many sacrifices along the way. Maybe, it was just a foolish idea. Maybe the dream and the passion they shared was really their calling.

Eventually they made up their minds that they must follow that dream. Shelly quit her job and worked full time—and then some—on the farm. Mark continued to work in the shop nights and farmed days. Sleep was a luxury they seldom allowed themselves. The young couple had the usual challenges one would expect. There were the usual uncertainties with the weather, markets, and disease. Mark and Shelly struggled for years, but eventually they made a sound business out of what was once a miserable failure.

Was the secret to their success hard work? Not really. Lots of people work just as hard. Was it managerial brilliance? No. They were bright enough, but no brighter than many. Was it good luck? No, it was more than luck. In fact, what made these two a success was more than hard work, brains, and luck.

Mark and Shelly never compromised their sense of hope. Never underestimate the power of hope.

Prayer: This Day I will cherish my most precious possession—my sense of hope. For when I am armed with hope, nothing is beyond my ability.

. . . and whoever lives and believes in me will never die.
—The words of Jesus as recorded
in John 11:26

It was a Saturday in May a long time ago. I was a member of a Cub Scout pack that had taken on a community-service project. A couple of dozen of us were raking a neglected and unkempt cemetery. We were giving the old cemetery a Memorial Day sprucing up. As I was raking among the weathered stones, I saw a marker I have never forgotten. I cannot remember the name of the deceased, but the message has never left my mind. Chiseled in the granite stone were these words:

1846–1856
Died going west

Of course, the fact that the lad who lay beneath that stone was my age added to the mystery. But, the words "Died going west" have long haunted me. How did the boy die? Was it an accident? Drowning? Diphtheria? Cholera? Typhoid? Had he been born frail and the trip was too much for him? And, where had he come from? The Ukraine? Ireland? New York? Where was his family going? California? Kansas? Illinois? Or was their notion of west somewhere near Kalamazoo? Those three words—*Died going west*—have been the yeast of much wonder.

We can only speculate about the lad, and many questions will forever go unanswered. One thing is certain: his parents never returned to his grave. The first crop they planted in the Midwest prairie soil was their own seed—their ten-year-old son. How a mother's heart must ache from leaving behind a child whose grave she would never visit again. The father must have felt that he left part of himself behind in an unfamiliar place. As a parent, I cannot imagine the grief of leaving a child behind.

Over the years, I have given much thought to that family who passed through my hometown a hundred years before my time. As Memorial Day draws near, I think about those three words—*Died going west*. The comfort I find is knowing that the Good News of Jesus Christ has turned our "left behind" into "gone ahead."

Prayer: This Day I pray that all the sorrow others bear in those who have been *left behind* will be celebrated as *gone ahead in Christ.*

Children begin by loving their parents; as they grow older they judge them; sometimes they forgive them.

—Oscar Wilde

Today marks a special day in my life. It was on this date I first became a father. My daughter's birthday is not a red-letter day on most calendars (save a few in our family). Yet, as any parent knows, it marks an important passage in my life.

The most important and lasting mark we will ever make on this world is our contribution to the gene pool. That surely does not mean that all other toil is useless or trivial. It means that a part of us now spans the bridge of time. We have joined the parade of generational perpetuity.

It is a bit strange that the most important contribution to our species is also the one for which we are the least prepared. Unfortunately, children do not come with an instruction book. The best we have is to copy the model our parents gave us. Here is the rub: the model our parents passed on to us now has many pages of addendums that roughly fall into a category called "what I will never do when I am a parent."

So, we take our flawed model, with its addendums, and a few ideas we saw on Oprah Winfrey, and we try to be good parents. Of course, our children almost immediately begin to write their own addendums and borrow from other contemporary sources. The net result is that we all somehow manage to keep the species moving along the trail of human endeavor.

What may be the most satisfying to any parent is to quietly watch your child as a parent. You know the pitfalls. You already know the addendums they have scrapped. And you, as silently as possible, watch another generation get out the indelible ink and begin to write about your child—"When I am a parent, I will never . . . ."

Cheer up, dear child of mine, for one day you, too, will be so blessed as to quietly watch your children's children fumble with the most important job they will ever have. Isn't God a trusting soul?

Prayer: This Day make me worthy of the greatest trust you have ever placed in me—my role as a parent. Today, help me to lovingly care for one of yours.

> *Now faith is being sure of what we hope for and certain*
> *of what we do not see.*
>
> —Hebrews 11:1

We will call him Peter. He was not the Peter who entered the empty tomb on that first Easter morning; rather he was another Peter who lived twenty centuries later. Peter was a mechanical engineer—one of the best. Somehow Peter survived some of the fiercest Nazi bombing of WWII. He was an officer in the British Royal Air Force that was stationed on Malta. Some have called the RAF on Malta "the Forgotten Few." There was no way for the British to supply those brave men. They were obliged to endure without food, medicine, or supplies of any sort for many months. Peter once said there were no rats and no garbage cans on Malta. Somehow he survived.

In his early thirties, Peter was attending graduate school in Montreal. He noticed some health problems that were later diagnosed as a disease that would one day completely debilitate his entire body. Peter had Multiple Sclerosis. Peter's dream was to be an engineer, and he was not about to let some nervous disturbance stop him.

It was a time when our society in general, and big business in particular, had little compassion for hiring the physically challenged. Peter kept his MS a secret and overcompensated in other areas.

In spite of his physical challenges, Peter became the head of Research and Development of one of America's "Big Three" automakers.

An uncompromising sense of hope knows no limits.

Prayer: This Day is limitless because it is lived in hope. Today, the certainty of what cannot be seen is still very real in hope.

*God made him who had no sin to be sin for us, so that in him we might
become the righteousness of God.*

—2 Corinthians 5:21

Marble season is a special time of the year. Many marble seasons ago, I worked out a trade with a classmate, Burton Wilder, for a huge, massive, red, white, and blue-striped boulder. It was as big as a baseball. It must have weighed a pound and a half. I had never seen such a magnificent marble before. I was mesmerized by its size and color. It had a few dings in it. It was not perfect, but it was perfectly magnificent

I traded my mostest, specialist, bestest-ever marble for the big boulder. Actually, it was worse than that. I traded three steelies, three cat's eyes, and these three crystal boulders, plus my bestest boulder for it. Ten marbles for just one.

I was delighted. I put my newly acquired marble in my desk. Over the next hour and a half, I found reason after reason to lift the lid of my desk just to look at that beautiful lunker. I could not wait for the next recess so that I could show off my new lunker. Recess came and I casually rolled it out in a game of "take away, no nothings." My opponent was the best shooter in the entire school. The big lunker made an easy target for him. He pulled out his very best steelie boulder and whap! He hit my newly acquired lunker dead center. The chipped up beauty split right down the middle. Right then was when I wished I had been alone, because I wanted to bawl, but not in front of my classmates.

I had made a mighty poor exchange. I had traded off ten good marbles for a chipped up, half cracked old lunker. Worse than that, it now lay in two half-round pieces like a melon sliced by a Samurai sword. I had made a mighty poor exchange.

Paul talks about the great exchange and how Christ exchanged our brokenness for reconciliation. It is good to know that life's most important exchange cannot be broken, withdrawn, or destroyed.

Prayer: This Day I will fully recognize what it took to exchange my brokenness for salvation. It is a new game today because Christ traded his unblemished life for my chipped and broken life.

For God so loved the world that he gave his one and only Son, that whoever believed in him may have eternal life.
—The words of Jesus as recorded in John 3:16

My early religious formation included a lot of tough preaching. Week after week, with a smug look on his face, the preacher would give us a checklist of ways we might have shown our rottenness. I suppose it was good for us, and he meant to help us get out of a state of denial.

He would ask, "Did you say anything hurtful to another this week?" Usually I did pretty well in that department.

"Did you steal from another?" No! Hey, I'm doing ok!

"Did you kill, covet, or use the Lord's name in vain?" Well, the kill and covet was no problem, but there was that once . . . that shouldn't count.

"Did you have one—yes, even one—lustful thought this week?" Oops! This 16-year-old might be in trouble here.

Then there was the grand finale—the one question that was the clean-up hitter that drew in all of us who had managed to slip through the "Rottenness Test." With an even smugger look, he would ask, "Was there any place you could have done more?" That did it. Between the 16-year-old lust and "could have done more," I was as rotten as the rest of them. There was no question that I was rotten and I ought to be ashamed.

One day we called a new pastor to our little church. Pastor Tom Alston stepped out from behind the pulpit, stretched out his arms, and the first words that came from his mouth were, "I want you to know that you are very special in the eyes of God."

That was the end of the "Rottenness Test."

Prayer: This Day I know God loves me. Even when I miss the mark, God still loves me. Why? I do not have to know why, he just does.

A little more than kin, and less than kind.
—William Shakespeare

My family has not produced a resident hero. We had no General Jones at Gettysburg. We have no big league slugger or a minor league grounds keeper. No Jones in the White House, the Senate, the Congress, or the Supreme Court. We have not produced county commissioner or township supervisor. We are not a bunch of abysmal failures; we are a family that longs for a resident hero.

We have brushed with greatness a couple of times. My Scottish grandmother had a sister who married an English aristocrat. The couple served the royal crown in India. I grew up hearing the stories of my great uncle Jim and aunt Meg and their lavish lives as servants of the king in the land of Gandhi.

It was years later, while studying humanities in college, that it dawned on me: My uncle Jim was one of the 20,000 Englishmen who enslaved 20 million Indians. My brush with greatness was just flushed down the toilet of human dignity and the cause of freedom. Good old uncle Jim was a good guy, but he had his fingerprints on the worst sort of imperialism.

I was crushed, but I still had hope. I still had my connection with the Texas patriot, Sam Houston. Sam Houston shared my grandmother's family name. He was a distant cousin many times removed. Sam Houston was an authentic and undisputed American hero. Old Sam would never enslave the people of India. No one could take that away from my heritage. But, once again my search for a family hero ended in disappointment. I read a couple of Sam Houston biographies that pointed out that good ole Sam Houston were a fierce patriot and a defender of Texas freedom. He was also a womanizer, a drunk, and an opportunist of the most unfavorable sort. Darn it, Sam! You let me down! You destroyed my last vestige of hope for having a hero in my pedigree.

My hope was to have a hero, and all I got was flawed folks. That sad fact is probably true for most us.

Prayer: This Day I will take ownership of my flawed self. Today, I will hand the remnant of my flawed soul to the only One who can truly mend it.

The greatest of faults . . . is to be conscious of none.
—Thomas Carlyle

Old Bill had done it all—or so he said.

"Braseball? I came this close to making it to the Phillies when I blew my arm. If it hadn't been for the pitching coach, I would have made it."

"Gold? I panned gold in the Yukon. Came this close to striking it rich. If it hadn't been for my partner who cheated me, I would have been a rich man."

"Banjo? I was on my way to playing at the Grand Old Opry, when my agent ran off with the female vocalist."

"Race cars? I was on my way to Indy when my head mechanic turned up the fuel pump and I blew an engine."

At the supper table one night I said, "Old Bill sure has had a life. He almost made it to the big leagues, he panned gold in the Yukon, he played the Banjo, and he just about drove in the Indianapolis 500."

My dad said, "Did Old Bill tell you that?"

"Yes."

"Let me tell you about Old Bill. He has never been out of Lenawee County except for the time he went to Detroit during the war for an Army physical, which he flunked."

My heart sank. I said, "But, Dad. Old Bill said he had done all those things!"

"Well, son, you know now why they always call him "Bologna Bill!"

Old Bill was a masterful liar. But there was something else hidden in his made-up stories: He always blamed someone else for his failures. Life's disappointments were always someone else's fault. And that is the saddest story of all.

Prayer: This Day will see no blaming. Today, I live beside my disappointments.

"Do not be afraid."
—The words of Jesus as recorded
in Revelation 1:17

Fear is a mixed bag. Fear can be healthy, unfounded, toxic, life saving, destructive, or helpful.

My grandmother lived in an old farmhouse that had a wood and coal furnace that was just one size smaller than a Pittsburgh blast furnace. It could take a whole log. There was a register in the first story floor just above this mammoth furnace. That register would get hot! I well remember tripping on the carpet and falling on that register. I had branded into the palms of my hands: CHILOTHEE IRON AND FURNACE WORKS. I feared the register, and you can bet I walked around it at a safe distance after that day.

That was *good fear*. It was a healthy respect of something that could harm me. A recovering alcoholic has a healthy fear of taking that first drink. The gambling addict has a healthy fear of placing that first bet. The diabetic has a healthy fear of chocolate cake. The easily tempted has a healthy fear of being in the wrong place at the wrong time. More than one potential criminal has been kept straight for fear of being caught. Did you ever notice how your driving improves when you look in the rear view mirror and see a State Police cruiser following you? It has a way of keeping you honest. Good fear can preserve life.

Of course, there are unfounded fears and fear that cripples your resolve. Fear can destroy dreams and potential. Fear is a two-edged sword that cuts both ways. The world can be a fear-filled place. And it is hard to argue that some fear is toxic and some fear is healthy. Strangely, the greatest fear of all often goes unseen and completely unnoticed. It is the fear of complacency. It is forgetting who you are and whose you are.

Fear little that life brings to your door. But, do fear forgetting to invite God in.

Prayer: This Day is going to be lived fearlessly. Today, I will sort out that which cripples my spirit and that which keeps me safe. I will opt for the safe and reject the fear that destroys.

I praise you because I am fearfully and wonderfully
made; your works are wonderful,
I know that full well.
—Psalm 139:14

June is National Dairy Month. So, it is fitting that at least one day begins with a cow story.

One spring day two cows were grazing in a lush pasture adjacent to a busy highway. As they were munching along, they heard the roar of a big diesel semi tractor speeding down the highway. The sound caught the cows' interest and they looked up from their grass lunch to watch the big rig pass by the pasture. It was a flashy, stainless steel tanker with big red letters on its side that said:

CLOVERLEAF DAIRY
DRINK MILK
HOMOGINIZED   PASTURIZED   VITAMIN FORTIFIED

One cow turned to the other and said, "Sure makes you feel inadequate, doesn't it?"

Ever feel inadequate? No doubt you have had your moments when your self-assurance was bankrupt. You do not feel you have what it takes to meet life's challenges. Maybe your inadequacy has been so draining that your self-doubts have moved to self-loathing. Feelings of inadequacy are not unusual, nor are they particularly helpful. They can digest our resolve, decay our good intentions, and eat at our spirits from within. Feelings of inadequacy deny the basic essence of creation and rebuff the truth of our having been created in the reflection of the face of God. Inadequacy is the starter dough of self-loathing. To doubt oneself, to despise any part of our humanly wonder, or to live in a world of inadequacy is to say, "God made a huge mistake in me."

Take a tip from the cows when you feel a twinge of inadequacy coming on. Let it pass and go back to what you were doing.

Prayer: This Day no negative internal voice will slow me down. The world has its own chorus of negative caution; I need not add to it. For I know that together, God and I can rise to any occasion that life brings my way.

For it is by grace you have been saved . . . it is a gift of God.
—Ephesians 2:8

Louie's father was abusive and often absent from the family. Louie told of the time his father lined his mother and his brothers and sisters up along the basement wall and held them at attention with a loaded shotgun. Eventually, Louie's father dropped out the picture altogether. Young Louie was introduced to a constant parade of one miserable loser father figure after another. These were men who seemed to take delight in making Louie's life even more miserable.

Louie found there was a way of temporary escape from all this misery—drugs. He joined that parade of wasted youth that has but four choices: insanity, prison, death, or recovery. He dropped out of school; he wandered the streets, dabbled in petty crime, and grew sicker. One day he drove a car off the road and into a bridge abutment. After a half-dozen surgeries, he wore a gruesome scar on the side of his face and a leg that was about three inches shorter than the other leg.

I had lost track of Louie, and then one day he showed up at my home (or, at least, someone who looked something like the Louie I knew). But this young man was wearing a suit and tie. He was smiling. He was clean—inside and out. He had a grin on his face that was as infectious as any I have ever seen. He said, "I have something I want to tell you about!"

My curiosity was aflame. "Sure, Louie, come on in. You look great. What is going on with you?"

Louie paused for a moment, "I have made a discovery!" He paused again. "I have found Jesus!"

I was hugely skeptical. I had heard Louie's solemn promises before. I had seen his best intentions at work before. Yet, something was clearly different about the grinning young man in the tweed suit who sat at my kitchen table. Louie was transformed. He had experienced a spiritual awakening that had changed him completely. Call it what you will—born again, saved, awakened, renewed, transformed, changed, or converted. Louie now had a life. The gift of God was at work in Louie!

Prayer: This Day I will refuse to estimate the wonder that God can do. Today, I will live in hope of that wondrous work.

What the inner voice says, Will not disappoint the hoping soul.
—Johann Schiller

At first, he thought it was only his imagination, but it was not imagination. He heard a nagging voice that kept saying, "Stan needs your help. Only you can help. Go to him and offer your help." The man tried to ignore the voice. He thought the whole thing was nonsense. Next, he tried to deny the voice. "Stan who?" he asked. None of this worked. The voice persisted.

The man had heard the coffee shop stories about how Stan was out of control. How booze had taken over his life. How Stan's wife had left him, his parents had disowned him, and how he was living on the edge of oblivion. He had heard that Stan had tried to take his own life in a drunken rage. It was a mess the man did not want to deal with—one best left to the professionals. But still, the voice continued in his mind: "Stan needs you. Go to him and help him."

The man argued, but the *still, small voice* would not let up. "Come on, you know that only you can help. Go to Stan. Offer your help."

So, the man went—but not to Stan. The man went to another friend, a man he trusted and knew as a close friend and mentor. He told the friend about the nagging voice that kept urging him to visit Stan. The friend's response surprised him. The friend said, "You, too?"

That settled it. Since both of them had heard this same urging and nagging, there must be something to it. Against their better judgment, and much to their personal discomfort, the two men went to see Stan. Timidly, they knocked on Stan's door. An emaciated and ragged looking shell of a man came to the door. Their approach was simple and straightforward. The man said, "Stan, we came because we care for you." The friend said, "Can we help?" That conversation began a twenty-year friendship, which ultimately helped return Stan to a life of restoration. By listening, Stan was restored and the two men were changed forever.

Prayer: This Day I will not ignore the still, small voice within. Today, I will listen, and I will act.

> *"The rule is, jam tomorrow, and jam yesterday—*
> *but never jam today." "It must come sometime to*
> *`jam today,'" Alice objected. "No it can't,"*
> *said the Queen. "It's jam every other day:*
> *today isn't any other day, you know."*
> —From the Walrus and the Carpenter,
> by Lewis Carroll

Do you remember those connect-the-dot coloring books? There were dozens of dots, each with a number that you connected in numerical order. When you first looked at the series of dots, the finished product was not visible. As you drew your line from dot to dot, a picture began to emerge. The fully—finished project remained incomplete until the last two dots were joined.

Our faith journey is a lot like a connect-the-dot picture. We are the sum total of our human experience. The victories and defeats we experience shape who we are as people of faith. Our successes and setbacks, our sweet moments and bitter times inform who we are as people of God. Our study, our prayer life, our sense of community, and our caring for others help connect the dots on our unfinished picture. No particular happening defines us in total. We are a work in progress.

We are God's unfinished business.

Prayer: This Day dare not be frittered away aimlessly. For today is another dot on my faith journey. If it goes poorly or if it goes well, this one day will not define the whole of life. Today well-lived is my goal.

You are the ones who justify yourselves in the eyes of men,
but God knows your hearts. What is highly valued
among men is detestable in God's sight.
—The words of Jesus as recorded
in Luke 16:15

I came across a book entitled *The Life of Christ* at a yard sale. It was on a table with a few boxes of other books marked fifty cents each. It was in good shape, but obviously old. I bought the book simply because I liked the title.

As I thumbed through my new library addition, I noticed the name of the book's author. The author was A. Layman. It was not A. Layman as in Alfred Layman. It simply was the A (as an article of speech) Layman.

Most of us like celebrity. We long to be noticed. We relish applause, even though we cultivate an embarrassed look on our face and a "Who, me?" kind of mock surprise. We like attention. We like recognition. We hunger for acknowledgement, even when we claim we value anonymity.

Do you think you could write a four-hundred-page book and sign it "A Layman"? Could you sculpt a mountain, compose a symphony, or discover a vaccine for AIDS and sign your life's work "anonymous"? Most of us probably could not or would not be able to do that.

The book, *The Life of Christ*, was sorely outdated. It reflected a theological and cultural time that was long ago. However, it was worth far more than fifty cents. The message I discovered on the title page—by A. Layman—was invaluable. It had a lot to say about this one man or woman's humility.

As any good book, it caused me to think. Would that I could be so humble!

Prayer: This Day I pray that my spirit be quiet, my soul be content, and my accomplishments go comfortably unnoticed. Today, I will more than just say that I gladly labor without expectation of recognition.

A community is like a ship; everyone ought to be
prepared to the helm.

—Henrik Ibsen

An old family picture album, entitled, "Spring, 1939" holds a full-page picture of about thirty or thirty-five old steel-wheeled tractors lined up in a huge semi-circle. In its stark black-and-white imagery, it was hard to say if the tractors were red, orange, or the proper John Deere green. It is a grand picture of another time. It features a panorama of not only tractors, but of men in bibbed overalls casually leaning on their tractors. Each man had a hand tugging on his overalls' suspender and the other hand cupped around a pipe full of well-pressed-down tobacco.

On the back of the picture it said, "Dad's Work Bee, Spring, 1939." The names of all the men were written in pencil on the back of that picture. There was Ray, Lester, Ernie, Graham, Pete, Bob, Chancy, Forest, Floyd, and a dozen others. All these were familiar names to me in my youth. These were the younger faces of men I had known as old men in my youth. I read the names aloud as if reacquainting myself with the past.

The steel-wheeled men were the neighbors who came to plant my grandfather's crops in the spring of 1939. Earlier that winter, my grandfather had a serious accident with a buzz saw that left him obliged to live out the remainder of his life and to farm 275 acres of land with just a right hand. The neighbors—thirty or so of them—gathered one day to plant his crops. This was the picture of the men with their steel-wheeled tractors who came that spring day to help a neighbor in need.

Modernity brings change, and that is both good and unavoidable. But, of all the institutions that have seen change in the face of modernity, none has been more challenged than our sense of community. Those men in bibbed overalls knew they were part of something bigger than themselves. If tragedy befell one of them, it impacted each of them. The steel-wheeled men of a half-century ago knew they had to keep their dues paid. Why? Because, one day they, too, would be in need of another's help.

Prayer: This Day I pray that I am capable of being part of something bigger than myself. Today, I wish to be immersed in community.

Always try to keep the main thing the main thing of life.
—David Tyler Scoates

The postmaster asked Tom to replace his mailbox. So Tom purchased a new mailbox and a 4x4 cedar post. He began the project by squaring up the 4x4 post. Unfortunately, the post slipped and he cut his finger. Tom set off to the emergency room for a couple of stitches and a tetanus shot. All patched up, he came home and set to the task once more. This time, while he was nailing the box to the post he missed the nail and hit his finger with the hammer. It began to bleed. So, he wrapped his sore finger in a piece of cloth and went back to work. He was spading the hole for the post with two heavily bandaged hands and completely missed the posthole and hit his foot with the digger. It drew blood, so back to the emergency room he went. This time there was no need for a tetanus shot—just stitches.

Tom was not a handyman, but he was a determined man. He was going to set that new mailbox. After all, the project was nearly done. What more could go wrong? He carried the mailbox, now nicely mounted on the cedar post, to the hole he had dug. In one mighty stroke of determination he raised the post over his head and slammed it into the posthole. The only problem was that he had turned the mailbox just right so that as the post went into the hole, the mailbox hit him on the back of the head and knocked him out!

The mailbox had cost him stitches in his hand, a lost finger nail, stitches in his right foot, a tetanus shot, and a lump on the back of his head.

In all of this disaster, my guess is that it was hard for Tom to keep "the main thing the main thing." It was hard for Tom to stay focused while patched from head to toe, and sporting a lump on the head.

Even if you are not as clumsy as Tom, staying focused is an issue for every one of us. Life has its distractions. In the busyness of daily living, it is hard to make sure we keep first things first. Keeping "the main thing the main thing" of life takes some concentration. It also takes some conversation with God. Why not ask God what is the "main thing" for you today?

Prayer: This Day I will try to keep focused. I will try to keep what engages me most God's main thing.

Today is Flag Day. A number of years ago, the popular television comedian, Red Skelton, recorded his version of the Pledge of Allegiance. Several hundred thousand copies were sold and Skelton's version of the Pledge of Allegiance was read into the Congressional Record.

Red Skelton's pledge:

"**I**"—me, an individual, a committee of one.

"**Pledge**—dedicate all of my worldly goods to give without self-pity.

"**Allegiance**"—my love and devotion.

"**To the flag**"—our standard, Old Glory, a symbol of freedom. Wherever she waves, there is respect because your loyalty has given her a dignity that shouts freedom is everybody's job.

"**Of the United**"—that means that we have all come together.

"**States**"—individual communities that have united into 48 great states. Forty-eight individual communities with pride and dignity and purpose, all divided with imaginary boundaries, yet united to a common purpose, and that's love for country.

"**Of America and to the Republic**"—a state in which sovereign power is invested in representatives chosen by the people to govern. And government is the people and it's from the people to the leaders, not from the leaders to the people.

"**For which it stands. One nation**"—meaning, so blessed by God.

"**Indivisible**"—incapable of being divided.

"**With liberty**"—which is freedom and the right of power to live one's own life without threats or fear of some sort of retaliation.

"**And Justice**"—the principle or quality of dealing fairly with others.

"**For all**"—which means it's as much your country as it is mine.

Skelton adds:

Since I was a small boy, two states have been added to our country and two words have been added to the pledge of Allegiance—"**under God.**"

Prayer: This Day may we live up to the words "with liberty and justice for all." May our pledge be as a godly people, bonded in a common cause that includes all your children as true brothers and sisters.

*Yet a time is coming and has now come when the true worshipers will
worship the Father in spirit and truth, for they
are the kind of worshipers the Father seeks.*

—John 4:23

The nervous lad may have been fifteen years old. The pink pimple or two that his youthful face bore were mostly disguised this day by the flush of embarrassment. Clearly, he did not want to be standing in front of the small congregation leading them in an opening prayer. But, today was Youth Sunday, and he had drawn the straw that put him in front of the gathered people.

The teenage boy stood on one foot, then the other, as he nervously swayed before the people. It was as if he were shifting his position to find a posture that made him invisible. He bowed his head, cleared his dry throat, and as he looked at the floor he said in a quavering voice:

"Let's pray."

"Hi God. (*pause*) 'er I guess ah we just want to ask you (*pause*) 'ta help us (*pause*) 'er worship better today (*pause*). That's about all. Amen."

The lad's prayer was both painful and true. It was painful to watch his struggle, to witness his ill ease, to observe the anguish that public scrutiny had caused him. It was painful for him and for all of us. His prayer was also true. The boy's point that we need divine help in our worship is the heart of worship. Placing our broken selves before God to ask for healing takes help. Coming before God to praise His inexplicable mercy begs for words that are beyond us. He had spoken the truth.

Leave your thee's and thy's behind. Forget your eloquent metaphors. Silence your brilliant tongue. Squelch the articulate. Simply pray simply.

Prayer: This Day the quiet of my heart will shout. Today, the words I use to proclaim God's goodness will be like a kitchen-table conversation with an old friend.

God saw all that he had made, and it was very good.
—Genesis 1:31

Suppose you had a twenty-dollar bill that was crumpled and ragged. Suppose the bill was faded, crinkled, and had a corner torn off. Suppose it was stained and frayed. Would it still be worth $20.00?

Of course it would still be worth twenty bucks. Currency has unchanging value. A twenty is always a twenty no matter how shabby it gets. You can fold it, crumble it, stain it, or tear it in two and it still is worth twenty dollars.

We are a lot like a crumpled twenty-dollar bill. No matter how we look, what we have endured, or how shabby our lives have become, God does not devalue us. We still have the same worth to God. Sure, crisp new bills have a pleasing feel to them. They are nice to flick out and snap before spending. But, a drab old twenty still has the same value.

It is good to know that our stock value before God does not fluctuate with the whim of the market place.

Prayer: This Day I will try to be worth the investment God has made in me. Knowing that His Son purchased my stock options and my futures on the cross tells me that I am very precious to God.

Every individual is representative of the whole . . .
—Malcolm Muggeridge

I am a Garrison Keillor fan. I try to listen to his *Prairie Home Companion* radio show as often as possible. I love to read about his mythical hometown of Lake Woe-be-gone, Minnesota.

One of Keillor's stories about Lake Woe-be-gone is about a traveling salesman who came to the town with the zeal of Harold Hill, the Music Man. Instead of inspiring them to organize a band, this salesman inspired the townspeople to build a living American flag for the Fourth of July. He sold them hundreds of red, white, and blue baseball caps. The plan was for everyone to put on his or her baseball cap and to stand in a grid on the morning of the Forth of July in such a way that the stars and strips were visible from above as one of the largest ever American flags.

But, there was a problem. Since every citizen of Lake Woe-be-gone was in the flag, there was no one to observe the flag. Then one of the townspeople had an idea. If one person broke ranks and went up on the roof of Koglan's Buick garage, they could see the living flag in full splendor. Well, almost full splendor except for the one place in the flag that person had left as a void.

So, in the summer's heat, one by one each baseball-capped piece of the living flag broke ranks and went up on the roof of Koglan's Buick garage to look down on the flag. The trouble was that every onlooker saw an incomplete flag. His or her part of the flag was missing.

Every single member of a community matters to the whole.

Prayer: This Day I will do my part. I will set aside my individuality for the great wonder of common union we call community.

NOT PERFECT: JUST FORGIVEN.
—Seen on a bumper sticker,
author unknown

Clubs have them. Fraternities and sororities have them. Political parties, labor unions, and professional societies have them. In fact, every imaginable institution has them. What do they have in common? They have requirements for membership.

We fill our need to belong as members of a family, a clan, a tribe, a political party, or some other sense of community. Red Wing jerseys, banners, and bumper stickers say, "I belong." The American flags that have become so apparent since September 11 are a patriotic statement, but they are also a way of saying, "Here, I belong."

What is the basic requirement for membership as a follower of Jesus Christ? It is not one of those fraternal or maternal organizations where you have to be nominated by a member in good standing. You do not have to have studied at a particular school or university. Requirement for membership as a follower of Christ does not demand a particular political affiliation. Neither does it expect a level of social or economic requirement. Surely, membership does not demand perfection.

Membership as a follower of Christ is much simpler than that. As much as we would prefer one of the former requirements, the fact is that the single standard to become a follower of Jesus Christ and to gain membership in Christ's church is to be a repentant sinner. Jesus said, "I did not come to call the righteous, but sinners."

Too many see the church as a museum for the prefect rather than a hospital for the sinner. You have heard it sarcastically and bitterly said, "And you call yourself a Christian?" It hurts. It hurts because the pointed intent is directed at one's shortcomings. And as painful as it is, that is exactly what it takes to be one of Christ's followers—shortcomings, flaws, and brokenness.

Welcome to the club!

Prayer: This Day will hear my voice of joy. Today, I will delight in my membership as one of God's broken who is mended in Christ.

The Rules for Being Human.
—By Cherie Carter-Scott

1. **You will receive a body.**
   You may not like it or hate it, but it will be yours for the entire period of this time around.
2. **You will learn lessons.**
   You are enrolled in a full-time informal school called Life. Each day in this school you will have the opportunity to learn lessons. You may like the lessons or think them irrelevant and stupid.
3. **There are no mistakes, only lessons.**
   Growth is a process of trial and error. The "failed" experiments are as much a part of the process as the experiment that ultimately "works."
4. **A lesson is repeated until learned.**
   A lesson will be presented to you in various forms until you have learned it. When you have learned it, you can then go on to the next lesson.
5. **Learning lessons does not end.**
   There is no part of life that does not contain its lessons. If you are alive, there are lessons to be learned.
6. **"There" is no better than "here."**
   When your "there" has become "here," you will simply obtain another "there" that will again look better than "here."
7. **Others are merely mirrors of you.**
   You cannot love or hate something about another person unless it reflects something you love or hate about yourself.
8. **What you make of life is up to you.**
   You have all the tools and resources you need. What you do with them is up to you. The choice is yours.
9. **Your answers lie inside you.**
   All you need to do is look, listen and trust.
10. **You will forget all this.**

Prayer: This Day I will live by the simple rules of life. Today, I will try to make my life less complicated.

My heart leaps up when I behold A rainbow in the sky:
So was it when my life began; So it is now that I am a man;
So be it when I shall grow old, Or let me die!
The child is father of the man; And I could
wish my days to be bound each to each
by natural piety.

—William Wordsworth

One of the men who served in President Lincoln's cabinet had a son who nagged his father insistently to take him fishing. The father always had an excuse why he could not go fishing. He repeatedly said he was far too busy, too tired, and too preoccupied for such nonsense. Finally one summer day he could not stand the boy's pestering any longer. He set everything aside and took the lad fishing. After returning home, the father penned the following entry in his diary:

June 21, 1864— I took my son fishing today. The weather was rainy and cold and totally inclement. We caught no fish. In every respect it was a completely wasted day.

Years later, a biographer who was researching the cabinet member's life, noted that the son had also made a diary entry on that same day. It read:

June 21, 1864— Father and I went fishing today. It was the best day of my life!

Prayer: This Day I will endeavor to live up to the most sacred trust God has placed in me. Today, I see my role as a parent as the greatest trust God has placed in me.

> *The day is yours, and yours also the night;*
> *you established the sun and the moon.*
>
> —Psalm 74:16

This day is a special day. What makes this day so special? Today is called Mid-summer day. It is also the first day of summer. Today will offer the longest day of sunlight and the shortest night of the year. The life-giving and nurturing rays of sunlight are at their zenith today. Since light and life are inseparably entwined, the blessing of living creation is most evident on this day.

There is another interesting aspect to this day. If you live somewhere other than near the north pole or near the equator, at precisely noon today your shadow is the shortest of any time in the year. The darkness you cast on the earth in the form of your shadow is at its ebb tide at noon today. For that moment, you blot out less of the sun than any other moment of the year.

Consider your short shadow from another perspective for a moment. It is not how much sun you blot out, but how much of God's warmth and goodness you absorb. As you ponder your short shadow today, think of it as the most-warmed, the most-blessed, indeed, the most-alive moment you will know this year. Embrace that moment on this day as the nearest you will stand in the light of all creation. Ignore the tiny dark blob on the ground that you cast and quietly drink in the blessing of the One who loves you and gives you life.

This is a good day to look up and say, "Thank you, God!"

Prayer: This Day I will drink in the wonder of God's love. Any shadow that walks beside me is notably small today. But, when compared to God's love, it is puny every day.

I will praise you, O LORD, with all my heart;
I will tell of all your wonders.

—Psalm 9:1

Michael Williams was from a broken home. Working two part-time, minimum-wage jobs, Michael's mother was barely able to put bread on the family's table. He was a bright student, but the stark economic blight that gripped the family made college an impossible dream. So, upon graduation from high school young Michael joined the United States Navy. He trained as a seaman and was assigned to one of the Navy's most modern nuclear submarines. The sub to which he was assigned carried sixteen nuclear warheads. Part of the ploy of a missile-carrying sub is the use of its underwater capability to keep its exact location a secret. Thus, these missile-bearing subs remain submerged and undetected for up to ten-week intervals.

Although Michael had never been a religious person, ten weeks under the ocean gave the young man a long time to think about things that would otherwise go unquestioned. During one of those submerged stints, at 200 feet below the ocean's crest, Michael began to wonder about the meaning of his being. He pondered what his purpose was in life. If he were never to step off that submarine, would the world ever notice? What difference had he made in the life of another? Michael shared his concerns with another sailor. His friend remembered that before boarding the sub, he had been given a Bible. Thinking it might help, the friend gave that Bible to Michael.

Michael Williams said that as he read that Bible, the Holy Spirit descended through 200 feet of water, penetrated the titanium hull of that sub, and entered his heart. Today, it is no longer Seaman Michael Williams. Today it is Michael Williams, PhD. Dr. Williams is the Associate Professor of Old Testament at Calvin Theological Seminary. It all began when a lonely sailor asked, "What is the meaning of my life?"

Prayer: This Day I will ponder what God has in store for me. When I hear God's call, I will be ready to respond as if my life depended upon it. After all, it really does!

"In the same way, let your light shine before men, that they may see your good deeds and praise your Father in heaven."
—The words of Jesus as recorded
in Matthew 5:16

Rick Warren, the author of *The Purpose Driven Church*, makes an interesting point about how small things make a big difference. Warren says that the grand chandelier that hangs elegantly over his dining room table is not as important as the night-light that lights his way to the bathroom in the middle of the night.

Warren's point is a simple one: small things that seem unimportant make a big difference in our lives. His comparison is directed at big, showy programs and ministries that may look impressive, but are ideal places for the individual to get lost. Warren believes that small group ministries attend to more needs than mega-programs.

Do you suppose the "Chandelier Believer" is the one who knows all the perfect biblical quotes, can recite centuries of doctrine, and offers prayers that stun the angels' ears? Maybe the "Night-Light Believer" is the one who is still cautiously searching the way, praying with a bit of uneasiness, and has no idea what doctrine even means. Maybe the "Chandelier Believer" uses his or her faith on special occasions, while the "Night-Light Believer" focuses on the daily trudge through life.

Most of us would prefer to be "Night-Light Believers." There is comfort in company. Besides, night-lights require low maintenance, and they need less dusting and cleaning. The night-light is friendly, while the chandelier can be formal and stuffy. Night-lights are warm and always present, while chandeliers can be cold, intimidating, and rarely turned on.

Jesus said, "Let your light shine," but he did not say that even small lights could not illumine the darkest corners. Let your light shine, no matter how spectacular or how small its glow.

Prayer: This Day my light will shine. It may not be the biggest, the brightest, or the flashiest, but hopefully it will light another's way.

"Go now and leave your life of sin."
—The words of Jesus as recorded
in John 8:11

A Texas lawmaker has proposed a coupon book for speeders. His idea is to allow motorists to purchase coupon books in advance in denominations from fifteen dollars to several hundred dollars. If the motorist is caught speeding, he or she can simply tear off the appropriate amount of the fine, hand the coupons to the officer, and drive away (hopefully slower).

Not surprisingly, the Texas State Police think this is a ridiculous notion. They insist that their business is law enforcement and not fees collection. They are concerned that more speeding would lead to more highway carnage, and no amount of fee collecting could ever assuage the additional suffering and bloodshed. Other lawmakers feel the same. In fact, there seems to be little support for the speeding coupon scheme.

The idea is a wacky one. Stripped of its nonsense is the idea that we can receive absolution in advance. Basically it is saying, "I intend to break the law, so I am seeking pardon in advance." It is a kind of prepayment for bad behavior or the ultimate "get-out-of-jail card."

Some theologians have proposed that the cross is all about absolution in advance. Regardless of one's sin, Jesus Christ has already paid the price in advance. Therefore, we are free to sin at will. *Not so!* Jesus said, "Go and don't do that again." When Paul considered the matter of absolution in advance, he asked, "Will our grace increase if our sinfulness increases?" Obviously, his answer was also a resounding, "No!"

The cross (and maybe one day the Texas State Highway Patrol) offers forgiveness for any sin. But, the two differ sharply. The cross is grounded in repentance and forgiveness, while the speeding coupon book is based on intent. In a sense, the cross of Christ is a coupon book that has been given to every repentant heart. But, these coupons are invalidated by intentional misconduct. As Jesus said, "Go now and leave your life of sin."

Prayer: This Day I will embrace the gift of forgiveness. But, just because I am forgiven once of all separation, I will not push the issue too far.

*May the words of my mouth and the meditations of my heart be pleasing
in your sight, O LORD, my rock
and my Redeemer.*

—Psalm 19:14

Words are such fascinating things. They convey feelings, knowledge, and ideas. Our choice of words says a lot about how we feel about a particular matter. For example, in the midst of an election campaign, a candidate who carefully chooses his or her words can put a favorable spin on what might seem like an irrefutable negative fact. One candidate might name an act as cautious wisdom, while the other might label the same act as callous ruthlessness. Of the same act, a third party candidate could say that inaction was the best reaction.

The business world chooses its words wisely. A house trailer becomes a mobile home. An expensive two-year-old car is not call "used." If it is expensive enough, it is called "previously owned." The airline industry has given us "an intrusion of space" instead of "two planes smashing into each other." And, in the matter of war, a patriot to one is another's terrorist. One country's thug is another's freedom fighter.

The words we choose to name an idea or thing has a lot to say about how we hope others will perceive, embrace, or act upon that idea or thing. Our words inform others and reveal how we think, what we believe, and what matters to each of us.

Listen to the words you choose. They might have something to say to you.

Prayer: This Day I will listen to the words of my mouth and the meditations of my heart. I will ask: What nuance do they reveal? What am I really saying? How do I really feel?

Then I heard the voice of the Lord saying, "Whom shall I send? And who will go for us?" And I said, "Here am I. Send me!"

—Isaiah 6:8

Random airplane seat assignments are one of life's serendipitous events. You never can tell who might sit in the seat next to you. Of course, there are those seat partners who do not want to be disturbed, and those who do not want to be conversational. However, here is one of life's unique opportunities to meet a fellow traveler.

I once sat beside a young Vietnamese woman. Her name was Meimei (me-me). She told me she was going to San Diego to finish her M.B.A. degree. Meimei told me she was born in Vietnam and her earliest memories were of the frightening sounds, the unthinkable sights, and the acrid stench of war. Her father was a fighter pilot who survived many missions. He had two brothers who were not as lucky. She told me a Christian church had sponsored her family of four. The generosity of this church had lifted these four pitiful refugees out of despair and brought them to this land of hope. "How different my life would have been if it had not been for the goodness of that church. I would probably not have lived, and I surely would not be completing a graduate degree," Meimei said.

Our plane landed in Chicago, and we went our separate ways. I had a deep feeling of satisfaction in knowing I was part of a faith community that continues to make a difference in people's lives. Here, in this young woman, was the presence of God's goodness freely given by caring Christians.

As I boarded my connecting flight to Los Angles, my next seat companion was reading a book entitled *Winged Serpents and Dragons: In Search of Our Reptilian Past.* The man turned to me and said, "You might like this book. It clears up the whole pack of lies that Christianity has fed us for the last 2,000 years."

Sometimes God reveals his handiwork, and sometimes he show us how much there is yet to be done.

Prayer: This Day I will balance the goodness and life-changing power of Christ. I will also keep a keen eye on what life changing is yet to be done.

"But we had to celebrate and be glad, because this brother of yours was dead and now is alive again; he was lost and is found."
—Luke 15:32

We were five, maybe seven miles from the lodge. It would not have been so bad if we were on a highway a half-dozen miles from a warm fire and the supper table. We were miles from camp, deep in a cedar swamp in the Maine wilderness. There were no roads, and surely no streetlights. If you drew a deep breath and stood as quietly as you could, all you heard was the faint sound of a brook and the distant rumble of an airliner on its way to Europe. As the sun slipped lower on the horizon, the closing of light surrounded us. The possibility of a night in the woods was rapidly becoming more real.

The guide turned to me and said, "Well, I've got some good news and some bad news. The bad news is that we are lost. The good news is that we are sure making good time!"

His grim humor did not ease my concern. I will never know how he managed it, if it was luck or skill, but within ten minutes of his good news/bad news announcement, we stepped out onto a logging road that took us to the truck. Supper, a warm fire, and a lumpy mattress were welcome that night!

The gospel of Jesus Christ is called the Good News. It is well named—especially when you are lost.

Prayer: This Day will be a Good News day! Why? Because I was once lost and now am found.

Jesus Christ is the same yesterday and today and forever.
—Hebrews 13:8

We often think of the ancients as primitive people. We see them as bungling and unsophisticated folks who wandered aimlessly through the desert or the forest.

Think again! Our forebears were keenly attuned with their world. They used their senses in ways that are beyond our imagination. The world was big, uncharted, and a mysterious place for them. But, they were patient observers. They patiently watched the moon and stars. They quietly observed the tides, the seasons, the blooming of flowers, the run of salmon, the birth of fawns, and the shape of oak leaves. They were in harmony with the ever-changing world around them. They did not understand themselves as shapers or controllers, but as patient observers.

Their observations were notched on sticks, scratched on cave walls, painted on pottery, and told around campfires. They chronicled the smells, the sounds, the sights, the tastes, and the feel of their world. They forged a sense of order, fashioned community, and tried to explain the world around them. They recorded the ever-changing world, its rhythm, its predictable, and its unpredictable nature. It must have been a daunting task. Yet, they patiently watched and retold.

What a debt we owe those who came long before us. And, what an apology we owe them for thinking of them as aimless wanderers.

More than that, what a blessing we have in the unchanging Word of God in an ever-changing world around us.

Prayer: This Day I will step back a moment and consider the grand scheme of things. I will ponder my role in the ever-changing world. I will reconsider my drive to reinvent. I will find solace in the harmony of God's unchanging Word.

> *All this is from God, who reconciled us to himself through Christ and*
> *gave us the ministry of reconciliation: that God was reconciling the*
> *world to himself in Christ, not counting men's sins against them. And he*
> *has committed to us the message of reconciliation. We are therefore*
> *Christ's ambassadors, as though God were making his appeal through us.*
> —2 Corinthians 5:18–20

The Greeks thought a child was born as a blank slate. Whatever that child became was shaped by what the world taught him or her. Today, we believe there is much that is imprinted on our souls. We have genetic tendencies. We are born with inherent yearnings. We are not completely blank slates at birth.

Yet, the Greeks were not all wrong. We are not born with prejudice. A child does not understand hatred or racism. We have to learn how to hate. We have to be taught how to separate ourselves by color, race, and ethnicity. Social barriers are not imprinted on a child's psyche. The child is without hate, but, tragically, the world is a willing teacher that is fully capable of tutoring the innocent mind.

The church has much to say about reconciliation. We think of reconciliation in terms of what theologians call the "ontological divide." That is a fancy word that means the great chasm between God and humanity. We are intent on healing the separation that keeps us apart from God. We long for reconciliation and a bridge that spans the great ontological divide.

What about our reconciliation with one another? What about healing the wounds of hate? What about dismantling the barriers that keep us estranged from one another? That bridge between God and humanity can never be built while the work force is itself separated.

Reconciliation begins when we wrap our arms around the innocence of a child and teach that child that we are one in Christ. It begins when we keep those precious minds free from hate. We build that bridge one child at a time.

Prayer:　　This Day I pray that I will be a worthy ambassador of reconciliation. I pray that no child ever sees in me a reason to hate.

> *Humor is a prelude to faith and laughter*
> *is the beginning of prayer.*
> —Reinhold Niebuhr

Mid-summer is huckleberry time in the North Country. Picking huckleberries has to be the sweatiest, most mosquito-infested, and tedious way to spend a summer afternoon. The work is monotonous, but the yield of a huckleberry pie makes the couple of hours of labor worthwhile.

One summer day, I lathered on some Off Mosquito Repellent, got a plastic pail, and headed for the huckleberry patch. I waited until evening when it was a bit cooler. All was going well. The berries were in their prime. The little plastic pail was filling up. Then, without any provocation or warning, I heard the unmistakable guttural growl of a bear. Either I had stumbled onto the bear's favorite huckleberry patch, or I was somehow in between a she-bear and her cubs. Neither was a good place to be. That one growl was all it took. I headed for my truck with my little plastic pail only half-filled with huckleberries. Pie would have to wait for another day.

The bear and huckleberry incident reminds me of the story of another man who came face-to-face with a bear in the woods. He and the bear looked into each other's eyes. The man closed his eyes and prayed, "Dear God, make this bear a Christian that is filled with love and peace."

There was a quiet moment. Then the bear fell on his knees and said, "Dear God, I give my heartfelt thanks for the meal I am about to receive."

Prayer: This Day I will rejoice with gladness, for life is too short to avoid mirth. I will celebrate the gift of laughter by laughing long and hard.

> *Their end is destruction; their god is the belly;*
> *and their glory is in their shame . . .*
>
> —Philippians 3:19

There is no such thing as glorious shame. Shame is such a futile god. To wear one's shame as a badge of courage and honor defies God's hope for us. Shame refuses to acknowledge God's presence in our lives. Shame is a waste of time that can atrophy our spirits and sap our strength. Shame has no place in a believer's heart.

We occasionally mistake shame for guilt. There is a huge difference between guilt and shame. To admit guilt is to say, "I made a mistake." To embrace shame is to say, "I am a mistake." Shame destroys, while guilt can be the embryo from which new life is born. Recognizing that a mistake has been made can lead to change. Believing that I am flawed, inferior, or worthless can only lead to more destruction. Mistakes happen, but as a child of God, I can never be mistaken for a mistake.

Prayer: This Day I will see my shortcomings and flaws as reason for change. Beginning this day, I will never again see myself as a divine mistake.

Reason is God's crowning gift to humanity.

—Sophocles

A man went to see his doctor for his annual physical. The doctor said, "You are in sorry shape! You need to lose weight. I want you to begin a vigorous exercise regimen today. Start by walking ten miles every day and then call me in a week."

So a week later the man called his physician and said, "I have walked ten miles every day this past week—just like you told me, Doc. Now I am seventy miles from home, what do you want me to do now?"

Sometimes we misunderstand life's directions. Sometimes we fail to listen and sometimes we just fail to understand. It would be a good strategy to always ask, "Does this make sense?" Life's directions ought to balance reason, God's Word, our experience, and the traditions that have been passed down to us. So, it is always a good idea to be sure to check your luggage to see if you have remembered to pack your common sense before you set off on life's journey.

Prayer: This Day I hope to balance reason with God's will. Today, I pray that my journey will make sense and please God in seeing that His will is alive in me.

To ask a question is to look foolish for a moment.
To never ask is to be foolish forever.

—Anonymous

An esteemed horticulturalist spoke at a garden-club meeting. The learned horticulturalist spent much time expounding on the benefits of old horse manure as plant food. After the lecture, the expert asked if there were any questions. One of the novice gardeners said, "Yes, I have a question. You said old horse manure was the best plant food we could use on our gardens. I want to know just how old the horse should be?"

Ever ask a stupid question? Maybe that is a stupid question itself. To never ask is to remain always uninformed. To ask, even though there may be some hazards in asking, leads to knowledge.

When you read God's Word, pay particular attention to the question marks. Whenever God is asked a question, divine wisdom follows. In God's Word, a question mark means, "Hear up! I have something important for you to know."

Prayer: This Day I will boldly ask, even though my ignorance is showcased in my question. Today, I will throw caution and vanity to the wind as I seek God's will.

. . . one nation, under God, indivisible with liberty and justice for all.
—From the Pledge of Allegiance
to the flag

U nder God: much ado has been made about these two words. The strict constitutionalists claim the phrase steps over the division of church and State. They see the inclusion of these two words as heaping religion upon a free people. They are offended and indignant.

The Christian world is also offended and indignant that anyone would even suggest that we are a nation not under God. Many claim that we were founded on Christian principles and that allegiance to God has a revered place in our patriotic spirit.

Christians ought to be offended and indignant about the language we embrace as a free people. But, the phrase that should offend us most is not "under God." We should be most offended that liberty and justice for all is not always the rule of the land. As long as cultural, social, economic, and ethnic barriers still keep some poor, disenfranchised, and rejected, there is not universal liberty and justice. The heart of God is more deeply concerned in liberty and justice for every one of his children than who is above all.

Prayer: This Independence Day I will do my part to bring liberty and justice to all. I will begin with how I love, treat, and respect others.

Grace is where service begins.

—Anonymous

A troubled believer once prayed to God a prayer of lament. "Why, O God, do you allow some to be poor and oppressed? Why do you let injustice rule so many lives? Why do the corrupt continue to prosper and the righteous go without reward? Why is there so much suffering, hunger, humiliation, and sorrow in this world? Lord, can't you do something?"

There was a firm, but gentle voice that quietly said, "I have done something. I sent you!"

How easy and delightful life would be if God instantly took care of every sorrow, every injustice, and every hurt. What a grand world this would be if every table had more than enough bread. That would be heaven on earth! Yet, it would be a life without much purpose or meaning. God has given us a better deal than heaven on earth. God has given us purpose, significance, and worth. God has made us servants who are the world's difference-makers. That is grace, trust, and significance all rolled into one.

Prayer: This Day I will rejoice in my role as the hands and the arms of Christ. I will understand my vocation as Christ's servant to be one of grace, trust, and the most important job I'll ever have.

> *Work as if you would live a hundred years,*
> *Pray as if you were to die tomorrow.*
> —Benjamin Franklin

We are part of a work in progress in which all work has a future hope. A community builds a library, hospital, school, or church with the knowledge that it will serve those who are yet to be born. Future hope is part of a sense of community. Work that lacks future hope is grossly unsatisfying. Had there been no future hope in those who came before us, we would have inherited a sorry world.

Conversely, if we always look to the future as the only place of hope, we waste the joys of today. Consider the poor soul who dreams about the far off happiness he will have when he finally gets the new car, new boat, bigger home, or promotion. The dreamer's hope is always in acquiring, getting, and having. But, hope placed merely in things is also hugely unfulfilling.

The joys of today and the hopes of tomorrow are not easy to balance. Perhaps Franklin understood it best in seeing the urgency of the present as it relates to a future hope. If we live today in concert with God's will, tomorrow's hope will be certain.

Prayer: This Day I will live in the moment as I focus on God's will for me. As I go about this day, I will labor diligently for a better tomorrow for those whom I'll not likely meet in this world.

Be careful what you pray for. You just might get it!
—Anonymous

It sounds a bit harsh and contradictory, but prayer is a dangerous thing. The most dangerous variety of all prayers is the "bargaining prayer." The bargaining prayer is a prayer that goes something like this:

> "Lord, if you will just help me out of this mess, I'll do anything you ask."

The hazard of a bargaining prayer is that God is likely to hold up his end of the bargain and we are quick to forget our part of the deal. If you intend to bargain with God, then you must know that God takes his commitment seriously and expects the same from you. Indeed, prayer can be dangerous, especially if you are not willing to be committed to your part of the bargain.

A safer prayer might be to simply ask, "What is your will for me today?" Of course, if you ask for God's will in your life, you will need to be ready to follow out God's will. That, too, can be risky and dangerous. When compared to the risks of going it alone, asking for no help, seeking no guidance, making no promises, and expecting nothing from God, then prayer begins to look less dangerous. Life has its risks, but life without prayer is truly dangerous.

Prayer: This Day I am taking a bold risk. Today, I will live dangerously. Today, I will seek God's will and the strength to carry it out.

O! my offense is rank, it smells to heaven; It hath the primal eldest curse upon it, A brother's murder!
—From Shakespeare's *Hamlet*

Sin, brokenness, and separation have a way of making life smelly. There are all manner of ways to mask the odor of sin. We can deny it. We can ignore it. We can blame others. We can call it a habit, an addiction, or a compulsion. But, it still makes our lives offensive. Forgiveness without Christ is like one of those pine-tree-shaped air fresheners that hang from your car's rear view mirror. It has a way of overpowering the stench of life, but the source of the stink remains.

Air-freshener forgiveness fails to resolve the source. It just covers up the stink. The journey becomes tolerable, but the problem remains. The smell is masked by a sickly-sweet pine fragrance, while the offense still smells to heaven. Air-freshener forgiveness ignores the source by merely covering up the stench.

God has seen to it that there is a way to reconciliation through Jesus Christ. The cross of Christ removes the source of the offense rather than merely masking its odor. The brokenness, separation, and resulting stench are dissolved in Christ. That which offends God is gone, forgotten, forgiven, and remembered no more! That is the gift of God in Jesus Christ.

Prayer: This Day I will clean house with Christ. No more air-freshener cover up for me, for today I will begin anew with Christ.

Today is the first day of the rest of your life.

—Anonymous

Portia Nielsen writes of her life experience in a short autobiography entitled, *My Life in Five Short Chapters.* Nielsen writes:

Chapter 1

I am walking down a street. There is a big hole in the sidewalk. I fall in the hole. I am lost. I am confused and bewildered. I try desperately to get out of the hole. After much struggle, I eventually get out of the hole.

Chapter 2

I am walking down the same street. There is a big hole in the sidewalk. I fall into the hole. It is not my fault. Someone else is to blame. I struggle for a while and find my way out of the hole.

Chapter 3

I am walking down the same street. There is a big hole in the sidewalk. I fall in the hole. It is not my fault. It is a habit. I get out of the hole.

Chapter 4

I am walking down the same street. There is a big hole in the sidewalk. I walk around the hole.

Chapter 5

Today I take a different street!

Prayer: This Day I will avoid the choices of the past that have been destructive to my life. Today, I will choose that which honors God and brings me solace, peace, and hope.

For revenge is always the delight of a mean spirit,
of a weak and petty mind.

—Juvenal

Revenge ought never be sweet. It is the primal mark of a mean spirit that can only find satisfaction in retribution. Revenge rejoices in another's misfortune or injury.

For the follower of Christ, there is no joy in revenge. To be sure, as Christians we are not perfect. We are not saints. Oh sure, when a driver speeds past you on the highway, gives you a dirty look, and mouths words you cannot hear but fully understand, a bit of rage wells up inside the best of us. That rage finds a twinge of cheer when we see the one who has offended us pulled over by the Highway Patrol a mile or two down the road. That is human. To wish the speeding driver would crash into the next bridge abutment is revenge. There is no quarter for revenge in a forgiven heart.

It is part of being human to quietly draw a bit of pleasure when one finally gets his or her earned comeuppance. The perfect squelch does bring a twinge of satisfaction and helps to once more reassure us that good will be rewarded and evil will be punished. But revenge is entirely another matter. Revenge is lived-out hatred.

Revenge gives life to hate. It blots out one of the most basic of all principles of peaceful coexistence—live and let live. Revenge saps our spiritual energy. It blocks the flow of God's grace into our lives. It separates us by wishing ill upon another. Revenge is just another name for hate.

Prayer: This Day I will give up any joy I thought that revenge would bring. Today, I will live and let live.

Eat not to dullness. Drink not to elevation.
—Benjamin Franklin

Moderation is not an easy word for most of us. After all, if one of a thing is good, then it should follow that ten thousand of the same thing is ten thousand times better. Our world has a way of dismissing moderation as weak-willed, uncommitted, or unfocused. Too often life's motto is, "Excess is best!"

Excess has had its price. We have the greatest abundance of food and the most obese nation on earth. We have the highest incomes and the most debt. We have the most leisure time and claim to have no time to waste. We enjoy the finest medical care and suffer with the poorest health. We are the best informed, yet still make poor choices. Excess has not treated us kindly. As a nation, we work more hours, have less time with our families, suffer from ill heath, divorce more frequently, and pay an ever-escalating cost for the notion that excess is best. Excess is not necessarily best.

So, how do we celebrate moderation? Perhaps it is captured in the bumper sticker that states:

Live simply that others may simply live.

Prayer: This Day I will use less so that others have more. Today, I will practice moderation, genuinely try to get by on less, and delight in having done so.

> For God so loved the world He gave His only Son, so that everyone who
> believes in Him may not perish but
> may have eternal life.
>
> —John 3:16

Life has its hazards. One of life's most volatile hazards is to love another. The safest way through life is to never love another. The surest way to be absolutely certain you never encounter life's hazards is to never allow yourself to become vulnerable to another's love. Never commit to another's trust. Never thrive on another's affection. Never let your deepest and most hidden self be seen by another. That is the surest way to avoid hurt.

Though avoiding love is the safe way through life, most would agree it is a ridiculous and unworkable strategy. We have been fashioned as vessels of love. God loved us into life. God showed us what it means to be loved when we are unlovable. God even loved us before we were put into our mother's womb. And, God fully knows the risks that go along with loving others. After all, "For God so loved the world . . . ."

Prayer: This Day I will take the ultimate risk. Today, I will allow myself the vulnerability of loving and being loved.

*"So do not worry about tomorrow, for tomorrow will worry about itself.
Today's trouble is enough for today."*
—Jesus Christ quoted
in Matthew 6:34

Writer Robert Burdette updates the words of Jesus in The Golden
Day. Burdette writes:

> There are two days in the week about which and upon which I never
> worry. Two carefree days, kept sacredly free from fear and apprehen-
> sion. One of these days is Yesterday . . . And the other day I do not worry
> about is Tomorrow.

Why spoil a good day before it begins? Is not worrying about tomorrow a way of tainting the promise, hope, and opportunities that
the unseen day brings? And even if our worry did not compromise
tomorrow in any way, it surely is a futile waste of energy.

Yes. Jesus is right. Today has challenges enough of its own. The
energy we waste on worrying about tomorrow only takes away from
our ability to live in this day. The end result is that today has been
spoiled with worry and tomorrow has been compromised by doubt.

Prayer: This Day I will focus only on today and see its twenty-four
hours as all I can handle. Today, I will live in today.

If you are going to pray, then do not worry. If you choose to worry, then do not bother God with your prayers.

—George Knapp

George Knapp was my maternal grandfather. He was perhaps the wisest man I have ever known. I have met more learned men, but none has the wisdom of Grandfather Knapp.

Grandfather was a man of sturdy faith and no stranger to adversity. As a young man, he was a seminary student studying for ministry when he lost his eyesight. Some time after leaving seminary, his vision slowly returned. He married, began farming, and started a family. While he and his wife were expecting their first child, she fell ill and died. He married my grandmother, purchased a hardware store, and once again started a family. His first-born son died before he was a week old. The hardware store was lost in the Great Depression. He watched my grandmother successfully battle cancer twice and lose the ultimate battle in her third bout with the disease.

In all that adversity he remained a man of profound faith with a fervor for prayer. Grandfather's theology was one of simplicity. He believed that you cannot simultaneously pray and worry. Either you hand your worries over to God, or you choose to keep them to yourself. Worry is tangible proof that you have not fully abandoned your cares to God in prayer.

Prayer: This Day I will fully surrender my troubles and worries to God. Today, I'll keep no worry in reserve, because I have given it all to God.

God hears that small, still voice within.

—Anonymous

Mickey was a five-year-old child. Mickey's mother was pregnant. The young boy was filled with excitement! Every night when Mickey's mother tucked him into bed, Mickey said good night to his new brother or sister. It became a nightly ritual. Mickey's mom would read a bedtime story to Mickey and then sing a song to him. Then Mickey would place his hands on his mother's swollen belly and say, "Good night" to his new sister or brother. Sometimes Mickey would sing to his unseen sibling.

The big day finally arrived. Mickey's sister was born, but not without serious difficulty. There were complications. The infant was rushed to a major medical center and placed in the Neo-Natal Intensive Care Unit. There, for the next five days, the tiny girl barely managed to cling to life. The doctors began to prepare the family for the inevitable. Their daughter would not likely live.

Mickey wanted to see his sister. The doctors and staff were much opposed to a child entering the ICU. What if a germ followed Mickey into the sterile environment? What if he disrupted the quiet facility? Finally, they decided no harm could come from Mickey's two-minute visit with his dying sister. Mickey was given a mask and gown and led into the room where his sister's nearly lifeless form was wrapped in a tiny blanket. Mickey walked up to the crib and began to sing:

You are my sunshine, my only sunshine. You make me happy when skies are gray. You'll never know dear how much I love you. Please don't take my sunshine away.

Some of the nurses called it "Mickey's Miracle." Some said it was only a coincidence. Some just did not know what to say. Two days after Mickey's visit with his dying sister, the family that had been preparing for a funeral took their now-healthy daughter home. She had heard a familiar voice of love.

Prayer: This Day I will listen to that small, still voice within me. Today, I will know that God hears the silence of my heart.

. . . if I say to the Pit, 'You are my father,' and to the worm, 'My mother,'
or 'My sister,' where then is my hope?

—Job 17:14–15

Consider the lowly earthworm. It has been said that life as we know it could not exist without the earthworm. The worm eats organic matter and turns it into soil. The soil nourishes vegetation, which in turn feeds plants and animals. Neither plant nor animal life could be sustained without the work of the worm.

The worm toils in community, works anonymously, and with a sense of humility. Never do you hear of worms slithering out on strike, taking graft, or failing to keep their promises. Worms quietly keep the planet fed and the soil restored.

We have much in common with worms. The Word of God tells us that out of dust we have been fashioned and to dust we shall return (Genesis 3:19). It is not an especially comforting thought, but on our return to dust, our physical bodies will pass through the belly of a worm.

I am not sure I especially like that idea. Oh, it is not the community, anonymity, or the humility part that I dislike. It is not even the dust unto dust part that I find unpleasant. What causes me uneasiness is that our time on top of the heap is one of such urgency and is so precious that we dare not waste a moment. As part of this ongoing cycle of life, here is where we need to really make a difference. Now is the time—before dust falls!

Prayer: This Day I will be sure that the lowly things of life matter. Today, I will savor the moment and embrace life as precious. Today, I will make every effort to make a difference in another's life.

Go figure!

—Unknown

(A word of caution: do not take the following too seriously)

Much has been said lately about the rocketing costs of prescription drugs in the United States. Some of our citizens have to choose between heart medicine and rent. Escalating costs of medical insurance puts a severe hardship on those who self-pay for health coverage, and on the employers who have to cough up the quarterly premiums. It has become a huge dilemma.

A few have discovered a solution (of sorts) to this conundrum. They cross the border to Canada and stock up on a six month's or year's supply of prescription drugs at a fraction of the cost that a like prescription would cost in the U.S.A. Somehow the Canadians have found a way to market prescription drugs much cheaper than their counterparts in the States.

It's amazing that these prescription-seeking Americans cross paths with Canadians who are on their way to the United States to buy lower cost cigarettes! Someone in Washington ought to give this some thought. Why don't we trade cigarettes to the Canadians for heart medicine? Perhaps it would have a two-fold impact on our nation's health—cheaper drugs and fewer cigarettes. We might balance our trade deficit. We could help our economy, our national health, and please our neighbors to the north in the bargain. There has to be a problem somewhere in this equation. It is just too simple and makes far too much sense.

Prayer: This Day I will not take myself too seriously. I will laugh, seek joy, and delight in life itself. I will also pray for those who have to choose between heart medicine and rent.

K.I.S.S. (Keep it simple stupid).

—Unknown

We go to great lengths to complicate life when, in fact, the simple things of life matter most. Keeping life simple does not come naturally to most of us. We have to work at it. And, having to work at simplicity is in itself a complicated paradox.

Thomas Merton was a theologian, deep thinker, and writer. Merton penned a number of devotionals, poems, and essays that explore the depth of our souls and our most intimate relationships with God. Merton was once asked, "What is the most important bit of knowledge you would like to teach your students?" He said, "The most important thing in life is to close doors quietly. Do not go through life slamming doors!"

The hotel magnate, Conrad Hilton said that the most important thing in life is to always put the shower curtain inside the shower.

Keeping life simple, uncomplicated, and uncluttered is an art. The real skill is to simplify life in the simplest way.

Prayer: This Day I will strive for simplicity and pray that I do not complicate the process of simplification. Today, I will quietly seek simplicity.

The Spirit of the Lord is upon me, because He has anointed me to bring good news to the poor. He has sent me to proclaim release to the captives and recovery of the sight to the blind, to let the oppressed go free, and to proclaim the year of the Lord's favor.

—Luke 4:18–19

Karl Barth (pronounced Bart) was a German-born, 20th Century theologian. Barth was a man of brilliance who helped define the post World War II Christian church. He was both a deep theological thinker and a man of profound faith in the face of global hatred and war. A lot can be said about Karl Barth as a Christian thinker, a man of faith, a brave voice in a time of war, and an example of living one's faith.

It can also be said that Barth could take the simplest idea and complicate it to the extreme. His writing is deep, complex, and nearly unreadable. He seemed to have a penchant for run-on sentences. For Barth, if a ten-cent word would do, why not use a ten-dollar word? Better still; why not use a few dozen ten-dollar words?

But, Barth had his moments when clarity and simplicity seeped through. Consider this:

The Gospel is intended to comfort the afflicted, and to afflict the comfortable.

Thank you, Karl Barth, for this one line of clarity and simplicity.

Prayer: This Day I will give thanks for the comfort God has given me in the Good News of Jesus Christ. Today, I will also delight in the Good News as a prod to serve, to love, and to care for others.

Omnipresent: to be everywhere at once.
Omnipotent: to be all-powerful.
Omniscient: to be all knowing.

—Webster's Dictionary

God is omnipresent, omnipotent, and omniscient. God alone is in all places, has all power, and knows all. That is a bigger idea than I can wrap my mind around!

Suppose we could somehow fully understand the whole being of God. Suppose we could fully grasp God's omnipresence, omnipotence, and omniscience. What if we knew all there is to know about God?

At first, that sounds like a grand idea. There would be no more lingering doubts. Knowing all there is to know about God would solve all the mysteries of God. Suddenly the paradoxical side of God would be clear. We would have all wisdom and all power. But, is that really such a comforting idea?

If we could contain the whole of God in our minds, then we would have reduced God to a human mind. Then our need for God would cease, because we would have the mind of God and, thus, we would be God. Here is the really scary part: the whole of God would be limited to my puny, little, mortal mind. Wouldn't be much of a God would he?

No. The paradox, the mystery, and the beyond-my-imagination must remain in place. That is what keeps God being God and we mortals being who we are. It really is better that way. Still, I think God rather delights in our musing, pondering, and wondering.

Prayer: This Day I will be content in letting God be God. Today, I will delight in the wonder, the paradox, and the mystery.

A lucky person is one who goes through life with three good friends.

—Unknown

Benjamin Franklin once said there are three faithful friends—an old wife, an old dog, and ready money. There is a twinge of cynicism in Franklin's choices. His choice of an old wife is a bit patriarchal. Not all are dog lovers. And ready money can turn out to be more of an enemy than a friend. I am not sure I fully agree with Franklin's choices.

So, what is an old friend? An old friend once told me that a true friend is someone who knows all about you and still likes you. A true friend has the ability to see beyond your faults. A friend is one who can appreciate you when you are at your most vulnerable moment. A true friend is one who loves you when you are unlovable. To have even one person who understands and accepts you in these terms is truly remarkable. To have three is amazing.

But, take heart. Having three such friends may not be as difficult as it sounds. Do you remember when you were in Sunday school and you sang the song, "What a Friend We Have In Jesus"? There is one friend who loves us when we are unlovable, knows about us and accepts us for who we are, and deeply appreciates us when we are most vulnerable. That one is Jesus Christ. There, we have reduced the task by one third, for we do have a friend in Jesus.

Prayer: This Day I will be a friend to someone. Today, I will accept another, look beyond their flaws, and truly care.

God heard the boy cry.

—Genesis 21:17

The story of Abraham casting his son, Ishmael, and the boy's mother—Abraham's mistress, Hagar—into the wilderness is a troubling tale. It is a story that shows the dark side of the human condition. It is the story of a fractured family. Abraham looks like an unfaithful husband and a heartless father. Sarah allows jealousy to rule her decisions. Hagar is an example of a disposable commodity that can be used and cast aside (not a good model for how to treat women).

You have to wonder what Abraham was thinking. What was Sarah thinking? What was Hagar thinking? In fact, given all the people on this planet whom God could have chosen to be the father of His chosen people, why such a dysfunctional bunch? What were you thinking, God?

The whole cast of characters are flawed folks. This would be an impossible story to embrace if it were not for five words—*God heard the boy cry*. Those five words reveal a unique quality of God. God listens, the heart of God is moved, and God responds. The story has a good ending because God heard the boy cry. Beyond that, God was filled with empathy and he brought about a comforting conclusion. Some call that the Good News. I call it the *very* Good News!

Prayer: This Day I will let God hear my voice. Today, I will call out because I fully know that God listens, God cares, and God responds.

Be still, and know that I am God!

—Psalm 46:10

Stillness is not a virtue that comes easily. We are a bit inclined to clamor. We probe, we question, we march, we picket, and we demand. We ask God "What is the meaning of this or that?" We sometimes say, "God, if you are there . . ." There comes a tragic low in every life when we begin a doubting prayer with words that go something like this: "God, if you really are God, and if you really do care . . ."

Clamor, doubt, and wonder are all familiar to God. More than a few have shaken their angry fists at God and said, "Why me, O Lord?"

God has to have gotten used to such racket. Though it is seldom discussed and rarely admitted, we all have our moments when we think we could do a better job of being God than God is doing. When the spiritual storm calms, we feel a bit foolish. We wonder how God can put up with our rage, our doubt, and our questioning.

The psalmist touches on this in those familiar words: "Be still, and know that I am God!" Quiet the clamor. Settle down. Cease the doubting. Just knowing is enough!

Prayer: This Day I will be still. And, hopefully, from that stillness my knowing will begin.

> *Just remember, God will never give you*
> *more than you can handle.*
>
> —Unknown

We have all said it. We have all relied upon it. There is a measure of comfort in those words. God will never give you more than you can handle. Are you ready for a real shock? Don't believe those words. I know, it sounds like blasphemy. These are almost sacred words—almost, but not quite. The second real shock is that these words do not come from the Word of God.

Think for a moment what kind of God is the sole proprietor of misery? Consider a God who measures out misery, despair, brokenness, sorrow, and grief. Consider a God who knows your limits and then delights in testing them to within a millimeter of your breaking point. Such a God is one who sees us as ants and poises a gigantic foot over our bodies and then applies just enough pressure to squeeze but not smash. That is not the God of grace I understand.

God is not the author of misery. Here is how it ought go:

Just remember, there is nothing you and God cannot handle together.

Life has its storms. There are tornados, hurricanes, earthquakes, cancer, and car wrecks. God does not hand out this misery. God is present to us in our misery as friend, companion, and healer.

Prayer: This Day I will walk with God in the certain knowing that together we handle all that life might bring to my door. Today, I will not have to go it alone.

For I am convinced that neither death, nor life, nor angels, nor rulers,
nor things present, nor things to come, nor powers, nor height, nor depth,
nor anything else in all creation, will be able to separate us from the love
of God in Christ Jesus our Lord.

—Romans 8:38

Today we begin a seven-day series I call "Spiritual Nothings." A book entitled "Spiritual Nothings" would not likely be a best seller. Yet, the knowing that nothing can ambush, derail, or destroy our faith is of imperative importance. The first Spiritual Nothing is this:

NOTHING will ever separate us from the love of God.

God's love is without measure. It is without condition. It cannot be earned. It will never be withdrawn. God is in the business of loving his creation. If you wonder what proof there is that God might just one day change his mind, then consider the price God paid. God sent his Son, Jesus Christ. God has a lot at stake.

God will love you when you are unlovable. God will love you when you are old, confused, bankrupt, ugly, unemployed, brokenhearted, or angry. Oh sure, God may be a bit disappointed in our behavior at times, but nothing will ever separate us from God's unconditional love.

So, the first "Spiritual Nothing" is that nothing will ever come between you and God that will cause God to withdraw His love. That is a good beginning.

Prayer: This Day I will bask in the absolute knowing that *nothing* will ever cause God to withdraw His love for me. Today, I will try my best to love others with the same unconditional terms.

The power is like the working of his mighty strength, which he exerted in Christ when he raised him from the dead and seated him at his right hand in the heavenly realms, far above all rule and authority, power and dominion, and every title that can be given, not only in the present age but also in the one to come.

—Ephesians 1:19b–21

NOTHING will ever separate us from the grace of God.

There is a sense of nothingness in God's hope in Christ. The nothingness is that in all creation, for all time, in every nation, and among all people, nothing will erode the hope of Christ. God's love and grace that has been made known to us in Jesus Christ will forever endure.

Few things in life are forever. Ideologies come and go. Empires rule for a time, then fall away. Dynasties all have an end. Fashions thrive, then fade away. There is not much in life that we can point to and say, "This is eternal." In fact, there are few models of forever.

Part of the Good News is that *nothing* will ever separate us from the grace of God. That includes anything we do, anything that happens within nature, and anything that changes politically. God's grace, and God's grace alone is eternal, inseparable, and enduring.

Some call that the Good News. The fact is it is *very* Good News!

Prayer: This Day I will quit doubting, wondering about, and questioning God's grace. Simply because it is divine grace, it defies explanation. So, today I will be content to relish in grace rather than try to fully understand it.

My dear children, I write this to you so that you will not sin. But if anybody does sin, we have one who speaks to the Father on our defense—Jesus Christ, the Righteous One.

—1 John 2:1

NOTHING you can ever do is greater than the cross of Christ can forgive.

There are those who say, "I can understand forgiveness for the common varieties of sin, but I have gone beyond the norm. My sin is unforgivable." The cross of Christ is sufficient to mediate any shortcoming any one of us can dream up.

Believing that the cross has some limitation has a way of diminishing the grace of God we know in Christ. It is biblically unsound. And it trivializes the gift of Calvary. To think that Christ is only capable of resolving tiny separations makes his suffering and resurrection no more than a home remedy for a severe illness. The cross of Christ is not a tourniquet or a Band-Aid for minor hurts. The cross of Christ is sufficient to bring about reconciliation for any sin.

The second Spiritual Nothing is knowing that nothing is bigger than the cross of Christ.

Again, some call that the Good News, when it is really *very* good news.

Prayer: This Day I will reconsider the scope of the cross of Christ. Today, I will marvel at its magnitude.

The virgin will be with child and will give birth to a son, and they will call him Immanuel—which means, "God is with us."

—Matthew 1:23

NOTHING is greater than God's ultimate hope for reconciliation we know as the Incarnation.

The life, death, and resurrection of Jesus Christ is a onetime, unrepeatable, event. If you are waiting for a better deal, it will not happen. If you think God will reconsider his ultimate hope for reconciliation, forget it. Christ will come again as Scripture says, but there will be no other Christ-event of the scope and nature of that one-time, 2,000-year-ago happening. The Incarnation is a one-time happening.

Consider all that went before the Incarnation of Jesus Christ. This was no accidental occurrence. This is God's ultimate hope for reconciliation after a long string of disappointments. First, the personal relationship in the Garden of Eden did not work out. So, God tried to start all over again in the Noah saga. That did not work out. Then God personally selected a man named Abram and made a special covenant with him. That, too, failed. Then God delivered his people when they were enslaved in Egypt, thinking they would always remember his goodness. They soon forgot. Then God gave them the Ten Commandments through Moses. They broke them. Then God sent prophets. The people did not listen. Then God said, "Maybe they need a book of instructions." So, God had his special people record all he had revealed. The people argued with the book and the authors.

One day God said to himself, "I guess there is nothing left for me to do but go there myself." God came—just once.

The fourth "Spiritual Nothing" is that nothing is greater than the Incarnation of God in Jesus Christ.

Prayer: This Day I will more fully comprehend what God has done for me in the life, death, and resurrection of Jesus Christ. Knowing fully that I will never fully know, I will be content to accept rather than to explain.

Praise the LORD, all you nations;
extol him, all you peoples.
For great is his love toward us,
and the faithfulness of the LORD endures forever.
Praise the LORD.

—Psalm 117

NOTHING will ever cause God to break His promise.

God is wholly invested in creation for the long haul. Think about the covenants God has made. There will never be another flood to destroy all creation. God kept his word (Genesis 9:11). God told Abram that from this day forth, he would be their God and they would be his people (Genesis 12:2–3). God kept his word. God lifted up a young shepherd named David and promised to make him a strong and faithful ruler. God kept his word (2 Samuel 7:1ff). In fact, in every incidence of God making a promise, he has kept his word. God can be trusted!

The ultimate covenant is the Incarnation. When Jesus said, "This cup is the new covenant in my blood," he was speaking to people who had a long history of a God who was a faithful covenant-keeper (1 Corinthians 11:25).

God has, still does, and always will keep his promises. That is why it is called a covenant. That is *very* good news!

Prayer: This Day I will cast off any shadow of doubt that concerns God's reliability. Today, I will take ownership of my role as covenant-keeper in all my daily affairs. I will give thanks for the model that has been set before me.

Heaven and earth will pass away, but my words will
never pass away.
—The words of Jesus Christ as recorded
in Matthew 24:35

NOTHING will ever destroy the church of Jesus Christ.

Often the Book of Revelation is read as a doomsday horror story. Some see it as a forewarning of the coming apocalypse. They read it as an end-of-the-world Judgment-Day catastrophe. For the doomsday soothsayer, this is hearty stuff.

There is another way to understand the Book of Revelation. It is one of promise and hope. The entirety of the forewarning, the impending doom, and the threatening disaster are no match for the enduring hope of the church of Jesus Christ. The promise of a shining holy city that emerges from the ash heap of despair is a message of hope.

But, is this just an optimist's speculation? Is this merely a positive thinker's hope? Not at all! The overarching truth of the gospel of Jesus Christ is that his church will emerge victorious. That victory has been proven time and time again. The church has endured crisis after crisis and has withstood them all. Some ill-conceived ideas have heaped hurt upon others. Some probably seemed like a good idea at the time. Some were only thinly disguised evil in the guise of holiness.

Countless tragedies have been placed at the church's door. The history of the church is a long litany of corrupt, evil, immoral people bringing their greed and lust to the church. One needs look no further than recent headlines to understand that Christ's church still endures the harm of imperfect servants. A lesser mortal institution would be no more than a footnote to history. Not so with Christ's church.

There is good news in all of this brokenness. Paul says, ". . . in all these things we are more than conquerors through him who loved us" (Romans 8:37). Again, out of Spiritual Nothingness comes good news!

Prayer: This Day I will live with the assurance that Christ's church will emerge victorious. Today, I will focus on how my gifts can bring about that victory.

Jesus did many other miraculous signs in the presence of his disciples,
which are not included in this book. But these
are written that you may believe that Jesus is the Christ,
the Son of God, and that by believing you may
have life in his name.

—John 20:30–31

NOTHING is stopping you from the love, grace, and forgiveness of God
through Jesus Christ.

No sin is too big for God's grace. There is no worry that you will outlive the church of Jesus. God keeps his promises. So, there is nothing that stands as a barrier between you and total reconciliation with your Creator. However, there is an "if" clause in all this—*if* you believe in Jesus Christ.

Some rainy day when you need a good indoor project, look up the most often used verb in the Gospel of John. You will find it is "to believe." For John, believing is everything. The only prerequisite for God's love, grace, and forgiveness is believing that Jesus is God's Son sent to redeem all humankind. Remember, it was John who wrote: "For God so loved the world that he gave his only Son that whosoever believed in him would not perish but have everlasting life" (John 3:16).

With that belief, the "Spiritual Nothings" become "Spiritual Some-things." Rejecting Christ plunges the nothings into nothingness. If you want to make something out of nothing, just believe.

Isn't that simple? Better yet, isn't that just another way of shouting the Good News?

Prayer: This Day I will believe. Today, I will begin to understand that God's love, God's grace, and God's forgiveness is not something that happens to me if I am lucky. It is mine merely by believing.

But seek first his kingdom and his righteousness, and all these things will be given to you as well.

—Matthew 6:33

It was the kind of day in which everything went wrong. If it were a machine that could break, it broke. If it were an animal that could get sick, it hovered near death. If it were a marketable commodity that could drop in price, the bottom fell out. It was the kind of day that comes along now and then without reason, expectation, or antidote. Just when I thought nothing else could go wrong, a brightly painted van drove into the driveway. That is just what I need right now—an uninvited salesman. The man drove up to the barn and stepped out of his van. He wore a cheerful smile and said, "Hello," in a way that made you believe he was truly glad to see you. He asked, "How are you fixed for hardware supplies—bolts, hacksaw blades, hand tools, and welding rods?"

"Well, we have a supplier who keeps us stocked. But thanks anyway."

"I'm mighty glad to know your needs are being met. But, if I can ever help in any way, here is my card."

He handed me a business card that looked much like any other business card, but this was no ordinary card. All it said was Matthew 6:33 in big, bold letters.

"What is this?" I asked.

With a jolly chuckle the man said, "Well, son, that's the order of all things. Now you have yourself a real good day." He got in his van and drove off.

I stuck the card in my shirt pocket. There it rested, but my mind did not rest. I wondered what Matthew 6:33 was all about. When I went in for supper that evening, I opened the Bible to Matthew 6:33. **"But seek first the kingdom of God and all his righteousness, and all these things will be given to you as well."** How did that stranger know I had put the empire of Jerry before the kingdom of God that day?

Prayer: This Day is a kingdom-building day for God. By putting God first, I will keep my priorities in order.

Give, and it will be given to you. A good measure, pressed down, shaken together, and running over, will be poured into your lap. For with the measure you use, it will be measured to you.
—The words of Jesus as recorded in Luke 6:38

The Old Sleepy Eye Flour Company in Monmouth, Minnesota, was a marketing innovator. In the late 19th century, the Old Sleepy Eye Company began putting earthenware pitchers in sacks of flour. It was the first Cracker Jack prize in a box scheme.

The pitchers came in fives sizes—half pint, pint, quart, half gallon, and gallon. The bigger the sack of flour you bought, the bigger the earthenware pitcher you received. The pitchers were creamy white with a dark blue cobalt silhouette of the Indian, Old Sleepy Eye. They were quite attractive, but cheaply made. The company thought the public would be delighted with the pitchers.

A huge backlash occurred and sales plummeted. Someone discovered that the heavy earthenware pitchers displaced more flour than the value of the pitchers. If fact, the company had tried to trick their customers by selling 96 pounds of flour and a 4-pound, cheaply made pitcher.

An interesting epilogue to the Old Sleepy Eye story is that those cheap pitchers have become collector items. In today's market, a mint set of five pitchers would fetch from $2,500 to $3,000!

When Jesus talks about pressed down, shaken together, full measure, he is saying, "My grace is boundless."

Prayer: This Day I will give out in the same measure I hope for in return. Christ's full measure will be my standard scale.

The best liar is he who can make the smallest
amount of lying go the longest way.

—Samuel Butler

A couple opened a donut shop on a street where two other donut shops were located. They immediately recognized they were faced with stiff competition. So, they decided they needed something special to attract business. They took what money they could scrape together and had a sign painted that read:

THE BEST DONUTS IN THE WORLD!

Seeing the new sign, the proprietor of the next donut shop on that street had a bigger sign commissioned that read:

THE BEST DONUTS IN THE ENTIRE UNIVERSE!

The next morning, the owner of third donut shop took a crayon and piece of cardboard and put a sign in his window that said:

THE BEST DONUTS ON THIS BLOCK!

Truth can be a matter of perspective.

Prayer: This Day I will live as honestly as I can. Today, I will consider what others hear when I think I am being honest.

In the same manner, after supper he took a cup, saying, "This cup is the new covenant in my blood, which is poured out for you. But the hand of him who is going to betray me is with mine on the table. The Son of Man will go as it has been decreed, but woe to that man who betrays him."
—Luke 22:20–22

Have you ever given any thought to who might have been at that Last Supper with Jesus? Think about it. There might have been many—perhaps dozens. Exactly how many we will never know. But, there were at least thirteen gathered there in that upstairs room celebrating a traditional Passover meal.

Who were these people, and what had they done to deserve a seat at this, the most important supper ever served?

There was Peter who would deny even knowing Jesus—not just once, but three times before the next dawn. There were James and John, a pair of power-hungry brothers who bickered constantly about who was the most deserving. There was Thomas who was filled with doubt. There was Matthew with his checkered and corrupt past. There was Judas who had already betrayed Jesus to the Roman authorities. Then there was a handful of lukewarm followers who would scatter when the chips were down and not appear again until it seemed safe. At best, they were a bunch of losers!

Yet, losers or not, Jesus offered each of them the cup of salvation. Not one earned the right. Not one stood out as righteous. Not one was a model of moral decency. Yet all were served.

This gives me hope. I do not have to be perfect to receive Christ. I cannot earn the privilege. It is not the just reward for righteousness. Simply put, Jesus accepted them in their imperfect condition.

There is a name for that. It is called grace. And that explains why a seat has been saved for you and for me at that table.

Prayer: This Day I will give thanks for the mercy and grace that is mine in Jesus Christ. Today, I will especially cherish God's grace, because I know I do not have to be perfect to be loved by Christ.

"Whoever believes and is baptized will be saved."
—The words of Jesus as recorded
in Mark 16:16

One of the great debates that grew out of the Reformation surrounded the sacrament of baptism. Some felt that only the baptized would receive salvation. Others were not so sure and preached that the unbaptized could also see heaven. Some thought that infant baptism was acceptable. Others were bitterly opposed to baptizing babies and insisted on adult baptism after the candidate had reached the age of reason.

Still others argued that it was wrong to baptize anyone more than once. This group was called "Anabaptists." The Anabaptists felt a second baptism implied that the first had failed. They argued that a second baptism sent a message that doubted God's grace was present in the first baptism. Today's Baptist Church, The Disciples of Christ, the Mennonites, and others are descendents of the Anabaptist movement.

We are far removed from the passion these early reformers brought to the discussion. It all seems a bit trivial to most of us today. But, the matter is one of importance and ought not be too easily dismissed. Each of us needs to consider and remember our own baptism.

When I was a senior in seminary, I visited the Holy Lands. It was my intention to be baptized in the River Jordan at the same bend in the river that is believed to be the place where John the Baptist baptized Jesus. The day we visited that site, the temperature was just above freezing and it was spitting snow. It was on the banks of the River Jordan, in the midst of a January snowstorm, that I decided the Anabaptists had a sound argument!

There are times when theology and practicality are in perfect harmony.

Prayer: This Day I will take time to remember my baptism. Today, I will recall the moment a new and clean slate was handed to me. Today, I will be especially grateful.

Now it is required that those who have been
given a trust must prove faithful.
—1 Corinthians 4:2

Bob Cox was a farmer. When he was a young man, he inherited an eighty-acre farm that had been "mined." Mined is a term that means robbed, abused, or drained of resources. This was as neglected a farm as any that laid outdoors. It had been said of this piece of land that if a rabbit wanted to walk across it, the poor bunny would have to pack its lunch or face certain starvation. But all that was to change under the tenure of Bob Cox.

Bob began to love that sorry farm back into life. He used every husbandry practice that was known to his generation. He took from it gently, and gave back generously. The eighty acres had been so mined that it took time for any progress to be noted. But, Bob was persistent. He just loved the land back into life.

Years passed and Bob became an old man. He had restored the land to a far more productive state than when it was initially cleared. What had once been junk was now a show place. The Michigan Cooperative Extension Service recognized what this gentle soul had done to this once-ragged farm. The M.C.E.S. named Bob Cox as the Soil Steward of the year. This is a prestigious award that is reserved for the finest custodians of the land. It is like the Congressional Medal of Honor of farming.

Bob was invited to the state capital to receive his plaque at a special banquet. Bob's acceptance speech may have been one of the shortest in history. He simply said, "All I ever wanted was to pass it on better than it was given to me."

What a world this would be if there were more who cared for creation in the manner of this simple farmer.

Prayer: This Day I will take ownership of my role as a steward of the land, the church, and my community. Today, I will do all I can with my piece of creation for the sake of future generations.

A new command I give to you: Love one another.
As I have loved you, so you must love one
another. By this all men will know that
you are my disciples, if you love one another.

—The words of Jesus as recorded
in John 13:34–35

A Christian was saying her evening prayers. She was upset by what she had seen and heard that day. She poured her heart out to God in an accusing manner.

Dear God,

Today I saw a hungry person with no coat sitting in a snowdrift. I saw a young mother buying boxes of macaroni and cheese with food stamps for her six small children. When I got home I turned on the television and there was news of millions dying in Africa with HIV/AIDS. There was a famine in India, war in Afghanistan, and another tyrant swallowed up another tiny nation. There was a robbery that took the life savings from an elderly woman. A wife was beaten, a drunk driver killed a carload of teen-agers, and another corporate executive stole millions from his company. Lord, there is so much suffering, so much hurt, and so much misery here. Why don't you do something?

There was a long pause and the gentle voice followed saying: "I have done something. I sent you!"

Prayer: This day and every day to follow, I will live out the Great Commandment that calls us to love one another. Today, I will recognize more than ever before that loving another takes more than words.

You stand your tallest when you stoop to lift a child.
—Unknown

Every child needs an Ernie Constable. Ernie was an elderly bachelor farmer who lived a mile or so from my home when I was a child. He was a robust man with enough laughter in his soul to fill a Big Ten football stadium. Ernie never married, so he became surrogate uncle to all the neighborhood children.

Ernie was well read. He could quote long passages from a half-dozen Shakespeare plays. He had a nearly complete collection of *National Geographic Magazines* that dated back to the late 1800s. He had an intense interest in the art, culture, politics, hunting, travel, and the world around him. There was only one Ernie. What made Ernie so special to the neighborhood children was that he was interested in us. In a time that still believed it was best for children to be seen, but not heard, Ernie wanted to hear us. Apparently Ernie heard plenty from me, because he nicknamed me "Blowtorch." He said I was an endless source of hot air (maybe Old Ernie recognized the preacher within me as a child).

More than once on a Saturday morning, Ernie would call my house and say, "Blowtorch, get on your bike and come on over. Today we are going to clean the junk drawer." Ernie's junk drawer was something to behold. It was a kitchen "catchall" that held all manner of treasures from elks' teeth to magnetic Scotty dogs. Cleaning Ernie's junk drawer was his way of saying, "Well Blowtorch, if you promise to take care of those Scotty dogs, I guess you can have them." I do not remember ever throwing anything away when we cleaned the junk drawer.

We have set aside days to remember and celebrate our mothers, our fathers, our loved ones, and our grandparents. We celebrate veterans, the flag, laborers, secretaries, and the pilgrims. I think we ought to set aside a day to celebrate the mentors of youth who model goodness to children. We need to celebrate the men and women who stretch young minds and listen to what children have to say. I think the world needs an "Ernie Day." But, perhaps before we go that far, maybe we need more men and women like Ernie Constable.

Prayer: This Day I will take time to show particular interest in a child. Today, I will pass on a glimpse of the wonders of the world to another generation.

We are human beings, not human doings.
—Robert Fulghum

One of my favorite authors is Robert Fulghum, the author of *Everything I Ever Needed to Know I Learned in Kindergarten*. Fulghum has a pithy way of passing on profound truths. His writing is laced with wit and common sense. He is one of those writers who makes me want to say, "That's right. I wish I had said that!"

As a popular writer, Fulghum travels a lot and meets many people. He has designed an unusual business card that he passes on to strangers he meets in his travels. The business card has just one word in the center of the card. It reads:

FULGHUM

He explains that the first question we ask a stranger is: "what do you do?" We look past the person and inquire about vocation. We seldom take the time to get to know the person before we want to know what they do for a living. Perhaps it goes even beyond that. Maybe we think that by knowing the vocation, we will know the person. And, by knowing the person's profession, we can begin to value or devalue the person at hand.

Fulghum reminds us that we are human beings. And, to know about one's vocation does not define the being, aspect of humanity. What one does for his or her livelihood merely speaks of their doing and not of their being. The "What do you do?" question is a subtle way of judging and valuing a stranger, because it overlooks the being within.

Prayer: This Day I will seek the being who does the doing. Today, the labor of another will not even begin to define that person.

No act of kindness, no matter how small, is ever wasted.

—Aesop

It is hard to disagree with Aesop. Even a small kindness can make a huge difference. But, what about those (hopefully rare) occasions when we show unkindness? Are they long remembered? What about those moments when we blurt out something we instantly wish we had not said? It happens to all of us. Most often, there is no malice at its heart; it just happens. Look in any greeting card store and you will find a section of cards that are designed to graciously apologize for some thoughtless act. If Hallmark and others can publish an entire category of "I'm sorry I said that" cards, then it must be a fairly regular happening.

It happens to all of us. Believe me, preachers are no exception! One day a woman was showing me a new doll she had purchased for her grandson. It was a Scottish doll named Stuart. She said, "And I think that is the Stuart tartan the doll is wearing." Before I could even think, I said, "No, that has too much green in it to be the Stuart tartan, and besides it is spelled Stewart."

I instantly wished I had remained silent. I had unwittingly dashed the woman's dreams. There was no repairing the damage. A Hallmark card would not fix it. A hundred "What a buy! What a find! I just know your grandson will adore it," would not heal the wounds of a smashed dream.

Tread lightly on others' dreams, passions, and excitement. For no act of kindness is ever wasted, and no smashed dream will ever go unnoticed.

Prayer: This Day I will make every effort to think twice and speak once. Today, I will try to applaud the dreams of others and treat them tenderly.

*Then Jesus came to them and said, "All authority in heaven and on earth
has been given to me. Therefore go and make disciples of all nations,
baptizing them in the name of the Father and of the Son and of the Holy
Spirit, and teaching them to obey everything I have commanded you.
And surely I am with you always, to the very end of the age."*
—The words of Jesus as recorded
in Mathew 28:18–20

The Great Commission is one that most of us would like to pass off
to someone else. Though we do not actually say it, we think, "Here,
you go tell the world about Christ. I just can't do it."

We think we are not capable proclaimers. This is a job that is best
left to preachers. Or, maybe a gentle way of living out the Great Commission is to fund missionaries or televangelists. Sometimes we think
the evangelical denominations are doing the job for all Christendom.
We shrug off the Great Commission by saying, "Let the professionals
tell the world about Christ, then it will be done right."

Sharing the Good News is every Christian's responsibility. It is not
an option. It is not reserved for the professionals. It is not the sovereign domain of the evangelical denominations. Telling others about
Jesus is our walking papers straight from Christ himself.

If you still say, "I just cannot do that," you might consider another
alternative. I do not know who said it, but here is a better way:

*We are told to tell the world about Christ, but use words only if absolutely
necessary.*

Prayer: This Day I will live in such a way that all who meet me along
life's way will readily recognize that Christ dwells within.
Today, I will model a Christlike attitude in all I do, in all I
say, and to all I encounter. This is no easy job, so I'm asking
for God's strength.

> *My words fly up, my thoughts remain below:*
> *Words without thoughts never go to heaven.*
> —From William Shakespeare's *Hamlet*

I would like to see the word "should" excised from the lexicon. Should is my least-favorite word, and, hopefully, among my least-used words. It is not profanity, nor is it a racial slur. Likely to most, the word "should" is quite innocuous. So, why my distaste? Why have I mounted a one-person campaign to rid the English language of this oft-used word?

I find "should" to be offensive, demeaning, or judgmental. In most contexts it is elitist, arrogant, and pompous.

Should coveys blame, as in, "You should have been more careful."

Should points out another's inadequacies as in, "You should try harder."

Should can be understood as shame. Consider: "I should have done better on the test."

Should is demanding—"You should always . . ."

Should is judgmental—"You should have thought of that before you acted."

Maybe we should think about using some other word, because we could live nicely without blame, shame, and judging. Oops, I did it again!

Prayer: This Day I will choose my words carefully. I will think about how I am heard and be a bit more sensitive about the feelings my words evoke in others.

Finally, brothers, whatever is true, whatever is noble, whatever is right,
whatever is pure, whatever is lovely, whatever is admirable—if anything
is excellent or praiseworthy-think about such things.
—Philippians 4:8

Resentments lead to rage. Rage leads to hate. Hatred atrophies your physical, emotional, and spiritual being. Thus, keeping watch of resentments when they are in their infancy is one of the keys to holistic wellness. Like any malignancy, early detection is the best cure.

A friend of mine once said, "When I feel a resentment building, I look in the mirror, and invariably on my forehead are the words: SPACE AVAILABLE—RENT CHEAP."

My friend's observation is sound. We are the landlords of what occupies space in our minds. To rent space to resentment is selling out to a poor tenant. Resentments, and all that inevitably follows, are often a matter of choice. Deciding what and who will take up residence in our minds is optional. Since the mind is such precious space, it ought to be reserved for the best leaseholders. To rent your mind too cheaply is turning a cathedral into a slum.

Prayer: This Day I will be more intentional about what occupies the precious space of my mind. Today, I will take inventory of my mental leases and do a bit of urban renewal if necessary.

There are many ways to be human.
—Dr. Linda Easley, Anthropologist

Every culture has found ways to organize its language, religion, economy, morality, taboos, and set of beliefs. Interestingly, every culture has addressed many of the same questions and have often come to remarkably similar conclusions. Of course, there are significant differences around the world. And, some cultures have proven to be more workable than others. Where we get stuck in this rich diversity is in believing that any one culture has a monopoly on the only possible way we address our humanness.

Consider our close cousins, the English:

When an Englishman says . . . In our culture it means . . .

When an Englishman says . . .	In our culture it means . . .
Serviette	Napkin
Cuddle up chaps	Gather in so you can hear what I have to say
Straight with	Immediately
Chips	French Fries
Crisps	Potato chips
Pie	Could be pudding
Pudding	Could be pie
Bonnet	Car hood
Boot	Car's trunk
Oh Crackers!	Darn it!
Smashing idea!	Great idea!
Bloody	An unflattering adjective
Motorway	Highway
Give way	Yield to traffic
Bangers and mash	Sausages and mashed potatoes
Chuckers	Filled to capacity
Mushy peas	Overcooked peas that are truly mushy!

Prayer: This Day I will be more open to diversity. Today, I will endeavor to learn from, to delight in, and to consider the worth of others. Today, I will embrace tolerance and pray for the same from others.

*James, a servant of God and of the Lord Jesus Christ, to the twelve tribes
scattered among the nations: Greetings.*

—James 1:1

There is a politeness in the western plains that is expressed in greeting a stranger. Sometimes it is a wave, a tip of the brim of a hat, or a slight nod. The exact manner of salute has regional variations. By whatever manner, though, no stranger is met on the highway of life without acknowledgement. It is a friendly gesture that says, "Hello" (or maybe "Howdy").

In the rolling western ranch lands of South Dakota the accepted greeting is the two-fingered wave. No, it is not a victory salute. The two-fingered wave is subtle and nearly involuntary. Two ranchers meet on the road. Each is intent on his mission—going into town for combine parts, fixing the fence in the back pasture, or checking a field of wheat. Their missions are individual and personal. Each of the ranchers has his hands on the steering wheel of his pickup in the perfect 10:00/2:00 position we were all taught in drivers' education. Each is deeply absorbed in the singularity of his mission, yet each is sensitive to the protocol of the prairie. Each rancher avoids eye contact, but acknowledges the other by lifting his index finger from the steering wheel.

The two-fingered wave says, "Greetings." It conveys a quiet hello, a silent "good to see you," and a solemn "Peace be with you." The two-fingered wave might say, "I want you to know I value your presence." It might also say, "Right now I'm too busy to stop and talk. But, be well until our paths cross again." Whatever it says, it is good to be acknowledged.

Prayer: This Day I will take no one for granted regardless of my busyness. Today, even in the midst of my mission, I will acknowledge all I meet with a hello—be it quiet or silent, I will make a sincere effort to acknowledge others.

I am the gate; whoever enters through me will be saved.
—John 10:9

There was a glut of wool in mid-19th-century Europe. Overproduction, cheap imports, and competition from cotton and silk caused the European woolen trade to fumble. The British, who had been the world's leading wool producers, felt the pinch more than any other country. Pressured by farmers and the textile industry, Parliament acted swiftly, though not brilliantly. In 1831, Parliament passed a law that demanded that all deceased British citizens be buried in wool. The dead would be garbed in wool or pay a fine that is roughly equivalent to $100 in today's economy. Some were so indignant about this ridiculous law that they made provisions in their wills to be buried in other than wool and have the fine paid by their estate.

The church became a willing accomplice in this ill-conceived idea. The priests would open the casket outside the cemetery before a burial to examine the deceased's clothing. If the poor soul was wearing other than a woolen suit, then entrance into the hallowed grounds was denied (at least until the fine was paid). Many churches built small roofed gates called liech gates at the entrance of the cemetery. Thus, the clergy did not have to stand in the rain and snow while he checked for wool clothing. The silly notion has long been repealed, but many liech gates still remain today at the entrance of English cemeteries.

When Jesus said, "I am the gate," he was not talking about the clothing on the corpse. Jesus was speaking about the life gate and not the liech gate. He was saying, "Think about your choices. Live in a loving relationship with one another. I am inviting you to enter through me."

Prayer: This Day I will live with intentional relationship with both God and others. Today, I will embrace and accept Jesus' invitation.

. . . when you pray, go into your room, close the door and pray to your
Father . . . When you pray, do not keep on babbling . . .

—Matthew 6:6–7

We were on our way to Israel. Three hundred or more of us were pressed into one of those jumbo jets that allows no more than four square feet per passenger. The plane was filled to capacity. The passenger list was an interesting and diverse mix of tourists, rabbis, and business people. We had traveled through the night, and now as the sun was breaking over the eastern horizon, there was a stir in the cabin. A hundred or more of the passengers began to poke around in the overhead luggage compartments and go through their carry on bags. At first, I was puzzled. Then it became clear what was happening. These were Orthodox Jews who were about to greet the new day with prayer. They were putting on their prayer shawls and phylacteries.*

About one-third of the passengers got up from their seats and went to the rear of the plane and looked out to the east in the direction of Jerusalem and began to pray in Hebrew. Initially, I was deeply touched by the prayerful commitment of these holy men. They read from their prayer books, chanted in Hebrew, and nodded in unison as they greeted the new day.

Then, it dawned on me. The isles were jammed with praying men. There was no way to get to the rest rooms. The balance of the plane's passengers (two hundred or so of us) were obliged to put our bladders on "parade rest" until the praying was over and the holy men had returned to their seats. Here was a case of one's religion ignoring the comfort and concerns of others. Here, prayer had become a spectacle.

I think that is what Jesus had in mind when he said, "Don't make a big thing of it. Talk to your heavenly Father in prayer as if you were speaking to your oldest and dearest friend. Do it quietly."

Prayer: This Day I will set aside a quiet time with God. Today, I will converse with God in prayer as if he were my oldest and dearest friend—after all, that is exactly who God is!

* A phylactery is a small leather box that is attached to a long leather strap. The box contains a tiny piece of parchment that is inscribed with a scriptural quotation. The strap is wrapped around one's forehead and spiraled down the right arm of an Orthodox Jewish man in prayer.

I have come that they may have life, and have it to the full.
—John 10:10

L ife can be endured, or life can be lived with fullness. Life can be a trudge, or it can be an abundant journey. Whether life is a trek to be endured or an abundant journey is largely a matter of perspective.

Often, the central focus of Jesus' ministry is seen as what becomes of us after we die. When this life is finished, the believer goes to heaven. Life's worries, trials, and sorrows are behind us and all that awaits us is harmony and tranquility. That is good news! How could anyone argue with the hope of eternal life?

Yet, the other half of the Good News is sometimes overlooked. The other half of the Good News is about what happens to us in the here and now. Eternal and everlasting life is good news, but abundant life in the present moment cannot be ignored. Salvation is not limited to a far-in-the-future-when-you-die happening. Salvation begins today!

What is the marker of abundant life? It is living with zest. It is embracing life, savoring it, and living with a sense of calm and joy. Zest is a good word for abundance. Zestful living is living with confidence, expectation, and hope. It is not about what awaits us in the future, but the abundance we share today as followers of Jesus Christ. Zestful living greets the new day with "Good—God it is morning!" Instead of "Good God, it's morning!"

Prayer: This Day I will live zestfully! Today, I will expand my understanding of the Good News and embrace the salvation of this very moment.

Therefore I tell you, do not worry about your life, what you will eat or drink; or about your body, what you will wear. Is not life more important than food, and the body more important than clothes? Look at the birds of the air; they do not sow or reap or store away in barns, and yet your heavenly Father feeds them. Are you not more valuable than they? Who of you by worrying can add a single hour to his life?
—Matthew 6:25–27

As best as I can tell, we pass through this life but once. So, why waste or compromise a second of it on worry? Of course, there are other ways to waste the preciousness of life. Resentment, anger, hate, and self-pity are all life-robbers. Overindulgence, greed, and a variety of vices can compromise life. But, worry seems to be the most universally accepted and the most commonly encountered life-sapper. Life is too precious to waste a second of it on worry.

A friend once told me that his philosophy on worry was simple. If I can fix it, then I have nothing to worry about. I'll just fix it. If the matter is something I cannot set straight, then all the worry in the world will never help. So, why worry? It is either within my power to change, and thus not a worry, or out of my power to change and therefore a waste of my time.

The Twelve Step people sum up the same idea in the oft-quoted Serenity Prayer. Here is worry put into perspective:

God, grant me the serenity to accept the things I cannot change, the courage to change the things I can, and the wisdom to know the difference.

Prayer: This Day I will sort out what deserves my worry energy. Today, I will not be surprised to discover that because of God's grace I have nothing worthy of my worry. The energy I would have put into worry, I'll used in a more productive way.

This life is worth living, we can say,
since it is what we make of it . . .

—William James

The late Joseph Campbell studied dozens, if not hundreds of cultures. He was intensely interested in how people defined the meaning of their existence and the purpose of life in their stories. Campbell compiled his findings in a massive work entitled, *The Power of Myth*.

When asked if there was a central theme or a universally shared concept of life that was shared by all, Campbell described it in this way: The commonality of all creation is the understanding that life is like a play. Not everyone has the best seat in the house. Some have an obstructed view, some are uncomfortable, and some may not see the whole play before they are obliged to exit. The hope of all creation is to live in such a manner that when the final curtain falls, you can say, "Now, that was some play!"

Campbell says that in studying any culture's stories you can uncover this single truth: "life is a grand play well worth attending."

Jesus Christ preached the same message, but in a slightly different way. In the Sermon on the Mount (Matthew 5:1–12) Jesus pointed out nine groups who were particularly blessed. For Christ, actively participating in life is the key to a rich and full life. To be a spectator was not enough for Jesus. But, James Campbell and Jesus agree—life is not something that happens to you. Life is what you make of it.

Prayer: This Day I will be an active participant in life. Today, I will step out from behind the spectator barricades and join the parade as a full participant.

No one has ever come to the end of his life and with deep regret said, "I sure wish I had worked harder!"

—Anonymous

We have been lulled into believing that we are defined by our labor. The more we work, the more we are valued. The more we are valued, the better person we must be. Therefore, the harder we work, the better we become.

Of course, that is not so. We all know that, yet everyone of us at some time becomes a willing participant in work-based worth. Have you ever prepared for a vacation and find that the two weeks preceding the vacation are the busiest of the year? And, when you come back to work after a vacation, have you ever been faced with such a pile of work that you wonder if the vacation was worth the effort? Sure you have. It happens to all of us.

Some years ago I had an experience that helped put work and worth into perspective. I had been a farmer for twenty-eight years. Every spring brought planting season. Hundred-hour-or-more work-weeks were common during planting season. I had to do it. If it were to be done in a timely fashion, then I had to do it. To compound the matter even further, there was a quiet matter of pride in being one of the first to complete planting. So, not only the crop, but also the perception of others was at stake.

I rented my farm to another farmer and took a third-shift job in town that last spring on the farm. One morning as I was returning from a night's work, I noticed that the renter had planted the entirety of my farm sometime in the night. As I drove slowly past the freshly planted cornfield, I became aware that in the overall scheme of things I was not remarkably important. The crop would grow without my labor, the world would not be plunged into famine without my expertise, and the Chicago Board of Trade would never note my absence. Clearly, my worth had to be found in something other than my labor.

Prayer: This Day I will focus on my real worth. Today, I will look at myself as a much-loved child of God and not merely as the laborer of an uncaring boss.

Your sense of humor is your spirit dancing.

—Fr. Martin

Have you ever watched a dour-faced preacher talking about the joy of Christ? The sober expression and the claimed joy seem to be a sorry mismatch. If a life lived in relationship with Christ is so joyous, it ought to follow that at least some measure of bliss would seep through.

A Jesuit priest friend of mine, Fr. Martin, claims that one measure of our relationship with Christ is our sense of humor. Fr. Martin insists that our sense of mirth is the barometer of spiritual wellness.

It is hard to argue with this opinion. Gladness, mirth, joy, happiness, and bliss are all markers of hope and serenity. Having been relieved of the burden of shame, worry, guilt, and hopelessness ought to show as happiness. Who wants a faith journey that is laced with drudgery? Who needs a Savior who makes you feel worse? Who would ever be attracted to a belief that promotes unhappiness? Thus, a dancing spirit that is gladly seen by all may be the most convincing way we can share the Good News.

We have been given a mandate to tell the world about the Good News of Jesus Christ. One way is to explain it. A far better way is to proclaim it. Let the dance begin!

Prayer: This Day I will allow the joy of Christ that is within me to be seen by all. Today, I will proclaim the Good News with gladness.

This above all: to thy own self be true, And it must follow, as the night follows day, Thou canst not then be false to any man.
—From William Shakespeare's Hamlet

I have never met a trustworthy person who did not have a sound self-understanding. Trustworthiness goes hand in hand with those who know who they are and what they are about.

Have you ever worked for or with someone who had an underdeveloped sense of self-understanding? Often, they are indecisive, unreliable, and undependable. One set of demands and expectations would be the rule of the day and the next day the exact opposite would be required. Understanding or pleasing such a person is like shooting at a moving target. You are never certain what to expect.

If trustworthiness begins with self-understanding, then the ability to take a critical look at oneself is the first prerequisite. Who am I? What do I do well? What do I do poorly? What are my likes and dislikes? Do I embrace an idea simply because it is popular? Can I be trusted? Am I self-seeking, filled with self-pity, or indifferent to others? Or, am I loaded with self-loathing? These are not easy, and no one can answer these for you. But, consider what is at stake. If you, who live with yourself every moment of life, do not know who you are and what you are about, then could any outsider ever guess the scope of you?

Trust is not a given. It has to be earned. And it begins by knowing who you are, what you are about, and a willingness to live contentedly with that knowing.

Prayer: This Day I will take a self-inventory. It may be hard work, so I am asking for courage, honesty, and the ability to take that deep introspective look at me.

So what?
—The Reverend David Tyler Scoates

David Scoates was one of my professors at the Crystal Cathedral School of Christian Communicators. He was the finest preacher I have ever heard. His command of language was unrivaled. He was a spellbinding storyteller. He had a commanding presence in the pulpit. I use the past tense, because David has written and preached his last sermon in this life. He now proclaims the Good News from heaven.

David Scoates gave me two words that changed my life as a preacher. The two words were, "So what?" On the surface, "So what?" sounds a bit flippant. Maybe some would say it even sounds arrogant or confrontational. What he was pressing each of his students to consider was the question, "Why is this important?" Just because Jesus said it or because it is a central truth that is recorded in God's Word is not always helpful. To proclaim the Good News, to challenge people, and to bring about the long-sought kingdom of God, the "So what?" question must be addressed.

Why ought I give to the poor? What difference does it make how I behave? Why is it important that I love others? So what?

The Reverend Scoates instructed each of his students to write those two words on a piece of paper and tape them to their computers. He asked us to always consider the "So what?" question as we begin, as we write, and as we preach. You would be surprised to learn how many seemingly acceptable sermons cannot pass the "So what?" filter. And, if these two words have such an impact on a ten-or-fifteen-minute sermon, just imagine if asked often enough how they might shape a life over seventy or eighty years!

Prayer: This Day is a "So what?" day. I will boldly and bravely ask myself if I am living merely by a familiar and comfortable pattern, or if I am making a difference.

> The Lord gave and the Lord has taken away;
> *May the name of the Lord be praised.*
>
> —Job 1:21

For many years it has been a July ritual for a half dozen of us to go walleye fishing in Lake Erie. The western end of the Lake Erie basin is called the "Walleye Capital of the World." I am not sure it is quite that remarkable, but I can say that is a place where I have spent at least one delightful day each summer for many years.

Some years ago, on one of these walleye adventures I cast my line into the lake and was reeling it in slowly when I began to feel a strange drag on my line. Walleyes are notorious quiet nibblers. They rarely strike with authority. So, the drag seemed much like another not-so-hungry walleye at first. Still not convinced that this was a hit, I set the hook just to be on the safe side. To my surprise I reeled in a rod and reel that some luckless fisherman had lost in the lake! No fish, but a good story. A dozen or so years have passed since my landing the rod and reel. That story has been retold every time we head out on the big lake.

An old cliché states that what goes around comes around. On a recent July walleye tour, I wound up, cast long and far, the rod slipped from my hand, and I watched it disappear into the dark waters of Lake Erie. Though not the same rod I had rescued from the lake years ago, I had given back to the lake that which it had given to me.

The Lord gives and the Lord takes away! Amen.

Prayer: This Day I will consider the great balance sheet of life. I fully expect that when the accounting is done, I will discover that the Lord has given much that can never be taken away.

> *Few love me.*
> *Many hate me.*
> *All respect me.*
>
> —Unknown author

I happened to see the above quote on a tee shirt. A young man in his mid teens was proudly wearing this bold statement. I suppose that at least in part, his hope was to invoke outrage or to be noticed. So, simply because I am reflecting upon it, his outrageous statement was somewhat successful.

Take a moment to consider the tee shirt's motto.

Few love me. How sad. To be unloved or unlovable has to be lonely. To be unloved is the ultimate of rejection. We are validated by another's love. We are encouraged, find our sense of worth, and grow our ability to love others by the gift of another's love. To be loved by few is sad.

Many hate me. Though it does not necessarily follow that many hate an unloved person, it is nonetheless predictable. To be hated by even one is hurtful. At the very core of our being is the desire to be liked. To be hated by many is the loneliest of the lonely.

All respect me. Really? Could it be that fear has been mistaken for respect? How does one so unloved and so hated gain the respect of even one? Perhaps the respect is not really respect at all. Maybe it is seeing the young man as a good example of a bad example.

The lad got what he wanted. He wanted to be noticed. That he accomplished. One thing he may not have hoped for when he pulled that tee shirt on that morning was my pity. He got that, too.

Prayer: This Day I will take particular delight in that fact that I am loved and respected. Today, I will quietly and prayerfully give thanks to all who make that love and respect possible.

*Therefore do not worry about tomorrow, for tomorrow will
worry about itself. Each day has enough trouble of its own.*
—The words of Jesus as recorded
in Matthew 6:34

A recent news release from a space observatory predicts that a huge asteroid is headed our way. The asteroid is no modest space rock. It is reported to measure one-and-one-half miles thick. Those who keep track of celestial phenomena predict that the asteroid is due to crash into earth in February 2019.

Scientists claim that this could bring a catastrophic consequence the likes of which the world has seldom seen. They remind us that at least one theory that explains the disappearance of dinosaurs is that one such asteroid slammed into earth eons ago. The resulting dust cloud destroyed dinosaur food and set the stage for the rest of us. Presumably, the dinosaurs did not have nearly two decades of forewarning.

So, what to do? We could worry about it for the next few years. That would not be particularly helpful. We could devise a plan to destroy it with some kind of super weapon and render it as harmless space dust. Or, maybe we could come up with a plan to alter the earth's trajectory so the collision is avoided. I am not so sure there is much we need to do or can do about this pending catastrophe.

On a slightly more encouraging note, the scientists did say they would carefully watch the asteroid over the next few years. They went on to say they needed to check their numbers carefully because it could miss us by a few million miles. I do not think I will spend too much time worrying about the asteroid. If I worry about anything, it will be the scientists' math.

Prayer: This Day I will remind myself of the futility of worry. Today, I intend to be worry-less.

Do not be afraid of what you are about to suffer.
—Revelation 2:10

Fear of the unknown is unfounded worry. Worry is toxic to our physical, spiritual, and physical wellness. Therefore, fear and its partner, worry, can destroy life.

Some fears are unfounded. But, some fears can be a wake-up call that nudges us into action. The World Health Organization met recently to discuss the HIV/AIDS crisis that is threatening global heath, economy, and life itself. No country has a greater HIV/AIDS crisis than Zimbabwe. Scientists tell us that one-third of that nation will die in the next decade. Seven million children will be orphaned by the resulting famine. Millions of children will be HIV positive. Compounding the problem even deeper is that Zimbabwe's total health care expenditure per capita is about $5.00—not enough to buy a bottle of Nyquil for each of its citizens. Looming on the horizon in Zimbabwe, and soon to follow in dozens of other nations on every continent, is the greatest pandemic since the Bubonic Plague in the 15th and 16th centuries.

Fear and worry will not turn the tide; compassion, concern, and love will. All the barriers that hold back the best the world has to offer this human suffering must be removed. Racial prejudice, fear, economic reservations, and moralistic judgment must not keep us from caring.

Maybe fear is not so bad after all. Fear may act as a motivator in this crisis. And just perhaps the greatest fear of all might well be that a future generation will look back on our time and say, "They could have done more."

Prayer: This Day I will live fearlessly. Today, I will consider the bravest act I can do is to care for another.

People are always blaming their circumstances for what they are. I don't believe in circumstances. The people who get on in this world are the people who get up and look for the circumstances they want, and, if they can't find them, make them.

—George Bernard Shaw

This probably belongs in a column under the heading, "Top This If You Can!" or "This is Outrageous!" There is an impending class action lawsuit filed against Wendy's, McDonalds, Burger King, and Kentucky Fried Chicken by a group of obese people. Their claim is that the four fast-food corporations failed to warn the public that their meals contained too much fat, sugar, and salt. The lawsuit is asking for an undisclosed amount of money for the wanton disregard that the fast food industry has for public health.

A similar lawsuit has been filed against Colt, Smith and Wesson, and several other small-arms manufacturers for the carnage that hand-guns cause the public. Of course, the tobacco companies have paid out billions to smokers who now claim to have had no idea that cigarettes were harmful to their health. A diabetic man in England has sued a dairy because the pint of their ice cream that he ate every day has led to his diabetes. I expect that one day someone in hell will sue the church for not having thoroughly warned them that the wages of sin is death (better I remain silent before I give them some new ideas).

What has become of personal responsibility? The fact is that we are creatures of free choice. Choices have consequences. End of subject!

Prayer: This Day I will celebrate the greatest choice of all—Christ as my Savior. Today, I will exercise my personal responsibility for the care and feeding of my soul.

I like pigs. Cats look down on humans. Dogs look up to humans. But pigs see us as equals.

—Winston Churchill

Who do you see as an equal? Not swine, I hope. Who we see as our peers is important, because our peers are a reflection of us. So, if you look to a pig as your equivalent, guess what?

A sense of belonging is inherent to every life. We belong to families, communities, clans, tribes, nations, clubs, political parties, and unions. We are Lions fans, Packer backers, Cheese heads, Spartans, or Wolverines. We are Christian, Jewish, Muslim, Hindu, or atheist. We are Congregationalists, Catholics, Baptists, Methodists, Presbyterians, or non-denominational. We join bowling teams, biker clubs, golfing groups, hunt clubs, and sewing circles. The list of possibilities is almost infinite. We are joiners. We join because it helps to fulfill our inherent sense of our need to belong.

It has been said that we are judged by the company we keep. There is much truth in that. Our associations, affiliations, and homage are the measure of who we are and how we see ourselves. Though it may not always seem apparent, the attraction we have for any given group satisfies a deep sense of self. This could be good news if you value your peers. If, on the other hand, you find your company unsatisfying . . . . Well, take a long, hard look—not at them, but at you!

Prayer: This Day I will celebrate my peers, for they are a part of me. Today, I will endeavor to be worthy of their affection, support, and friendship, for I am also their reflection of self.

*Jesus said to her, "I am the resurrection and the life. He who believes in
me will live, even though he dies; and
whoever lives and believes in me will never die.
Do you believe this?"*
—John 11:25

The scars of war still remain. Yes, you have to look for those scars, but they are still evident throughout Europe. The evidence might be a massive steel beam bolted to the side of a brick building to help stabilize it. There are whole sections of towns where fifty—or sixty-year-old buildings stand while adjacent communities have a rich mix of new, old, and ancient. These are the subtle scars left by the hundreds of thousands of bombs dropped in WWII. Of course, there are the countless monuments, markers, plaques, and memorial gardens that remind us in a more deliberate way of that tragic insanity.

Now and then there will be an intentional piece of wreckage that has been preserved as a reminder. London has several churches that were bombed and not rebuilt. Today, they stand as roofless, window-less walls. They are stark reminders of war's wrath.

Though I wholly agree that we must never forget the suffering of the past, nor the ugly side of war, I find those wrecked churches theologically unsound. They portray death, but show no hope of resurrection. The central message of Christ's church is the hope of resurrection. Where is the new life in four bombed-out walls rotting in the heart of a busy city?

There is one bright exception to these scarred memorials. Coventry Cathedral kept its bombed-out, 14th-century hulk and attached it to a modern cathedral. Here Christ dwells in death and life once more. Here resurrection is proclaimed alongside death and destruction.

Prayer: This Day I will live in hope. I will rejoice in knowing that the scars I bear, the hurts I have known, and the losses I have endured are all tempered by my life in Christ.

*As long as the sun and the moon shall last
The generous one shall never be empty.*

—Gaelic Proverb

Discussing the matter of generosity is an occupational hazard for me. Everyone expects a preacher to talk about giving. There are about as many collection-plate and money-grabbing preacher stories as there are lawyer jokes. So, I am aware that the reader may think this is just another "dig a little deeper, folks" essay. Not so.

We have a tendency to limit our generosity. We diminish true generosity by cultivating a patronizing attitude that judges the needy. We want to know if they are really needy and truly deserving. The problem with such judging is that we can always raise the bar of neediness. Generosity can be flawed if we demand something in return. Good manners on the receiver's part will always express gratitude. But, others' gratitude ought not be a condition of giving. The miserly spirit can corrupt true generosity if we think of our surplus as the source of our giving. True generosity comes from the first fruit picked from the orchard, and not from what is left over after all the other bills are paid.

True generosity offers an unexplainable paradox. The more you give, the greater you are blessed. I do not know how it works. I agree it does not make sense. But, the fact is that gravity does not make sense either, yet I fully depend upon gravity to keep from falling into space. I cannot explain how giving grows getting. That is why it is a paradoxical truth.

Generosity is like a well that taps into an aquifer. The more it gives, the greater its source. The well does not care who drinks from it. The well does not judge who pulls a bucket from it. The well does not demand to know if the water washes wounds, slakes a thirst, bathes a fevered child, or irrigates a patch of turnips. The well just gives forth and fills once more.

Prayer: This Day I will examine what drives my generosity. It may be a fearful exercise, so I'll need an added bit of courage, honesty, and faith. Today, I will give reason a rest and embrace the paradox of generosity.

> *What we anticipate seldom occurs; what we least*
> *expected generally happens.*
> —Benjamin Disraeli

Everyone loves to stumble into the unexpected. The unexpected helps spice up our lives. It is what keeps us from drowning in boredom. The unexpected can be frightening, and it can catch us so off guard that we are sent reeling in confusion. Horror novels and scary movies depend upon our appetite for the unexpected. Part of what makes the unexpected so delightful is that it comes when least expected (if that makes sense).

On a recent trip through the Highlands of Scotland, I stumbled into the unexpected. We visited Balmoral Castle where the royal family spends their summers. There is no question why they chose this particular spot as a summer retreat. The scenery is beyond words. Since the Queen was in residence at her Balmoral estate, the castle was closed to the public. It was Sunday morning and there was a church near the castle. The royal family often worships at this small country church. Many tourists, hoping to get a glimpse of the royal family, stop at this house of worship. So, for privacy's sake, it was no surprise that the doors were locked during worship that morning.

As I walked around the church, I heard the organ playing from within, and the sound of the congregation's singing slipped through some of the ancient cracks in the church's stonewalls. I would have guessed that their choice of music would have been some old dowdy hymn from a century or two ago, or maybe some Latin chant. What liturgical song of Christian hope drifted through the walls and into the Highlands that Sunday morning? *"Shine, Jesus Shine!"*

I never expected that the Queen and I had anything in common, but we do. She and I both like *"Shine, Jesus Shine!"*

Prayer: This Day I will especially delight in the unexpected. Today, I will pay particular attention to just how vast and delightful this world really is.

Haste Ye Back!
—From a Scottish folk song

A real Scotsman would say, "Aist ye bake!"
A Southerner would say, "You all come back now.
Ya hear?"

In the true spirit of word economy, a Yankee would say, "Come again."

Regardless of how it is said, the spirit of hospitality is to know you are always welcome, and you have a standing invitation for a return visit. True hospitality is a genuine desire to comfort the visitor.

Have you ever noticed how much of the gospel has to do with hospitality? The setting for many of the stories is someone's table or home. Washing the feet of a weary walker, oil or perfume to add to the comfort of a sweaty traveler, and food for the hungry far from home are all common themes.

When Jesus spoke to the multitudes on a hillside near the Sea of Galilee, he expressed hospitality. Jesus asked if anyone had thought to bring lunch (John 6:1–15). No one had given groceries any thought that day. Town was some distance away, and funds were limited. There was, however, a young boy who had a few fish and some loaves of bread. It has been said that the miracle of feeding the multitudes was not about the wonder of multiplying the five loaves and the two fish. The real miracle that day was the lad's willingness to share what little he had. Even a child had the spirit of hospitality.

Hospitality can be said in many ways:
"Haste ye back!"
"You all come back now, you hear?"
"Come again."
"Here is my lunch. Let's share."

Prayer: This Day I will hone my hospitality. Today, I'll share with another for the joy of it and I'll not be surprised if in my hospitality I encounter Christ.

They will beat their swords into plowshares and their spears into pruning hooks. Nation will not take up sword against nation, nor will they train for war any more.

—Isaiah 2:4

War has been one of Christendom's great struggles. On one hand, there is the urgency to protect world peace, to promote justice, to embrace freedom, and to abolish tyranny. On the other hand is the ugliness of war. The death and destruction that war brings is a profane assault on God's creation. It is a debate that every generation has had to face. We have a ways to go if we are to live out the words of the angel long ago who said to a bunch of shepherds one night, "Peace on earth and good will to all." Yet, tyranny that strangles hope, justice, and human dignity cannot be ignored. What to do?

It may be helpful to think of all society as a three-legged stool. One leg is authority. Another leg is economy. And the third leg is religion. The three are co-equals. Saw off any one of the three legs and the stool is no longer of any use. Each holds the other in check as it supports the common good. There have been times when any one of the three has assumed too much power. Wars have been started merely for economic gain, or to satisfy the ego and greed of some king. Religion of every stripe has had its darker moments in history (the Inquisition, the Crusades, and the September 11 radical belief that God wanted thousands to die are all examples).

In a perfect world, the swords would be forged into plowshares and the spears would all become pruning hooks. But, for now that is not to be. The best we can do to bring about lasting peace is to do our part in keeping a comfortable harmony, and yet a definite separation between economy, authority, and religion. That harmony can be breeched if it grows too close or strays too far.

I saw such an example of authority and religion having grown too close. Edinburgh Castle is the home of that lovely city's oldest building, a well-preserved church built in 1093. Ten feet from the church's door is a 16th century cannon that can lob three hundred pound cannon balls. That is too close for comfort!

Prayer: This Day I will pray for lasting peace. Since peace begins in our hearts and our homes before it moves to nations, I will begin with peace in my heart.

Then God said, "Let us make man in our image, in our
likeness, and let them rule over the fish of the sea and
the birds of the air, over the livestock, and over all
the earth, and over all the creatures that move
along the ground."

—Genesis 1:26

The notion that God created the universe and then put us in charge has caused more than a little controversy. The environmentalists and animal rights advocates argue that we have no right to govern. They bristle at the idea that we stand above all life in the hierarchy of creation. They point to thousands of years of egregious waste and destruction and say that we have done a poor job of living up to the trust God put in us. An even more radical voice says that God made a huge mistake in his choice of stewards. They claim all creation is equal. We share all creation equally. Thus, the wind, water, and vegetation belong to the deer, the ant, and the grub and not just to humankind.

I agree with the concept of equality. And, I think God agrees, also. Consider the Flood story. God instructed Noah to gather up two of every kind. Maybe Noah said to God, "Are you sure you want two of each? This would be a great time to get rid of mosquitoes. And, as an added bonus we could save future generations from Malaria. And what about scorpions, and rats, and cockroaches, and skunks, and wasps, and poisonous snakes? Who needs them, God?"

God said, "Noah, gather them all. The ones you like and the ones you dislike."

So Noah gathered them all, two by two.

God has a heart of equality. Maybe God knew we would make our mistakes, but God also knew that for the most part we would be obedient.

Prayer: This Day I will take ownership of my role in creation. Today, I will work hard be a steward of all creation, a caretaker of the weak, a friend of the unloved, and a voice for the voiceless.

After a while, those standing there went up to Peter and said, "Surely you are one of them, for your accent gives you away."

—Matthew 26:73

The scene is a familiar one. Peter is standing in a courtyard on the night Jesus was arrested. A local person came up to him and said, "You are one of them, aren't you?"

Peter said, "No. You have the wrong guy."

Then another thought she recognized Peter as one of Jesus' followers. "You are one of the people who was with the Nazarene."

Peter's response was a quick denial, "No. No. I am not one of them!"

Then several said to him, "Oh yes, you are one of them. Your accent gives you away."

Just then the rooster crowed and Peter remembered Jesus' last words to him, "Before the rooster crows, you will disown me three times."

Can you imagine what it would take for someone to recognize us as followers of Christ? What if someone looked at you and said, "You look like a Christian to me. Are you?"

What is there about you that would cause someone to recognize you as a Christian? Would it be a calm expression in the face of danger? Would it be your choice of words? Perhaps a gold cross on a chain around our neck? Would your accent give you away? What would it take for the world to know you are one of Christ's followers?

And, how would you answer? Would you say, "No. You must be thinking of someone else."

Or, would you say, "Yes. I am one!"

Prayer: This Day I will try to be more Christlike in all I do and say. Today, I will quit denying and begin to boldly proclaim the Good News.

*There is no worse lie than a truth misunderstood
by those who hear it.*

—William James

Misunderstandings are often at the heart of wars, divorce, corporate breakup, and hatred. Some misunderstandings have cultural or social genesis. Nuances and word meanings can have either comical or disastrous impact in relationships. Some are innocent, and others are carefully and intentionally crafted to only appear to say one thing yet mean another. Some are deliberately created to always allow the speaker to say, "That wasn't at all what I meant."

Communication is not always about words. We have heard of families that separate because one partner refuses to replace the cap on the tube of toothpaste. Many a domestic quarrel can be traced back to the position of the toilet seat after use. Or, how about the changes left by another driver on one's car radio, rearview mirror, and seat position? All seem like minor annoyances. But, are they really minor misunderstandings, or are these messages of indifference?

Some of the soundest marital advice I was ever given was from an elderly gentleman who had nearly sixty years of experience. He said, "Just always be sure what is being said is what is really being said. That means that you need to be a skillful listener and a thoughtful talker."

According to my old mentor's advice, St. Francis of Assisi had it at least half right when he said, "O divine Master, grant that I may not so much seek to be understood as to understand."

Prayer: This Day I am going to try with every fiber of my being to be a good listener. Today, I will work just as hard at understanding another as I would hope to be understood by others.

Life is real! Life is earnest!
And the grave is not its goal;
Dust thou art, to dust returnest,
Was not spoken of the soul.
　　　　　　—Henry Wadsworth Longfellow

I learned a simple truth from my late, dear friend, Dick Speed. **You have to have goals.** A goal-less life is one that ambles aimlessly through the years. Without goals, how can you ever determine if you have arrived at your appointed destiny? Goals are imperative. Dick taught me how to create and keep my list of goals updated. He suggested a list of "21 THINGS YET TO DO." Why twenty-one? Who knows? Some must be achievable so you can see progress. The list must be revised every January. Some need to stretch your imagination and may never be accomplished.

Having kept a list of "21 THINGS YET TO DO" for more than fifteen years, I can see the progress I have made. The biggest challenge is to limit the list to just twenty-one.

List of 21 Things Yet To Do

1. Write a book and submit it to a publisher.
2. Hunt and tag a black bear.
3. Hunt and tag a turkey.
4. Learn to fly fish
5. Restore an old tractor.
6. Drive the Zamboni machine at a hockey game.
7. Serve on a college board of trustees.
8. Save more.
9. Lead another, then another, then another, and after that another to Christ.
10. Teach preaching (homiletics) at seminary level.
11. Make a significant endowment to some worthy cause.
12. Visit a foreign country.
13. Finish the basement and landscaping at Clam River.
14. Learn to play the banjo
15. Help a hopeless drunk find sobriety.
16. Comfort a dying person.
17. Be the best son, husband, father, grandfather, and friend I can be.
18. Reread Moby Dick.
19. Try to understand Moby Dick.
20. Mend one fractured relationship (mine or another's).
21. Make sure Marilyn always knows how much I love her.

Prayer:　　This Day I will quit ambling aimlessly and focus on what really matters in life. Today, I will work diligently toward at least one goal.

Without this playing with fantasy no creative work has ever yet come to birth. The debt we owe to the play of imagination is incalculable.
—Carl Jung

Often, imagination is better than reality. Often, the reality never measures up to the imagination that is played in the theater of our minds. Sometimes it is better to hope for and dream about than it is conquer and own.

Consider this example. I think I would like to own a dog. I am not sure what kind of dog I would like, but in my imagination my mind keeps returning to one of our former farm dogs named Mose. Mose was a free spirit, filled with life, and had a boundless supply of energy. He was far from pedigreed, but more than made up for his curious lineage with an enthusiasm for life. Mose was well-mannered, docile, and always willing to please. I would like to find another Mose—that is the imagination part.

Now, the reality part. There is no other Mose and never will be. The reality is that I do not have hundreds of acres on which a new Mose can run. The new Mose would have to be walked. The old Mose was an easy keeper. No doubt the new Mose would bring a long list of personal demands. The new Mose would never ride in the pickup, the combine, or chase a rabbit. The new Mose would never have the opportunity to trot back to the field just to see how we were getting along with planting.

It seems clear to me that imagination far outweighs the reality when it comes to my owning a dog. I would once again discover that my expectation and my reality are a sorry mismatch.

It is a harmless exercise to have an imaginary dog. Now think about the wrecked lives that have not been content to live with imagination. Think of those who had to have the new career, the bigger boat, or the new spouse. Think of the disappointment and the hurt that comes from an unsatisfying reality. Feeding an imaginary dog is cheap when compared to the wreckage that having to have can cause.

Prayer: This Day I will bask in my imagination. Today, I will find solace, contentment, and joy in the theater of my mind.

> *In dog sledding, only the lead dog ever has a change*
> *of scenery.*
>
> —Anonymous

You can learn a lot about life from dog sledding.

1. A team of dogs pulling a sled is teamwork at its finest. What would be impossible for an individual dog is doable if they all pull together.
2. A big heart can outpull an uninterested stallion. Sled dogs are not large—usually under seventy-five pounds. What they lack in size, they more than make up for in heart.
3. Pulling together can be fun. Of course, the occasional rabbit or deer encountered along the trail would be great sport to chase, but commitment to the team and to the cause comes first.
4. Follow your leader. He or she became the leader for good reason.
5. Be a contented follower.
6. Dump the rider if you can. He'll cuss and yell, but the load is lighter. Besides, life is too short to take too seriously.
7. Rest when you can.
8. Summer is long, boring, and snowless. Run when you can.
9. Learn how to glare at the sled driver. He will step off and run alongside the sled if you shame him with a well-calculated glare.
10. Be still. Barking, yelping, and whining use too much energy.

Prayer: This Day I will try to learn something worthwhile from the world around me. Today, I will admit that I do not have a monopoly on wisdom, so I will pray to be teachable.

The LORD is my light and my salvation—
whom shall I fear?
The LORD is the stronghold of my life—
of whom shall I be afraid?
When evil men advance against me,
to devour my flesh,
when my enemies and my foes attack me,
they will stumble and fall.
Though an army besiege me,
my heart will not fear,
though war break out against me,
even then I will be confident.

I am still confident of this:
I will see the goodness of the LORD
in the land of the living.
Wait for the LORD;
be strong and take heart
And wait for the LORD.

—Psalm 27:1–3,13

Today, we remember a day that will be remembered for centuries to come. Today, we remember a day that irrevocably changed our lives. Today, we recall the innocence lost on an autumn morning in September.

How true the words of the psalmist ring. When life ceases to make sense, we look to the Lord. When we are plunged into life-changing events, we search for reassurance. When we feel most torn, it is the most natural of all human endeavor to look to the Great Healer.

The psalmist penned these words of hope in a time of duress and sorrow. Part of the message is a call for patience. There is a confidence that time will heal, good will be restored, and we will be a changed people. Changed not by bitterness and rage—oh yes, they still linger—but by a renewed strength found only in a lived-faith.

Prayer: Wait, O world that weeps. Wait, widows who mourn with no grave. Wait, children whose fathers will not come home from work today. Wait in the confidence and the hope that the Lord will restore. Wait, O world that weeps.

Make haste slowly.

—Unknown

Cows, deer, sheep, and a few others are ruminants. They are four-stomached animals that have digestive systems that require many hours of chewing. Ruminants usually eat harsh, branchy foods that must be chewed long and hard. I suppose that somewhere back in the times of our great-great-ever-so-great grandparents, God knew that ruminants would be another animal's lunch. So they gulp their rough forage in open spaces and then retreat to cover to spend the rest of the day chewing. It sounds like a boring way to spend that day. I am glad that I am not a ruminant.

However, there are times when it pays to ruminate, or as we say, "sit on it." Have you ever been upset and wanted to inform the world how upset you were? This is a good ruminating time. Nearly always, a night's sleep puts everything back in order. And, if all is still not well, we are better prepared to deal with the matter in a more rational manner. Sitting on it can save us much misery and embarrassment.

Do you suppose that is why cows, and deer, and sheep rarely offend anyone? Could it be that they have mastered the art of quiet reflection? Or, are they enjoying a long lunch?

Prayer: This Day, if need be, I'll sit on it. Today (and hopefully all days), I will reflect long and hard before I speak.

Be aware of the "taken away trap."
—Richard Carlson

In his book, *Don't Sweat the Small Stuff for Men*, best selling author, Richard Carlson, talks about the "Taken Away Trap."

Carlson describes the "Taken Away Trap" in this way: Suppose a man is hired by an employer to do a certain job. He is quite satisfied with the pay, the working conditions, and finds the work to be fulfilling. The man is given a two-week vacation each year. He works two years and takes his full two weeks each year. The following year his boss gives him an additional week of vacation. He is delighted and takes a three-week trip to Hawaii. We will call this scenario one.

Now consider scenario two. The same man is hired by the same company for the same pay and asked to do the same job. The only difference is in this scenario the man gets three weeks vacation per year. He works two years and enjoys his three weeks vacation each year. The following year, however, he was informed that next year he would only get two weeks vacation. As you can imagine, he is furious.

I suppose most of us would be unhappy with such a cut after three years of faithful service. But, consider the facts. In scenario one the man worked three years and received seven weeks of vacation. He was happy. In scenario two the same man was given eight weeks of vacation over three years and he was furious. He received more, but was ultimately disappointed.

It has happened to all of us sometime in life. We make a promise to a child that we find we cannot keep, and we are reminded with the heart-wrenching words, "But Dad, you promised!" The "Take Away Trap" is sometimes unavoidable. Even though the end result is better as in scenario one, others' feelings are always at stake. The "Take Away Trap" is part of life. Be sensitive to it.

Prayer: This Day I will make a sincere effort to keep all my commitments in good repair. Today, if another's feelings are unavoidably hurt, I will have the solace in knowing that I made my best effort.

Be thrilled when the job is difficult. Not everyone can do it.
—Unknown

Mrs. Spotts was my eighth grade algebra teacher. She was a strict taskmaster who demanded much of us. Hanging from the top of the blackboard in the front of her room, in large block letters for all see, was the following motto:

Be thrilled when the job is difficult. Not everyone can do it.

I can assure you that if difficulty is the measure of thrill, then it was a thrilling year!

I have encountered many mottos in classrooms, sports locker rooms, bumper stickers, and in church bulletins since I sat in Mrs. Spotts' algebra class. Most have been quickly forgotten. Yet this motto stuck. Somehow knowing that tough jobs are reserved for but a few does have a way of encouraging. To know that great challenges are not often part of a boring and unrewarding life has given me the guts to go on at times.

As I reflect on Mrs. Spotts' eighth grade algebra class, I must admit that I cannot recall the quadratic equation. I am not sure I could still solve a problem using the x/y slope formula. But, this I do remember: though not always thrilling, tough jobs make us better people. It is the tough of life that shapes us.

Thank you Mrs. Spotts wherever you are.

Prayer: This Day I will meet whatever challenges life brings to my door with the confidence that nothing will be greater than God and I can handle together. Today, I will embrace the tough rather than run from it.

If you confess with your mouth, "Jesus is Lord," and believe in your heart that God raised him from the dead, you will be saved.
—Romans 10:9

There was once a king who was a melancholy sort. He was plagued with bouts of depression and sadness. One day he decided he needed a court jester, or a court fool as they were called in those days. Perhaps the fool would cheer him up. So he held an audition to find a suitable court jester. Men came from throughout his kingdom. Finally one was selected.

The jester served the king well. He brought him much mirth and joy. Soon the king's mental health was fully restored. Years passed and the king decided he needed to publicly thank the jester for all the happiness he had given the king. So, a grand banquet was held to honor the jester. The king had a large medallion struck that said in bold type: THE GREATEST FOOL IN MY KINGDOM. The king placed the medallion around the jester's neck, and from that day on, the jester wore the medallion with great pride.

One day the king summoned the jester to his bedside. The king was dying. "Fool," said the king. "You have brought much joy to my life, and I thank you. But now I am going on a journey and I am filled with fear. Can you cheer me just once more?"

"What have you done to prepare for this journey?" the jester asked.

"Nothing. I have made no preparations for this journey." The king said.

Whereupon the jester took the medallion from around his neck and placed it on the king and said, "Here my Lord, you need this more than I. For I may be the greatest fool in your kingdom, but you, my friend, are the **biggest** fool!"

Prayer:　　This Day I will rejoice in my salvation. Today is the day of salvation and I will be glad in it.

The LORD is my shepherd, I shall not want.

—Psalm 23:1

It is good to know who you are. It is better still to know whose you are. To know that the Lord is the leader of my flock relieves me of the burden of having to be in charge. I am not the shepherd; I am one of the shepherded.

As a one-time farmer, I am not wholly delighted by the sheep imagery. Sheep are not my favorite of the domesticated animals. I think of sheep as weak-willed, watery-eyed, runny-nosed, and slow-thinking animals. They smell bad on rainy days. In fact, they don't smell that great on sunny days! Sheep are dimwitted souls who gladly follow a leader who may or may not have their best interest at heart. Sheep are the bottom-feeders when land cannot support cattle, corn, or alfalfa. They may be cute and lovable, but they have their definite downside.

My reticence regarding the sheep imagery notwithstanding, the idea of a shepherd is comforting. A shepherd watches out for the flock. He attends their every need. The shepherd knows where to find the best water, the greenest grass, and the hillsides that are free of poisonous weeds. The shepherd knows the way to the best shelters on stormy days. He watches the sky for threatening dangers. He keeps an ever-vigilant eye out for anything that might harm the flock.

Thus, because I have such a shepherd, "I shall not want" makes good sense. I can readily acknowledge my need for the shepherd. I guess I can be a sheep if that is what it takes to be so cared for and so loved.

Prayer: This Day I will rejoice in being part of God's flock. Today, I will be content to be a part of the flock, for it is here that I am loved, cared for, and moved along the safe path of life.

> *He makes me lie down in green pastures, He leads me beside quiet*
> *waters, He restores my soul. He guides me in*
> *the paths of righteousness for His name's sake.*
> —Psalm 23:2–3

Have you ever thought about why it is important for the sheep to be made to lie down in green pastures? It means there is such a bounty that the grass is sufficient enough to more than fill the sheep's bellies. Sparse grazing would demand that the sheep would eat a bit and then go lie down where there was no forage. This shepherd does not just let them rest in the lush field, but makes them lie down in green pastures. The imagery is not just enough, but more than enough.

This shepherd will not let his flock quench their thirsts from some stagnant pool. These sheep drink fresh water that moves quietly. This shepherd is intent that the flock has maximum creature comforts. His flock does not just get by on wilted grass, sleep on rocky hillsides, and drink foul, stale water. This shepherd insists on the best for his flock.

Why is this so important? This shepherd knows that physical comfort comes before spiritual comfort. A hungry, starving flock would have no desire for a restored soul. The same is true for us, because bread alone does not satisfy our spiritual hunger.

Here is a shepherd who cares for the whole of his flock. This shepherd practices holistic husbandry.

Prayer:　　This Day I will care for my physical self in the knowing that my soul is in harmony with my complete wholeness. Today, I will unselfishly look after me.

*Even though I walk through the valley of the
shadow of death, I will fear no evil,
for you are with me; your rod and
your staff, they comfort me.*

—Psalm 23:4

Life has its scary places. A trip to the doctor's office to hear the news about a recent biopsy is scary. Knowing that your employer is spending lavishly on updating a plant in South America is scary. Watching a son or daughter get on the school bus for the first time is scary. Visiting your mother or father and they cannot remember your name is scary. Life has its scary valleys. There is no way around them. You cannot go over them. You have to press on through the valley.

To walk fearlessly through all of life's scary valleys takes more than confidence and a positive outlook on life. To walk fearlessly demands faith.

The image of the shepherd with both a rod and a staff is easily overlooked. The rod nudges the sheep along when they might be paralyzed with fear. Linger in the valley too long and you become easy prey. The rod moves us along. The staff has a hooked end that pulls the sheep back from danger when they go too boldly.

It is that dual prodding and pulling back that delivers us from one end of the scary valley to the other. It is comforting to know that we do not walk alone, nor do we go without direction. When in the valley, there is a time to pull back and a time to move on. But, when traveling without a caring shepherd, it is hard to tell when to stand your ground and when to run for daylight.

Prayer: This Day I will know that I do not trudge that valley alone. Today, I will willingly be led or pulled back as the Good Shepherd guides me through the valley.

You prepare a table before me in the presence of my enemies.
You anoint my head with oil; my cup overflows.
—Psalm 23:5

Can you imagine the lump in your throat if you had to eat a banquet in front of your worst enemy? Suppose someone wanted harm to come to you. Do you think you could enjoy a meal sitting in the rifle sights of an enemy? I doubt it very much. Most of us would want to fix a quick roast beef sandwich and duck under some protective cover to gulp it down. The imagery of sitting down to a banquet table in the presence of enemies is a bold statement of confidence.

Since we know the shepherd wants no harm to come to the flock, this table is not a bait pile for your adversaries. God will never set you up to be destroyed.

No. The psalmist is saying God will protect you even when you are most vulnerable. Moreover, God will make you comfortable. There is oil to soothe your tired feet. Your glass will never be empty. The message is: Here, bask awhile in solace and peace. Fear not. I will offer complete protection and rest while you drink in the goodness of life.

Prayer: This Day I will live boldly and not timidly. Today, I will rejoice in the knowing that God wants me to embrace life in all its fullness. Today, I will live fully.

Surely goodness and love will follow me all the days of my life,
and I will dwell in the house of the LORD forever.
—Psalm 23:6

Perhaps no single verse in the entire Hebrew text speaks to the dual mercy of God better than Psalm 23:6. God's goodness and love are here and now in this life as well as eternal in the next.

In this closing scene of a passage that has gone from pasture, to stream, to scary valley, and to banquet table the final destination is named. In this saga of travel the eternal aspect of forever is promised. And do note: we do not merely go the Lord's house. We *dwell* there. We live there. Having been cared for in our most vulnerable times, this is believable. Having been protected in our scariest moments, this is comforting. Having been lavished when life presses in on us and threatens us, this is another chapter of a rich relationship with our Creator.

A life of faith and belief in Christ is not just about what happens to you after you die. If God's goodness and mercy were limited only to eternal life and a one-way trip to heaven, then faith would be a rather self-serving adventure. Faith is a lived experience that is part of every day. The fulfilling of basic needs, protection from life's tough passages, confidence in the face of adversity, and even a bit of luxury when least expected, are all part of this grand adventure. Truly it can be said, "All this and heaven, too!"

Prayer: This Day I will bask in the duality of God's goodness, for I am cared for and loved in both this life and the next. Today, I will see eternal hope as but another chapter of the same goodness that surrounds me this very day.

*I do not understand what I do. For what I want to do I do not do, but
what I hate I do. And if I do what I do not
want to do, I agree that the law is good. As it is,
it is no longer I myself who do it,
but it is the sin living in me.*

—Romans 7:15–17

What a dilemma. Does it sound familiar? Have you ever had a habit you wanted to quit, you knew you needed to quit, and yet you were powerless to do anything about it? Join the club. Most of us can relate to that.

I knew a man who was a heavy smoker. He was diagnosed with lung cancer. His doctor told him to quit smoking. His wife told him to quit smoking. His son and daughter told him to quit smoking. In fact, he said he wanted to quit smoking. Yet, he puffed away. The man knew what he wanted to do, what he needed to do, and what he had to do, but he was powerless to do it.

It is not easy to take ownership of powerlessness. We like to think we are in control. Powerlessness is just another word for failure. But there are times when we are out of control. Such was the dilemma of my smoker friend. Apparently, that same powerlessness was Paul's problem. I think Paul may have been on his way toward recovery. And, if my friend had had a little more time, he, too, may have found that same recovery. *The only known antidote for powerlessness is surrender.* That is when you come to the place where you can say, "I can't. God can. I'll let him."

That is surrender. That is the beginning of dealing with whatever it is that you know in your heart of hearts must change, but cannot find the power to change. This power through powerlessness is a paradox. It is saying, "Paradoxically, I am at my strongest when I am at my weakest. It is through surrender that I am victorious. I win when I lose."

Sorry, I cannot explain it either. If I could, it would no longer be a paradox.

Prayer: This Day I will seek victory in the midst of defeat, power in the face of powerlessness, and Christ where I need Him most. Today, I will gladly let go and let God.

When the Counselor comes, whom I will send to you from the Father,
the Spirit of truth who goes out from
the Father, he will testify about me.
—The words of Jesus as recorded
in John 15:26

When I was a boy of ten years old or so, a new Wrigley store had its grand opening in a nearby town. It was a huge store for those days, but would probably fit into any three or four aisles of today's superstores. I was amazed at the store's size, and the variety of goods it offered was beyond my imagination. This was our first experience with big-city marketing coming to small-town America.

What most amazed me was the store's automatic door. I was entranced by the automatic door opener. I kept stepping up to the door to see if I could catch it sleeping. I tried from the side angle and the door opened. I backed into it and the door opened. I ran and the door opened. Looking back, I must have looked like I had led a sheltered life to be so engrossed by an automatic door opener. Of course, today I understand how automatic doors work. When you break a beam of light, it activates the opener mechanism and the door opens. It is not magic.

The beam of light that is invisible is a good illustration of the Holy Spirit. I cannot see him. I cannot hear, taste, smell, or feel the Holy Spirit. But, like the automatic door opener he is sensitive to me and responds to me. Again, like the automatic door opener, the Holy Spirit is the unseen force that continues to open doors for me in life.

Prayer: This Day I will be sensitive to the Christ-presence that surrounds me. I will marvel in the knowing that his goodness is always near and still opening doors.

*Jesus answered, "I did tell you, but you do not believe.
The miracles I do in my Father's name speak for me,
but you do not believe because you are not my sheep.
My sheep listen to my voice; I know them, and they
follow me. I give them eternal life, and they shall
never perish; no one can snatch them out of
my hand. My Father, who has given them to me,
is greater than all, no one can snatch them out
of my Father's hand. I and the Father are one."*
—The words of Jesus as recorded
in John 10:25–30

A Hebrew man encountered a friend of his as he was on his way to the synagogue. His friend noticed that the man looked worried, so the friend asked, "How are you?"

"Not well at all," said the man. "I sent my son to Israel and he came back a Christian!"

The friend said, "Oh, I know just how you feel. The same thing happened to me."

So, the two men went on their way to the synagogue to pray together. While praying in the house of God, they said to God, "Lord help us. We sent our sons to Israel and they came back Christians."

To this the Lord replied, "I know. The same thing happened to me!"

Prayer: This Day I will invite a bit of laughter into my life. Today, I will not take myself seriously, but will allow the joy of living to shine through. I may even do something a bit outrageous!

> *The truth, namely, that the wrongdoing of one*
> *generation lives into successive ones.*
> —Nathaniel Hawthorne

Some years ago I saw a young black woman in her mid-teens wearing a sweatshirt that said:

> **You bet I have an attitude. My people worked 300 years without a pay check!**

No question, the young woman's bold statement to the world was correct. Who can argue with the facts? No one can tie a colorful ribbon around the suffering, the shame, the indignity, and the human carnage that we know as slavery. It is one of the most tragic and appalling chapters in history.

However, there is a dilemma here. How do we balance remembering the past so it is never repeated alongside living with a hateful attitude? How do those two reconcile with one another? Can we just forget and move on? Hardly. Must we forever bear the shame and own the misery of the past? No.

The deep sadness that is in the midst of all this is how this young woman's spirit has been atrophied by hate. Tragically, she, too, is a victim. Her chains are not forged of steel that chafes her wrists and ankles. Her binding is that of a compromised spirit. She is like the families of those who have lost a loved one to violent crime. They stand outside a prison in the dark of night while the execution is carried out on the one who brought so much hurt into their lives. When interviewed after the execution they will usually say, "Well, now after fourteen years, justice has been done and we can go on with our lives."

When someone robs another of fourteen years of life, then two assaults have been made. The young black woman was still chained, and the families of the murdered victim had also been robbed of life. Forgiving and moving on is not forgetting. It is the best we can do sometimes. It is living in the face of injustice.

Prayer: This Day I will work toward the delicate balance of forgiving and forgetting. Today, I will also be sure to recognize that forgetting dare not be denying.

To live a life through is not like crossing a field.
—Russian Proverb

An old friend who was as fine a woodsman as I have ever met once gave me this advice:

Walk a little. Look a lot.

He was giving me advice on deer tracking, but his point was a simple one—take time to observe the world around you. Too often, we have a tendency to rush through life. We hurry here and there. We demand faster cars and wider highways. We fly half-way around the world in a matter of a few hours, but complain about a ten-minute delay for our baggage to get to the terminal. We have faster computers, higher wattage microwave ovens, and ten-minute oil changes. We eat instant food and want faster-acting medicine for indigestion. Life is a blur!

My old friend saw the woods in its totality, because he took time to drink it all in. His was an unhurried commune with his surroundings. His slow pace allowed him to see what would have otherwise gone unnoticed. Just imagine how much life he observed in his lifetime. Just imagine how much more he packed into life by simply walking a little and looking a lot.

Prayer: This Day I will relish the world around me. I will walk a little, look a lot, and not be too surprised by all I have been missing.

---

*From everyone who has been given much, much will be demanded; and
from the one who has been entrusted
with much, much more will be asked.*
—The words of Jesus as recorded
in Luke 12:48

William Fairlie points out an amazing fact. He says that every canvass for charities reports that the best givers are from the poorest classes. Study after study confirms this dichotomy. Where the expectation ought be the lowest, the per capita giving is the highest.

> Fairlie says, "If we give because we feel that we have to give and we bemoan every cent of it, then it is like lost money to us. We count only the debit side of the ledger. On the other hand, if we give because it is a privilege to share with others thereby turning it around so that we are the ones receiving the blessing, then we have gained in assets what money can never buy."

Of course, he is right on track with his theology of giving. What still remains a mystery is why the poor have figured this out while the rich are still puzzled.

Prayer: This Day I will endeavor to see sharing as a privilege, for it is by giving that I receive most. Today, I will cultivate a generous heart in all things.

My son was dead and is alive again; he was lost and is found.
—From the Parable of the Prodigal Son:
Luke 15:32

We will call him Joe. Joe was born into privilege. Joe attended the best schools, wore good clothes, and vacationed in places other children only read about in *National Geographic Magazine.*

Joe worked hard. He married, started a family, and owned his own construction business. It is hard to say what caused Joe to change so dramatically, but over time Joe ceased to be the Joe everyone knew and liked. Sometimes he would just disappear. No one knew where he was or what he was doing. Joe's marriage and his construction business failed. But, interestingly, he always seemed to have money. What was up with Joe?

One day Joe did not come home again. His absences had become more frequent, but they never lasted more than a day or two. A month passed, then two months, and then six months and still no Joe. Joe's parents filed a missing person report with the local police—still no Joe. Months melted into a year, and a year became four years. One day Joe's father received a call from the police. "We think we have found your son."

Sure enough, on a cold January morning, Joe was found sleeping in a dumpster behind the J. L. Hudson's store in Detroit. He was emaciated, dirty, and bewildered. The once bright star had fallen into drugs, crime, and confusion. Joe had worked for the underworld doing whatever task they demanded. In return he got his drugs wholesale. This arrangement had worked until Joe became a greater liability to the crime organizers than he was worth. Now, Joe was just a shell of the man he once was.

A lost life you say? Well, do not be too hasty with your judgment. Fast-forward a dozen years and Joe's life has changed. Joe is the director of every substance-abuse clinic located west of the Mississippi River that one of America's major health providers operates.

Indeed, he was lost and is found!

Prayer: This Day I will practice persistence. I will never give up on another, call someone hopeless, or quit believing that God still finds the lost.

Avoid it, do not travel on it; Turn from it and go on your way.
—Proverbs 4:15

A man went to the doctor and said he had severe pain in his back. The doctor thoroughly checked him over and could find no organic problem. But the man was persistent.

The man stood up, twisted his torso into a near pretzel shape, and grimaced, "But Doc, it hurts when I do this."

The doctor calmly said, "Well, if it hurts when you do that, then don't do it."

Avoidance is a good strategy. Some condemn avoidance and say it is like an ostrich putting his head in the sand (actually animal behaviorists say ostriches never put their heads in the sand). Some say avoidance is the cowardly way around a problem. Some would argue that avoidance never solves the real problem. I have come to believe that avoidance is sometimes a sound solution. Sometimes, it is the only reasonable solution.

I went whining to a friend one time, complaining about how I had been ill-treated by another individual. I wanted sympathy, or at the least my friend's agreement. I got neither sympathy nor agreement. What I got was sound advice. My friend said, "If something or someone upsets you that much, then you better stay away from that thing or that person."

He was absolutely right! The world is filled with choices. One of those choices is, "Do I avoid it, or do I endure?" Think of it as an allergy. If a food causes a rash, avoid eating it. Avoiding a particular food is not a cowardly act or a non-solution. Think of a hurtful relationship as a spiritual allergy. Often, avoidance saves hurt feelings, bruised souls, and a rash on your well being.

Prayer: This Day I will see avoidance as a reasonable solution. Today, I will not ignore, but I also will not seek misery.

I can do everything through him who gives me strength.
—Philippians 4:13

One of my favorite books is Dr. Norman Vincent Peale's *The Power of Positive Thinking.* It may surprise you to hear that not every theologian agrees with Dr. Peale. Some argue that his positive-thinking model means that life-changing power is within your mind. They claim that such a notion removes, or significantly diminishes, the role of God in changing lives.

Such an argument misses the point entirely. Peale is precise about the source of positive thinking. He insists that God is a God of possibilities. There is nothing you can dream, imagine, or hope for that is greater than this divine strength. God alone is the source of strength that turns vision into reality. God is at the epicenter of positive thinking. If that were not so, then God would be a God of failure, discontent, and disappointment. Instead of a God of possibility, we would have a God of the improbable or the impossible.

I can do everything through him who gives me strength. Think about it. Believe it. Live it. Do this and you will have turned your vision into reality, your unlikely into probability, and your faith into action.

Prayer: This Day I will set aside negative thinking, because it diminishes the omnipotence of God. Today, I will dream outside the ordinary, because that is where God lives.

> *I imagined some horrible things in my life*
> *—a few of which actually happened.*
> —Benjamin Franklin

I once knew a father and son partnership that seemed to thrive on negative thinking. They were known in the neighborhood as Old Doom and his son, Gloom. Old Doom and Gloom could cast a shadow of doubt over the best of plans. They were constant complainers. The weather was too cold, too dry, too wet, or too hot. If they had a good crop, they complained about the cost of all the dryer gas it took to dry it. They whined about the markets and the government. Old Doom and Gloom were never pleased. All they could see was misery, discontent, and more woe.

Old Doom and Gloom brought a good measure of misery to themselves on two fronts. First, they alienated most of their neighbors. People did not want to listen to their constant complaining and their dreary outlook on life. So, they became lonely men. Second, they were so convinced that nothing good could ever happen to them, it seldom did.

They were a tragic pair. Success did not come their way. At least in part, they were the authors of this failure. They were so consumed in negative thinking that they had given energy to it. If you think that is a stretch, consider this: If there is truth to the idea of the power of positive thinking, then it would surely follow that negative energy flows from negative thinking.

If you can dream it, you can do it. Your dreams, your passions, your attitudes, and your hopes must be of success and not failure. How you think matters, because there is an amazing amount of energy between your ears.

Prayer: This Day I will deliberately avoid negative thinking. Recognizing how toxic negative thoughts can be, I will refuse to give them even an ounce of energy.

> *The only way to make a man trustworthy is to trust him; and the surest*
> *way to make him untrustworthy is to*
> *distrust him and show your distrust.*
> —Henry Lewis Stimson

Trust is vital to our being human. We trust our parents, our spouse, and our employers. We trust babysitters, surgeons, and barbers. We place trust in our church, our government, and our economy. We could not function without a sense of trust.

It is said that trust is earned. Is that really so, or is trust inherent and can only be lost or withdrawn? Consider this: A Maine hunting guide places an advertisement in a sporting magazine. For a given price, he will provide lodging, meals, and expert woodsmanship for a bear hunt. From that ad, you trust that the cabin will be clean, the food will be acceptable, and he has expert knowledge of the woods. All this is inherent trust.

But, this is only where real trust begins. At 2:00 PM, the guide transports his five or six bear-hunter clients deep into the Maine wilderness and places each of them in a secluded tree stand that is overlooking an active bear bait. There the hunter stays until dark (about 7:30 PM). Then the process is reversed. The guide returns to the five or six stands and picks up the hunters who are scattered over 5,000 acres of cedar swamp. It takes more than an hour to gather all the hunters and return them to the lodge. The last hunter on the return circuit sits in the woods until 9:00 PM or so.

You sit in total darkness, not more than thirty yards from a bait pile that is deep in bear-rich country. The sound you hear may be a bear rattling the pail that holds the bait. Maybe it is only a mouse or a skunk. You have never seen dark until you have been in a cedar swamp at 9:00 PM. Trust is knowing the guide will return to take you to a warm fire, a hot bowl of soup, and blessed light. Trust is also believing the guide is telling the truth when he says, "Bears seldom attack hunters." Trust is inherent, but could be lost in a millisecond if a hunter is left in the woods until dawn or eaten by a bear.

Prayer: This Day I will cherish the trust others place in me. I will understand it as precious and will do all it takes to keep it healthy and well placed.

*If anyone would come after me, he must deny himself and take up his
cross and follow me. For whoever wants to save his life will lose it, but
whoever loses his life for me will find it. What good will it be for a man
if he gains the whole world, yet
forfeits his soul?*
—The words of Jesus as recoded
in Matthew 16:24–26

How often have you heard someone say, "I guess this is my cross to bear"?

A battered spouse says it. A man living with HIV/AIDS says it. The parent of a child whose life is in shambles says it. The woman with cancer says it. The man whose job was just moved to South America says it. The wife whose husband is passed out on the floor after another late night bout with the bottle says it. Probably we have all said it sometime.

Listen once more to Jesus' words. He said, "If anyone would come after me, he must deny himself and take up his cross and follow me."

The verb is "to take up." It is not "to be heaped upon." The cross you bear is not the harsh hurts of life. It is not the loss of job, the withdrawal of another's love, or a debilitating disease you have contracted. The cross you bear for Christ is not the sorrows and hardships of life. Christ's cross is voluntary participation in another's affliction. It is caring for another. It is willingly serving and lovingly sharing with another.

Abuse, disease, economic despair, and hardships are not always the results of poor choices. The cross of human affliction is just the stuff that happens to you along life's way. It is the rigors of living. But, Christ's cross is optional! The cross of Christ is predicated upon God's love. It is because of Christ's choice to endure the cross, and our willingness to follow in the same selfless spirit of compassion, that the rigors of life are never terminal or eternal. Deciding to take up Christ's cross means choosing to care for another.

Prayer: This Day is a day of decision. I can decide to wallow in my misery, or I can decide to follow Christ and serve as his presence in another's life. Would that I decide to fully follow this day.

The Lord said, "Go out and stand on the mountain in the presence of the LORD, for the LORD is about to pass by. Then a great and powerful wind tore the mountains apart and scattered the rocks before the LORD, but the LORD was not in the wind. After the wind there was an earthquake, but the LORD was not in the earthquake. After the earthquake came a fire, but the LORD was not in the fire. And after the fire came a gentle whisper.

—1 Kings 19:11–12

The New International Version translates the voice of God as a "gentle whisper." Other translations call God's voice "that still small voice within." The psalmist says, "Be still and know that I am God" (Psalm 46:10).

Standing in the din of life and looking for that still, small voice within has to be among life's most perplexing tasks. It is not easy and is not a basic human instinct. Listening to the still, small voice within is a learned and practiced behavior that can only be realized and perfected by intentional repetition. Listening to the stillness of life is dichotomous to our noisy world. Commercials, traffic noise, ringing phones, and the thundering presence of all manner of sounds bombard us all the time. So how do we sort it all out and master the ability to hear the still, small voice within?

Consider the deep forest and all its sounds. There are squirrels chattering, birds chirping, and frogs doing their chug-a-lug chorus. Mosquitoes buzzing, wind rushing through the treetops, and a brook delightfully tumbling over mossy rocks. The forest is a calliope of sound. Suddenly all is still. Only the wind and the brook can be heard. The forest has grown silent. Why the stillness? A black bear is moving through the woods. The experienced bear observer has learned how to hear the nothingness of the woods. It takes a long time to learn the art of listening for no sound.

Listening for silence in a noisy place is a learned art. It is not the roaring voice of God that we hear. It is the still, small voice within that is the presence of God's whisper. Hear up! God has something to say.

Prayer: This Day I will strain my ears so I can listen to the still, small voice within. Today, I will be still before God and relish in the quiet of his whisper.

The scars of others should teach us caution.

—St. Jerome

John Rogers is a registered Maine Master Guide. He guides hunters into the Maine wilderness and fly-in fishermen to remote lakes. John is without question the finest woodsman I have ever met. He knows the way of the woods and all its creatures.

John has mastered the art of moose calling. In the fall, when the moose are inclined to romance, John takes to the woods to call a bull moose. His equipment is not cutting-edge technological marvels. John takes two coffee cans. He removes the top from one can and both the top and bottom from the other can. Then he tapes the two cans together end-to-end with electrical tape. He punches a hole in the bottom of the can and runs a cotton shoestring through the hole in the can. By wetting the shoestring and rubbing it between his thumb and forefinger, the can lets out a strange bellow. The coffee can and the shoestring sound like a deep base violin. While John works the coffee can, his eighty-plus-year-old father beats the brush with a stick to simulate the sound of a cow moose thrashing in the underbrush.

Often, the coffee can violin is more than the Romeo bull moose can stand. Often, the sound leads the moose into harm's way and someone's deep freezer.

Life can be a lot like the moose and the coffee-can violin. We can rush to false hope. We can place too much trust in the unproven. We can orchestrate our own undoing by impetuousness. We can blindly pursue without thought. A bit of caution would give the moose another summer or two. The same goes for each of us. Sometimes it is best to make haste slowly.

Prayer: This Day I will neither rush nor sit idly. Neither will I be filled with fear. Today, I will fearlessly move with deliberate caution.

For where your treasure is, there your heart will be also.
> —The words of Jesus as recorded
> in Matthew 6:21

One of my favorite television shows is *The Antiques Road Show*. For those who have never seen *The Antiques Road Show*, the show moves from city to city where people bring their old treasures to a large auditorium to be considered by a group of expert antique appraisers. As the show moves from one major city to the next, there is no telling what might turn up to be appraised. People pour in with jewelry, china, weapons, art works, Indian artifacts, furniture, needlepoint, and old toys to be examined.

Two categories of items are included in every show. One is the person who is sure he or she has something of value that turns out to be worthless. The other is the person who thinks he or she has a piece of junk that *is* worth a fortune. One is hugely displeased, while the other is surprised beyond words. One is sickened with disappointment, while the other is struck with delight. It is not uncommon for someone to have nearly tossed out what he or she thought was trash that turns out be a good down payment on a new yacht.

Life is a bit like *The Antiques Road Show*. Often, what we pursue with much enthusiasm, and place so much worth into, has little real value in life. And, that which we overlook or treat with casual ambivalence is what really matters. We work countless hours for promotions, new cars, faster boats, and bigger homes. We seek public fame, popularity, and the best fashions. Yet, we take good health, the love of another, and God's grace for granted.

When you give it some thought, it takes no expert, television crew, or auditorium to consider what really has value in life. In the *Road Show of Life*, it is good from time to time to consider and to appraise what really matters.

Prayer: This Day I will inventory what has real value in my life. Maybe I will be pleasantly surprised. Maybe I will be a bit disappointed. Either way, I will be better equipped to understand what really matters.

*I praise you because I am fearfully and wonderfully made; your works
are wonderful, I know that full well.*

—Psalm 139:14

Ralph Lemon was my father-in-law. He was a tool and die maker by profession, but his real passion in life was inventing useful items. Ralph had a wonderfully inquisitive mind that was laced with imagination. He was a quiet man and somewhat a loner. But, his splendid imagination was never at rest. That God-given imagination, that was so alive in Ralph Lemon, has quietly and anonymously touched nearly every life on this planet.

During WWII, the military developed planes that flew at higher altitudes than had even been thought possible. These high-altitude bombers could fly above the range of enemy anti-aircraft guns. However, there was a serious problem with high altitude flight. The atmosphere was seriously oxygen deprived. Somehow, a supply of oxygen had to be carried at these high altitudes. The source had to be lightweight and use little of the plane's precious cargo space. Compressed oxygen in a tank seemed liked the solution, but how could one inhale the oxygen that was stored at hundreds of pounds of pressure per square inch? Breathing out of the high-pressure tank would explode human lungs.

Ralph set to work on the solution. In one weekend, he devised the original diaphragm that meters out oxygen at a breathable pressure. Ralph Lemon was the first man to take a breath through an oxygen mask. Today's oxygen tanks are still equipped with the same basic device Ralph invented. Hundreds of millions of air passengers breathe air that has passed through one of Ralph's pressure controls. Millions more have breathed life-sustaining oxygen in hospitals through his invention.

Ralph was a tinkerer who would prefer to putter in his machine shop than fish, read, or see the Grand Canyon. He was an unassuming man who never sought fame. Yet, the gift of imagination God gave this gentle and quiet man lives on and continues to impact multitudes of lives in this world. It is good for all of us that he used his gift wisely.

Prayer: This Day I will inventory my God-given gifts. I will also check to see if I fully recognize the source of these gifts and how they are being used to make this a better world.

Do not confuse your needs with your wants.

—Anonymous

The lease on my truck was coming to the end of its contract. It was decision time. For about the same price, I could purchase the truck or turn it in to the dealer and lease a new truck.

I said to Marilyn, "I think I'll get a new one."

"Why would you want to do that?" she asked. "Why not just buy the one you are driving? It is in perfectly fine shape."

"Well, I think I need four-wheel drive. Maybe I will get called to a hospital in the midst of a snowstorm. Or, maybe four-wheel drive would be better to pull a boat up the boat launch."

"You don't have a boat." She reminded me.

"Well, I might have one someday. You can never tell."

As you can probably guess, I went ahead and leased a new truck with four-wheel drive. One day, I was on one of my hunting trips and came to a threatening stretch of mud on the trail. I reached over and with a twist of my wrist I switched the four-wheel drive button on the dash. The truck plunged right through the mud. As I chugged along in four-wheel drive I said to myself, "I wish Marilyn were here so she could see this. Then she would know just how much I need four-wheel drive."

I drove along for another half mile or so, and I noticed it was getting warm in the truck. In fact, it was more than warm. It was hot! I looked at the climate control button and discovered I had turned on the heater instead of the four-wheel drive!

What I thought I absolutely, unequivocally, and really needed, I only wanted.

Prayer: This Day I will diligently try to sort out wants and needs. God has given me all I need, and, better still, allows me to indulge in a few of my wants. What I really need to know is which is a want and which is a need.

Too much light often blinds gentlemen of this sort.
They cannot see the forest for the trees.
—Christoph Martin Wieland

Having spent a lifetime as a lover of the woods, and having introduced a number of others to the forest, I have come to understand how easily the trees can disguise the forest. The forest is more than a collection of trees. The forest is a living and breathing organism. It is a complex living being.

Moreover, the woods have much to teach us about life. It is an ongoing cycle of life that begets life. Some go to the woods to listen to the quietness of life. Some take to the forest to see what it holds that they might use. A few—a very few—discover the meaning of life therein.

As autumn unfolds around us, the season of harvest is at hand. Stores of nuts and seeds are being secreted away. Caterpillars are wrapping themselves in cocoons to emerge next spring as butterflies. Waterfowl are preparing for their long journey south. Deer are focused on conceiving spring's fawns. Autumn is a time of intensity, a time of harvest, a time of procreation, and a time of preparation.

New Englanders have the most exquisite autumns. They see the rush of fall and the beauty of the forest as part of God's ongoing promise. They balance the autumnal beauty with the brutality of winter. A New Englander says that October is God's way of saying, "For the harshness of what is to come, I am giving you this beauty so you will know I still love you."

Prayer: This Day I will pause to drink in the beauty of creation that surrounds me. Today, I will bask in its deeper meaning.

> *But because of his great love for us, God, who is rich in*
> *mercy, made us alive with Christ even when*
> *we were dead in transgression-it is by grace you have been saved.*
> —Ephesians 2:4–5

Some years ago, actress Bea Arthur had a popular television show called "Maude." Maude was an outrageous, outspoken, and difficult woman. She cared little about whose feelings she hurt or whom she managed to insult. Maude took particular delight in ridiculing her diminutive husband, Walter.

One of Maude's most-often-used comments to her husband was, "Walter, God will get you for that!"

The theology of Maude was a simple one of retribution. It is one that portrays God as one who delights in smashing us like an ugly bug on the sidewalk. A God who will get us for that (whatever that might be) is a God of puny grace. Such a theology holds us in check by fear. It is one that keeps us in line through dread of what horrible things might happen to us. It is one that wholly denies grace.

Grace is God's unmerited, unearned, and undeserved good favor. Grace is at the opposite end of the spectrum from Maude's "God will get you for that." Given our view of life and understanding of fairness, the theology of Maude probably makes more sense than God's grace. That is the wonder of it all. Grace cannot be fully understood. It cannot be explained. It does not even make sense. But, we do not have to understand it, explain it, or try to make it make sense. All we have to do is receive it.

As someone once said, "I don't just believe in God's grace. My life depends upon it!"

Prayer: This Day I will put aside any hint of fear of God's wrath. Today, I will embrace God's grace and, admittedly, be puzzled in it.

And the words of the LORD are flawless, like silver refined in a furnace of clay, purified seven times.

—Psalm 12:6

Adversity does not make us better people. Adversity does bring out unseen strength. It is not the tough times of life that makes us better. Tough times just have a way of bringing to the surface the strength that has been secreted away and kept out of sight.

We are like precious ore tossed into a furnace. The intense heat of the furnace is not the creator of silver or gold. The heat merely brings the precious metal to the surface. So, in the midst of life's hurts, challenges, or when you are standing knee-deep in despair, and someone tells you that suffering is good stuff because it makes you a better person, you do not have to believe it.

God does not use adversity to make us better. A loving God would never heap hurt upon us to make us better people. That is akin to child abuse. Rather, in the process of creation, God has already instilled in us all that it takes to endure whatever life might bring. Adversity merely brings that strength to the surface.

But, what about those times when you are spiritually bankrupt? What about the times when you cannot reach deeply enough to bring forth the strength the crisis demands? That is when God takes over.

A smelter would not put ore into a furnace and then walk away. The smelter stands by and is there to do whatever it takes to preserve the precious metal. It has been pointed out that when a goldsmith attends the furnace, he checks the crucible from time to time to see when the gold is refined to its purest state. The goldsmith's test is a simple one. He looks for the reflection of his face in the crucible. It is then that he knows the gold is pure. It is the reflection of God that adversity brings to the surface.

Prayer: This Day I will know that somewhere within me is the solution. Today, I will rely on God's strength within and know that He attends me even in the toughest of times.

You are only as sick as your deepest secret.

—Unknown

Secrets can be toxic. They are malignant tumors that sap our spiritual strength. Secrets wall themselves off in the deep recess of our souls and incubate there in a quiet and forgotten place, only to emerge when least expected.

Families that live with the mentality of, "Whatever you do, don't tell Dad," are spiritually sick families. An unfaithful husband who thinks that his secret liaisons are better kept quiet is setting the stage for his next affair. Wives who keep financial secrets from their husbands are stealing from both themselves and their marriage. Children who cheat on a math test to get good grades are failing in the only test that really matters. Churches that keep secrets are assured of having more secrets in the future. Secrets are toxic to business, governments, churches, and families. Consider the words of the Gospel writer John:

> *"If we confess our sins, he is faithful and just and will forgive us our sins and purify us from all unrighteousness. If we claim we have not sinned, we make him out to be a liar, and his word has no place in our lives"*
> (1 John 1:9–10).

Harboring secrets bars Christ from our lives. God's grace that we know in Jesus Christ cannot cohabitate with secrets. Christ is anxious to fill the void within us, but he cannot be a roommate with secrets. The only way to invite Christ within is to offer him a secret-less dwelling place.

Prayer: This Day I will do my best to get honest and rid myself of any lingering secrets. Today, I will invite Christ into my life and give him the least-cluttered room in the house.

The dream is the small hidden door in the deepest and the most intimate sanctum of the soul . . .

—Carl Jung

To say that Old Tom had lived a colorful life is like saying that the Pacific Ocean has a lot of water in it. Tom was born at the end of the great push westward. He was a rugged and adventurous sort who loved the great outdoors. Tom panned gold in the Snake River in Idaho. He worked in a lumber camp in Oregon. He trapped in the mountains of Colorado, worked in a copper mine in Arizona, and hunted the Bitterroot Mountains for bighorn sheep. Old Tom had worked in the copper mines of the Upper Peninsula of Michigan in their boomtown days.

Tom had endured much disappointment. He had lived through two failed marriages and a half-dozen dried-up business ventures. When I knew Old Tom, he was living with his aged mother and caring for her in return for food and lodging. Though his life was stuck in dismal stagnation, Old Tom was far from defeated. He had a big dream and future hope.

Old Tom had an adventurous dream. He would say, "One of these days things will change. And the minute it does, I'm out of here. I'm headed for the North Country just as soon as I can."

Tom's mother died. They sold the farm and settled the estate. Sure enough, Tom headed north. He went as far north as you can go and still be in the States. There, he bought a small cabin.

I went to visit Old Tom the summer after he had moved north. I found a dreamless, broken, and defeated man. The boomtown of his youth was now a ghost town. The copper mine had closed, and his friends had either died or moved away. The stream where he had caught big trout was dammed up. The woods where he had hunted was a clear-cut wasteland. Most of all, what was gone was Old Tom's spirit. Tom died before his second winter in the North Country. His cause of death was officially listed as "Heart Disease." He really died of dreamlessness. For Old Tom, it is better to live with a dream than to wallow in abject disappointment.

Prayer: This Day I will nurture my dreams and keep them well attended. Today, I will embrace the present moment as I invite the future.

Good, to forgive;
Best, to forget!
Living, we fret;
Dying, we live.

—Robert Browning

A pastor friend of mine, the Reverend Bill Genda, tells of seeing a car with a license plate that proudly and boldly displayed, "Pearl Harbor Survivor." Pastor Bill also mentioned that the car the man was driving was a Japanese import.

The driver of that car seems to have mastered the ability to forgive and move on. Surely, you have known someone who has carried a grievance around like a badge of honor. It is like putting a cement block in a gunnysack and carrying it every hour of the day. Carrying around hatred and past grievances is a full-time job. You never can put the weight of the sack down for a rest. Make no mistake about it, people do some horrible things to others. Few of us can get very far into life without having a few grievances that we could put in our gunnysacks of discontent. Some of us might need a U-haul to transport our grievances.

But, is the satisfaction worth the energy it takes to lug around a bag of grievances? Usually it is not. The unique thing about forgiveness is that the forgiver is often just as liberated as the forgiven.

I think the Pearl Harbor survivor who can drive a Japanese car has done a good job of carrying his sack for a while and then leaving it behind.

Prayer: This Day I will weigh the baggage I carry through life. Maybe, with God's help, I can lighten my load.

> *Some people look upon any setback as the end. They're always looking*
> *for the benediction rather than the invocation . . .*
> —Hubert Horatio Humphrey

Are you a quitter? Most people would vehemently deny any semblance of a quitter's attitude. Quitting is not part of our nature. We see quitting as a weakness. It is a sorry barometer of one's spiritual metal. To never quit is understood as toughness and a character asset.

However, there are times we are called to another place, another calling, or a different vocation. What if God really wants us to serve in some other capacity? What if our present calling, though rewarding, is only a preparation for some other venture? Or, what if the odds of success in our present job, marriage, or calling are impossible? Suppose there is no hope, and we stubbornly hang on just because we see quitting as a weakness? I once knew a man who pawned his wife's engagement ring to keep his failing business alive for one more week. We can carry all this to extremes.

What do you think God would say if he had a new job for us and we stubbornly and emphatically said, "No, I cannot do it because I do not want to be seen as a quitter?"

This is no easy matter. It is not one we dare rush into on our own. However, there may be another option. A General's army was roughed up in a battle and he ordered them to regroup. When asked why he retreated he bellowed, "We did not retreat. We are advancing in another direction!"

Consider advancing in another direction as an alternative to quitting. You do that by surrendering your will to the care of God. The matter is out of your hands. You are unburdened of any weakness. And, the matter of personal stubbornness will not be a barrier to God's will. Maybe God wants you to staunchly and stalwartly stay. Maybe God wants you to advance in another direction. Only by surrender will you ever know the difference.

Prayer: This Day I will listen for God's call by surrendering my will to him. Today, I will try not to get in God's way.

Therefore do not worry about tomorrow, for tomorrow will worry about itself. Each day has enough trouble of its own.
—The words of Jesus as recorded
in Matthew 6:34

Have you ever heard someone say, "Don't borrow trouble?" Sometimes we take on the troubles of others that do not concern us in any way. And, sometimes we look ahead and borrow our own future's potential troubles. Borrowing trouble is a useless waste of energy and has a way of sapping the joy out of the present.

A seminary student came to a place in his studies where he felt he was beyond his capabilities. What if I fail this Greek test? What if I cannot pass next semester? What if my senior year is too hard for me to comprehend? The student was filled with self-doubt, and he decided to leave the seminary. He packed his bags and went to see his mentor before he boarded a bus for home. The spiritual mentor advised the young student to take life in smaller bites. The seasoned mentor said:

> "Your only responsibility is for today. If you do all right today, then chances are you will do all right tomorrow. So unpack your bags and quit making it such a big deal."

Borrowing tomorrow's troubles never solves them in advance. Rather, it has a tendency to compromise today while you still have tomorrow's troubles to endure. Take life in smaller bites. After all, our only responsibility is for today. And a well-lived today gives us confidence in tomorrow.

Prayer: This Day I will focus on the present. I'll bite off just today and leave tomorrow for tomorrow's today.

They crucified two robbers with him, one on his right and one on his left.
—Mark 15:27

My friend, the Reverend Robert Carlson, had a vision one day that shaped much of his ministry. In his mind he was picturing the Hill of Calvary and its three crosses. It dawned on him that the three crosses etched three T's against the sky. What could those three T's signify? There were many possibilities. Bob Carlson gave the matter much thought. He seemed to recognize that this was not just mental musing. He sensed that somewhere in this vision was an important ministry-shaping message. But what could it be? Then it came to him—three T's—TIME, TRUST, and THANKFULNESS. The whole gospel is entwined within these three T's.

God is the author of all time. God was before time, and he accompanies all creation in all time. Time is God's and is God-given. Without God there would be no time.

Trust is our response to God. In a world that can fill library shelves with lists of mortal institutions that have failed miserably, the matter of divine trust is vital. When all else fails, there is no earthly reason for hope, and common sense and experience seem to point toward total breakdown, we can still trust in God. Trust placed in God is like no other. He is infallible, eternal, and inexplicable.

The third "T" is for thankfulness. Insofar as we have been given this time and trust, it is incumbent upon us to be a people of thankfulness. Our attitude of gratitude supports the trust and relishes the time that has been so graciously given. God gives us time. We trust in God's grace. And, in return, we unashamedly give our thankfulness.

When you look upon that hillside of ignominy and see the three crosses silhouetted against a gray sky, look beyond the suffering and see what is really there. It is the handwriting of a loving God spelling out TIME, TRUST, and THANKFULNESS.

Prayer: This Day I will celebrate, embrace, and take ownership of the three T's. May my time be used wisely, my trust be without reservation, and my thankfulness loudly proclaimed.

I warn everyone who hears the words of prophecy of this book: If anyone adds anything to them, God will add to him the plagues described in this book. And if anyone takes words away from this book of prophecy, God will take away from him his share in the tree of life and in the holy city, which are described in this book.

—Revelation 22:18–19

Sometimes, God's Word can be misquoted, misapplied, or used in wholly inappropriate ways. We have seen zealots use Scripture to validate outrageous behavior.

I once knew a man who had a tendency to take ownership of that which did not belong to him. Simply put, he made a practice of stealing. When caught, the dishonest man used a bit of convoluted theology. He said, "It is written that God helps those who help themselves. So, I was just helping myself to someone else's stuff!"

As you might guess, the outlaw's biblical excuse did not cut much slack with the judge. He got a hefty fine and a few weeks in jail. That is how civil law dealt with the man.

But, I wonder how God saw the incident? My guess is that the man's convoluted theology surely did not impress God. My guess is that God was hugely offended. I seriously doubt if God was amused. The light-fingered man may be facing double jeopardy. He may well have to deal with the judge and the Judge, for God's Word is not mocked.

Prayer: This Day I will diligently try to live in a manner that is pleasing to God. As the sun sets on this day, I hope to have so lived that God says, "Well done!"

No one sews a patch of unshrunk cloth on an old garment. If he does, the new piece will pull away from the old, making the tear worse.
—The words of Jesus as recorded
in Mark 2:21

By necessity, our forebears had to be frugal people. The pioneers were not wasteful folks. They made do with what they had. The Great Depression left those same scars of frugality on many lives. Later, WWII rationing brought sacrifices to America that added yet another layer of careful spending to our national fabric.

One place that frugality is evident is seen in quilts. A shirt was worn until its elbows were thin. Then the sleeves were cut off and it was a short-sleeved shirt. When that got too thin to wear, the still sound fabric was cut out and pieced together in colorful patterns to make quilts. Quilt-making is a fine art. Many have survived that are valuable family heirlooms. They deftly combine beauty, function, and economy.

A Christian's life is like a quilt. Through Christ, God has taken the scraps of our lives and given them purpose. He has given the useless bits of our being beauty. He has put together worth, purpose, beauty from the scraps of our lives. We seldom think of Christ as the Great Quilt-maker, but that is exactly what He is. He takes the useless and gives it worth. He takes the ugly and gives it beauty. He takes our singularity and binds us as community.

Prayer: This Day I will rejoice in the fabric of which I am but a tiny part. I will thank God for the Great Quilt-maker who has given my life beauty, function, and value.

We shouldn't teach great books; we should teach a love of reading.
—B.F. Skinner

Minnie Green was my first grade teacher. Mrs. Green was a widow who taught school during the day and helped her son publish a small town newspaper every evening. She had taught school long after the usual age of retirement. Looking back, I am now aware what a tedious and tiring life Mrs. Green had. There were times when the thirty or so first graders must have tried the poor woman's patience.

Mrs. Green taught me how to read. By that simple act, she opened the world's knowledge to me. If you can read, there are no barriers to what you can learn. It is not a stretch to say that Mrs. Green gave me the world's knowledge (or at least ability to acquire it if I so chose).

Mrs. Green lived well past the century mark. Near the end of her days on earth, I had the good fortune to thank her for the world she opened up for me. I said to her one day, "I am sure you do not remember me, but you are the woman who taught me how to read. I want to thank you." I felt better, and I think Mrs. Green did, too.

Today might be a good day to thank the person who taught you how to read.

Prayer: This Day is as good as any to attend to that which I have been putting off. I will tell someone thank you, I'm sorry, or I love you today.

> *Silent and amazed even when a little boy,*
> *I remember I heard the preacher every Sunday put God*
> *is his statements, As contending against*
> *some being or influence.*
>
> —Walt Whitman

I grew up in a shame-based theology. It was a church that practiced hard preaching. Every Sunday we were reminded that we might not have confirmed reservations for heaven. We were reminded that we were bold sinners and a fiery hell awaited us. We were reminded that we were a rotten lot. When the preacher of our little church got wound up, we were reminded of our rottenness.

But, not to worry; there was a way out. We had a weekly altar call so that anyone who wanted to reject his or her rottenness could do so. Many Sundays our tiny congregation was moved to tears as one of our number came forward to reject Satan and to get rid of this putrid scourge that had pock marked his or her life.

I cannot scoff at this harsh, shame-based theology. The fact is that we do some rotten things to one another. As a preacher I have come to recognize that most of us do not need a weekly reminder of our rottenness. The Good News is that most of us are really not that rotten. We are just imperfect. What we need more than anything is an understanding of the difference between imperfect and rotten. We also need to know that even if we slip from imperfect to rotten, there is still hope. God loves the righteous, the imperfect, and the even-less-than-imperfect.

Prayer: This Day I will take ownership of my imperfection. I will not wear it as a badge of blame or shame. I will be grateful that even in my worst moments, I am still loved and forgiven.

What is impossible with men is possible with God.
—The words of Jesus as recorded
in Luke 18:27

Ever get the impression that miracles do not happen to you? Do you see miraculous happenings as events of the long-ago past? Or, are biblical miracles the inexplicable actions of a less-scientifically-informed time? What about miracles? Are they real? Do miracles still happen? Are you a candidate for a miraculous happening?

The answer is a resounding *yes!* Miracles are real, they are present, and are available to you. The fact is, you can expect a miracle. Better yet, why not expect a lifetime of miracles?

Perhaps a slightly different understanding of miracles would be helpful. Jesus said that nothing is impossible with God. When we heap perplexing and seemingly impossible events into the "impossible-for-God" category, we rob God of his omnipotence. Declaring that God cannot bring about a miraculous happening limits God. It makes God puny. And even beyond that, casting doubt upon God's ability to act in miraculous ways implies that God needs us to validate his omnipotence. The fact is simple: God does not need our validation to be God. God can do quite nicely without our vote of approval. Putting mortal limits on God makes God small and wholly denies God's divinity, supremacy, and sovereignty.

Here is a better way to see miracles:

I can't.
God can.
I'll let Him!

Instead of merely believing in miracles, why not depend upon them?

Prayer: This Day I will do all I can to show God is limitless. Today, I will delight in awe that what seems impossible for me is effortless to a limitless God.

> *Be still and know that I am God.*
>
> —Psalm 46:10

As autumn ebbs and turns to the stark biting cold of winter, take a moment to consider the world around you. Stand still at your kitchen window as the sun comes up. Look at the leaves, both those on the ground and those still clinging to the oak tree. As you look, try not to think about how you have to get out there and rake and bag those leaves—just look. Look at the shadows the morning's sun casts on the lawn. What do they look like? Are they just gray blobs? Or are they delicate silhouettes of a maple tree's limbs pointing to the sky? Look at the moon that still shares the fading dark of night with the dawn of this day. Is it a tiny sliver, or is it full and robust?

Look at the mums. Aren't you glad you planted them? Think about the tulips and the daffodils you planted yesterday and how they will look next April. Think about the long winter sleep that awaits these bulbs. Think about the miracle of spring flowers breaking through what was once frozen earth. Think about the squirrel that sits on a limb looking at ten thousand acorns and wonders where to begin?

Listen a while. There is a far-off pheasant, a mallard, and a rooster greeting this new day. A dog is barking. A screen door slams. The dog is now silent. If you could just hear better, you would hear the satisfying lap of the dog licking his dish.

Listen to the silence. Look at the beauty. Be still.

Now, as you stand at your kitchen window, at the ending of a season and the beginning of this new day, ask yourself, "How is it, Lord, all this and heaven, too?"

Prayer: This Day I will deliberately pause. Today, I will drink in the beauty, bask in the wonder, and give thanks.

There is nothing in the world constant, but inconstancy.
—Jonathan Swift

Nothing is static. The world is in constant and perpetual change. Two recent studies looked at longevity. One focused on a group of individuals who had reached the century mark. The other study looked at couples who had been married sixty years or more. Both studies came to the same conclusion: people who cope with change live longer and stay together longer.

If change is inevitable and coping with it is beneficial, then it would seem that we have two choices. We can try to recreate the world and make it static, or we learn better change-coping skills. The first is impossible. Given the fact that all life must pause at this precise moment, static is out of the equation. We would have to somehow stop aging, invention, birth, marriage, death, disease, new employment, and human creativity. The list is endless and points to the fact that nothing is static. To use every resource to replicate or retrieve the past is not a solution. To maintain the status quo denies progress. Change is inevitable. Thus, learning better change-coping skills is a must.

You have heard it said, "Just roll with the flow." We can discover the embryo of new change-coping skills by not taking life too seriously. Learning how to deeply appreciate and revere the past, while still looking toward the future, is another option. Both of these can work, but there is one change-coping skill that stands above all others: **Live in this day.** Relish the present for how it encompasses the past. See it as an opening door for an exciting tomorrow. Embrace this day, for it is all you have. Neither the yesterday nor the tomorrow is ours. This day is all we have. Is it as good as yesterday? Probably. Will tomorrow be better? Maybe. But, a well lived today celebrates the best of the past and the hope of the future.

Let change flow as it will by not letting this day slip away. Avoid wallowing in yesterday or anguishing about tomorrow, for even this day is not static.

Prayer: This Day is unique. It will not pass my way again. I will welcome it, embrace it, and do whatever it takes to treat it for what it really is—a gift from God.

Let go and let God.

—Unknown

There are happenings along life's way that are hard to let go. Every one of us has been hurt in some way. Somewhere along life's journey a parent, a teacher, an employer, a friend, or a spouse has left scars of disappointment on us. The hurt may have come from an institution rather than an individual. A church, school, hospital, a lender, or government agency may have harmed us. The natural response is to harbor resentment against that person or institution. Many of these resentments make sense on the surface. The hurt may have been so life-shaping that it seems impossible to live beyond it. We take the resentment and stuff it in a suitcase and carry it with us everywhere we go. It becomes our baggage of life. Understandable? Yes. Reasonable? Absolutely not!

Resentment is ill will re-sent. Think about it. When another hurts us, either deliberately or unintentionally, we want retribution. We want to stamp the hurt "return to sender." It is part of being human. But, at what cost does that come? Maybe the price is too high. Certainly carrying a suitcase full of resentments is a high price. It takes too much energy. Such baggage holds us back in the race of life. And, it makes us weary, unpleasant, and unlikable people. Resentments can atrophy our very being. The cost of lugging resentments is just too dear. *Re-sending ill will never, never, never solve the original problem.*

There is only one liberating solution: put down the suitcase, unpack the resentment, throw the suitcase in a dumpster, and move on. Let go! How? By letting God carry the load. Turn your ill will that you would love to re-send into baggage left behind. Simply say, "Here, God, I can't carry this load any longer." Then move on.

Prayer: This Day I am not asking for the easy. Today, I want to be liberated from having to drag my baggage of resentments. I will need God's help, but first I will need the courage to set down my load of ill will.

He who has ears, let him hear.
> —The words of Jesus as recorded
> in Matthew 13:43

It is harvest time. Birds and animals of the forest are secreting away a cache of food for the coming winter months. Instead of building a storehouse of food, some carry their winter food along with them by packing fat on their backs. In nature, harvest time is a time of abundance. Only those who heed the warning of putting away for winter will survive.

The time of harvest is a small window. Time is short. The days are getting shorter. The weather is less favorable. The crop will not last forever. No one knows this urgency better than the farmer. Harvest time is the busiest of the year. Every move must count. Ever moment is precious. Like the animals of the forest, only the farmer who heeds the urgency will survive.

We were chopping corn silage one October. The dairy required several thousands tons of silage each winter to feed the appetites of the cows until spring grass grew. Tuck, the farm's foreman, always operated the chopper. Tuck was a master mechanic and could push any machine to its fullest capacity. He kept a constant flow of chopped corn pouring from field to silo.

One day Tuck said, "We got a bad sound in the chopper. She could blow any minute. I've looked her all over, but I can't tell what is making the racket."

This was a serious concern. The chopper was powered by a huge diesel engine that turned at high speed. If a shaft broke or a knife let loose, thousands of dollars of damage would surely follow (not to mention the loss of precious time). What should we do? Should we stop and tear down the chopper as a preventative measure? Or, should we keep going and hope for the best? We kept going. The next day I asked Tuck about the noise. He said, "All fixed."

"How did you fix it?" I asked.

"I just turned up the radio, and now I don't hear it anymore!"

Prayer: This Day I will not cover up that small, still voice within. Today, I will listen for God's voice.

A thing is important if anyone think it important.
—William James.

Fred O'Donnell is a wise man. Oh, yes, he is learned and well educated, but he has a wisdom that goes beyond mere academia. Fred has a hunger and curiosity for life, and he keeps that hunger well fed. He reads deep and complicated theology books for entertainment. He taught himself Greek so he could read the Gospels in their original language. Fred O'Donnell is more than intelligent. He is wise.

Fred O'Donnell belongs to one of America's fastest-growing groups. He is a cancer survivor. Fred's brush with death, the suffering that he endured through several runs of chemotherapy and a couple of bouts of radiation, shaped his wisdom. Fred would be quick to point out that his cancer gave him new insights, but the tuition he paid for this wisdom came at a high price.

Fred's wise philosophy of life is summed up in his home phone's answering machine message. In a cheerful voice Fred says:

> "Greetings! You have successfully dialed the O'Donnell residence. We are not here to answer this call, but since you have done such a good job of dialing, I want to share two important bits of wisdom with you. First, don't sweat the small stuff.
> And second, it is all small stuff! Now, if you still want to talk to us, please leave your message and I will call back. Be well!"

Fred O'Donnell is a wise man.

Prayer: This Day I will attempt to sort out what really matters. Today, I will get a big box for small stuff and a small box for big stuff.

*We must pay more careful attention, therefore, to what we have heard, so
that we do not drift away.*
—Hebrews 2:1

A young seminary student was having difficulty with his Greek class. In fact, he was failing. Worse than that, he was failing in two other of his five classes. The seminary Dean called the young man into his office to see if anything could be done to get the student's grades up.

The Dean explained the gravity of the young man's grade situation. He said he had no choice but to put him on probation. One more failing grade and he would have to drop out of seminary.

"But sir," the lad protested. "I have been called to be a preacher. It is God's will."

"Tell me, son, how did you happen to decide you were called to be a preacher?" asked the Dean.

"Well, one day I was working on the farm and I saw a huge cloud in the bluest sky I had ever seen. In that cloud were the letters P and C. I knew right then it meant Preach Christ. So, here I am."

The Dean sat thoughtfully for a moment and said, "I think in your case that P C means Plant Corn!"

Prayer: This Day I will listen intently to God's voice. I will make every effort to set aside my bias, my ambitions, and my personal aspirations as I listen to God's voice.

Stop judging by mere appearances, and make a right judgment.
—The words of Jesus as recorded
in John 7:24

Dr. Glen Miller is a distinguished scholar. He has had a long and notable career as a history professor in a number of colleges and universities. Most recently, Dr. Miller has served as professor of church history at Bangor Theological Seminary.

Glen Miller is a colorful character. He has a wit that knows no bounds. He is a brilliant storyteller and an accomplished lecturer. Dr. Miller has deftly balanced the delicate art of academic integrity with his students' interests. Glen Miller brings a bit of mirth to what could admittedly be a rather dry subject.

Having moved through the halls of academia for many years, Dr. Miller has been nominated for a number of prestigious awards. Many boards and university presidents have interviewed him over his thirty-plus-year career. Glenn Miller is no stranger to the process that goes along with scholarly politics.

Dr. Miller has discovered a way to make a quiet, yet bold statement in the interview process. He always wears bright red socks to an interview. It has even been said that the more prestigious the possible assignment, the brighter Glen's socks. He says, "If the color of my socks matter, then this is not an institution I wish to serve." The point he is trying to press is that our outside trappings are unimportant. It is his way of expressing his distaste for quick surface judgments.

Dr. Glen Miller knows a lot about church history. He also understands the danger of judging others.

Prayer: This Day I will take a hard and fearless look at my storehouse of prejudice and bias. Hopefully, today will begin a life that is free from surface judgments.

Since trifles make the sum of human things,
And half our misery from our foibles springs.

—Hannah More

In her stilted 19th century way, Hannah More said, "Don't sweat the small stuff" a couple of centuries before it became a popular cliché. One of our vice presidents called his four-year tenure to the nation's second highest elected office a grand misery. Misery often springs from the unimportant and the small stuff of life.

Misery wears many faces. It can be physical suffering. It can be political oppression. It can be poverty. Misery can be real or imagined. It can last a lifetime—maybe even for generations—or it can stay but for a while. Misery can be a private matter or one that is seen by all. Misery can atrophy your physical, emotional, and spiritual well-being. It can be a quiet annoyance no more threatening than a stone in your shoe. As in the case of an alcoholic, misery can be the result of making a poor choice. It can just as likely be the harsh and unprovoked act of another. Misery can be societal, as seen in slavery or racism. It can be private and individual, as seen in disease, serious injury, or birth defect. It can wear a cultural face, as seen in a community's response to HIV/AIDS. Misery comes in all of these and many more possibilities.

In many cases, there is little we can do about the misery we are obliged to endure. However, the overwhelming cause of misery is both preventable and curable. *It is the misery we create through the pursuit of the trivial.* We seem to have the innate ability to make a big deal out of nothing. The result is that our expectations and the end product is a disappointing mismatch.

Ms. More said it well when she said that half our misery is contained in foibles. Right on, Hannah! Don't sweat the small stuff and half your misery is no more.

Prayer: This Day I will leave the small stuff behind. Since this is no small task, today I will need God's help in knowing what really matters and what I can pass up.

Before all else, I am responsible for my own actions.

—Unknown

Substance-abuse counselors have long known that there are a number of triggers that can set a recovering client up for failure. Some of these are physical problems, and some are emotional. To help teach this list of triggers, they have coined an interesting acronym: H.A.L.T. It stands for hunger, anger, loneliness, and tiredness.

Do not get too HUNGRY. A complicated balance of insulin and sugar can cause a recovering person to be predisposed to recidivism. Hunger can be deadly to the recovering addict.

Do not get too ANGRY. It has been said that anger is a luxury one cannot allow oneself. Anger sets up an emotional powerlessness that renders the recovering person particularly vulnerable to relapse.

Do not get too LONELY. Loneliness is akin to abandonment. It works on one's emotional wellness in a negative way. The lonely person feels forgotten, rejected, and unworthy of another's affection. It can trigger such depression that the addict becomes defenseless against the next fix.

Do not get too TIRED. Fatigue leaves one weak. Exhaustion wears down the natural defenses that a clear and well-rested mind and body could easily muster. Tiredness saps resolve.

There they are: Hunger, anger, loneliness, and tiredness. Even though you may not be a recovering alcoholic, drug addict, or suffer from any one of several other addictions, the H.A.L.T. model of living makes good sense. Making any change in one's life demands a bit of self-care. Remember—before all else, you are responsible for you.

Prayer: This Day I will show myself how much I like me. Today, I will take ownership of the only person I can control—me.

. . . faith, hope and love. But the greatest of these is love.
—1 Corinthians 13:13

Today is Halloween. Most of us can remember at least one Halloween disguise from our youth. We can fondly recall the scary witch, the grotesque ghoul, or the silly clown we became long ago. You may have even won a prize for the best costume. Or, perhaps you won the apple-bobbing contest. Maybe your fondest memory of past Halloweens is the enormous bag of treats you hauled in. Hopefully, your Halloween memory is not one of some outrageous prank. My fondest Halloween memory has nothing to do with costume, candy, or tricks. Mine goes back to the sixth grade, and rather than the usual bag of sweets or Howdy Dowdy costume, mine has to do with a peanut-butter sandwich. Peanut-butter sandwich, you ask? How could that be?

It was that awkward age. I was a sixth grader—not yet an adult and surely not a child. Costumes were optional, and I absolutely refused to wear a silly costume that day. I pretended that Halloween was just another day, yet deep down inside I still longed for a bit of the magic that goes with Halloween. My brothers got on the bus that morning with their costumes packed neatly in a grocery sack. I carried only my books and my lunch in a brown paper bag.

When I opened my lunch that day at noon, there were two peanut-butter sandwiches my mother had cut out with a cookie cutter. They were round pieces of white bread with jack-o-lantern faces and peanut butter oozing through the eyes, nose, and smile of the top piece of bread. I was keenly aware that she had taken time to craft these special sandwiches. Her mornings were not easy. She had three lunches to pack and breakfast to prepare for several hired hands. Yet, she took time to lovingly make a jack-o-lantern peanut-butter sandwich.

I have eaten more than a few peanut-butter sandwiches over the years, but none are memorable or remarkable in any way, save those two sandwiches. What made them so special? They were packed with love.

Prayer: This Day I will look for some way to make the mundane extraordinary for another. Today, I will show rather than say, "I love you" to someone who really matters in my life.

> *. . . everything goes on as it has since the beginning of creation.*
> —2 Peter 3:4

Who is your furthest back person? Whom have you met along life's way that was the earliest born? Was it a great-grandparent? Was it your hometown's oldest citizen? Who have you met that spans the most time?

I am not sure who my furthest back person might be. I had three great-grandmothers and a great-great-grandmother I met as a child (only one of whom I can say I really remember). Perhaps my furthest back person was a woman I met in Grand Junction, Colorado, in the mid-1960s. Her name was Mrs. Holson. As an infant, she and her family migrated west from St. Louis in a covered wagon just after the Civil War. Along the way, the wagon train was attacked and several of their number were killed. When I met her, Mrs. Holson had passed the century mark.

Perhaps when Mrs. Holson was a child, an elderly grandparent had held her and bounced her on his or her knee, looked into the child's innocent eyes, and delighted in the babe's quizzical smile. Perhaps that person was ninety or more years old. That would have put that person's birth date well before the American Revolution. So, Mrs. Holson's furthest back person and my furthest back person combine to span all of American history. Just two conversations bridge the whole of this nation's time. If I have the good fortune to live a full life and hold a child in my later years, then I, too, will be part of that link that could conceivably reach another century.

All this is mind-boggling and may seem a bit pointless. However, it does clearly illustrate that we are part of an ongoing, unbroken circle of life that bridges the past with the future. None of us, or any particular point in the spectrum of time is the finished product. Creation is an ongoing and unfinished event. God did not merely create and then absent himself from creation. God continues to create, to foster change, and to shape an ever-changing world. The only unchangeable, ever-present, and unmovable presence is the Creator himself. All else is merely process.

As you greet this new day, see yourself as a part of that bridge.

Prayer: This Day I will see myself as an important link in the ongoing creation begun by God. Today, I will hold a child and keep that link in good repair.

For I am the least of the apostles and do not even deserve to be called an apostle, because I persecuted the church of God. But by the grace of God I am what I am, and his grace to me was not without effect.
—I Corinthians 15:9–10

John Newton composed one of the world's most-recognized hymns, *Amazing Grace*. Like Paul, John Newton was no stranger to God's amazing grace. He began life as a seaman and worked his way up to the rank of ship's captain. His cargo was far from noble and honorable. Newton captained a slave ship. He hauled human cargo from Africa's west coast to Great Britain to help keep the slave trade auction houses filled.

Caught in a devastating storm off the coast of Africa, Newton was filled with fear. He prayed that he and his crew would be spared. The seas calmed and Newton, good to his covenant with God, turned the ship around and headed back to England with an empty hold. The ship's owners were furious, and you can be sure that ended his career as a ship captain. It also began his career as a preacher and hymn writer. Newton composed and published several hundred hymns.

John Newton's grave marker in Olney Church cemetery succinctly sums up his biography. It reads:

John Newton, clerk, once an infidel and libertine, a servant of slaves in Africa, was, by the rich mercy of our Lord and Savior Jesus Christ, preserved, restored, pardoned, and appointed to preach the faith he had long labored to destroy.

John Newton knew just how amazing God's grace could be.

Prayer: This Day I will not settle for average grace, good grace, or remarkable grace. Today, through Christ, I expect and have need of one kind of grace—amazing grace!

The LORD is my rock, my fortress and my deliverer;
my God is my rock, in whom I take refuge.
He is my shield and the horn of my salvation,
my stronghold.

—Psalm 18:2

I am fascinated with the impact that media has on our thinking. We have little voice in what is reported. It is a bit like feeding time at the hog trough—whatever the farmer shovels in, the hogs gladly consume. We gobble up the sordid details of politicians and their sexual affairs. We hunger for the latest court testimony in high-profile cases. We clamor for the newest tidbits of outrageousness in the lives of sports, music, and movie stars. The more bizarre it is, the deeper the coverage, and supposedly the greater the appetite of the public.

There is a lack of proportionality in media coverage. It seems that the amount of ink and the importance of the story are incongruous. For example, we have heard much about the outbreak of West Nile Virus. This is not meant to trivialize the suffering that West Nile Virus has caused. In some cases it can be fatal. Sometimes, it causes permanent brain damage and disorientation. Protection against the possibility of contracting West Nile Virus through mosquito bites is a must. But consider the numbers. There have been a few hundred documented cases of West Nile Virus, and most have not led to death. In 1918, more than 660,000 people died in the influenza epidemic. In the late 15th century, 25 million, or about one in every three citizens in Europe died from Black Death. Both influenza and bubonic plague are still viable germs lurking somewhere in the world. But, how long has it been since you have heard a word about influenza and bubonic plague?

Proportionality is missing in more than just medical coverage. In a world that has challenges aplenty, we sorely need proportionality. The information and the challenge dare not be a mismatch. The good news in all this is not to worry. Regardless of the epidemic, the global threat to world peace, or any nature of impending doom that goes either unreported or over-reported, God is still our rock, our fortress, and our deliverer.

Prayer: This Day I will take in all I hear with some reservation. Today, I will not fear no matter what the news.

I can do everything through him who gives me strength.
—Philippians 4:13

I could not help noticing the young lad. He was part of the wedding party, but he was wholly disinterested in the ceremony that was about to take place. He had been just as disinterested at the rehearsal the night before. The boy might have been thirteen or fourteen. He had an intellectual, studious look about him. Two or three ballpoint pens were stuffed in the shirt pocket of his tuxedo. He had a rather thick book, which seemed to occupy his interest far more than the upcoming nuptials and all the hoopla that went with it. Not in an unkind way, but in a factual way, the boy looked like a Hollywood casting of a genius.

The wedding was flawless and lovely. The music was moving and tender. The bride and groom were obviously very much in love and delighted to tell the world so. It was one of life's sweet moments.

During the blessing portion of the liturgy, I said to the couple, "May your challenges be few and your victories be many."

Immediately after the pronouncement and the recessional, while the happy crowd was milling around the newly married couple, the young boy came up to me and said, "I want to talk to you."

"Sure, what can I do for you?"

"I want to know how you can have a victory without a challenge? Ought they not be in equal proportion?" He asked.

He had me! I am not sure how I answered the young philosopher. However, when I bless a couple today I say, "May your challenges never limit your victories. And may they be many."

Prayer: This Day I will see my challenges as yet-to-be victories. Today, I will rejoice in the balance of both challenge and victory.

Therefore keep watch, because you do not know the day or the hour.
—The words of Jesus as recorded
in Matthew 25:13

My father had a splendid sense of humor. He ripped apart the English language at every opportunity and had a way of pretending it was purely accidental. Many of his analogies were colorful, pointed, precise, and, I might add, not likely to be heard from the pulpit.

He took particular delight in inventing new sayings. His imaginative mind was at work all the time. Many of his sayings were gleaned from his farming background, his observations of human nature, and a quick wit. Once he saw a neighbor pulling a large combine with an especially small tractor. He said it looked just like an ant pulling a loaf of bread!

On another occasion, he commented on one of his sons not showing the best table manners. He said, "You eat just like a peach-orchard hog." I guess that meant chewing too noisily.

Perhaps his all time classic was a trip to the doctor's office when he was not feeling too well. The doctor wanted him to have some tests and then they would decide the course of treatment. "What did the doctor say?" I asked.

He answered in a matter-of-factual sort of way, "I probably shouldn't buy any green bananas until we see how this comes out."

Prayer: This Day I will appreciate the urgency of life, but I will not fret in its brevity. Because of my faith's hopeful and secure future, I can buy green bananas.

But grow in the grace and knowledge of our Lord and Savior,
Jesus Christ.

—2 Peter 3:18

If we could somehow completely eliminate child abuse and neglect, what would be the worst that could happen to a child? It might surprise you, but tying your child's shoelaces is the next worst thing that can happen to a child. You probably never thought of tying a child's shoelaces as a form of abuse, but it surely does have a crippling impact on a young life.

Tying your child's shoelaces is a way of keeping him or her from growing up. It stifles the child's maturity. It robs the youngster from the sheer delight of accomplishment. Remember your son or daughter's ecstatic joy when he or she first said, "Look Mom, I tied it myself!" And, tying your child's shoelaces keeps you in control. It is a subtle way of withering adolescent progress.

Patiently standing by while your four-year-old wrestles with a bow-knot is not easy. Watching a child fumble with a lopsided shoelace almost makes you want to buy Velcro straps or loafers on your next trip to the shoe store. It may be one of the hardest restraints a parent has to endure. You are in a hurry. It would be far more time-efficient if you tied the shoe. But, if you tie it this time, you will feel compelled to tie it the next time. Where and when will it end?

I once watched a mother cut her son's New York strip steak while he patiently waited. The son was a 225-pound varsity football line-backer! When will it end? Or, where does self-sufficiency begin? It begins when you say, "Let's see if you can tie your shoelaces today." It may be the most loving (though not the easiest) thing you do today for your child.

Prayer: This Day I will step out of the way and let my child fumble a bit. Today, I will lovingly, quietly, and patiently watch my child become the person God has begun in this special gift of life.

As Jesus was walking beside the Sea of Galilee, he saw two brothers,
Simon called Peter and his brother Andrew.
They were casting a net into the lake,
for they were fishermen. "Come, follow me," said Jesus,
"and I will make you fishers of men."
At once they left their nets and followed him.
—Matthew 4:18–20

The twelve disciples: Peter, two men named James, John, Andrew, Philip, Bartholomew, Matthew, Thomas, Thaddaeus, Simon, and Judas. They are the twelve disciples. Unless you are a biblical scholar, it is unlikely you know much about several of these twelve men. Bartholomew, Thaddaeus, Philip, and one of the two men named James are seldom mentioned and remain quite obscure. They could be called the "lesser known disciples."

Who were they? Why did Jesus select them from the crowd? What did they do? What did they say? What set them apart? How did they serve after the resurrection? What became of them? We simply do not know. Over the centuries, legend and folklore have surrounded these lesser-known disciples, but we know remarkably little about these men.

From what we know about a handful of Jesus' closest friends, here is what we can safely assume. They were common folks. Probably they were not highly educated. They were dedicated and willing to devote their lives to Jesus and to His ministry. They did not seek fame, had little interest in wealth, and, with the exception of one, had unyielding affection for Jesus.

There is one other remarkable attribute about these men. The Bible records, "at once they followed him." They did not say, "Let me get back with you on that." They did not tarry, mull it over, or procrastinate. They followed at once, immediately, and without delay. They made no great ado about it. They simply laid down their work and followed. Most of them followed in quiet obscurity—almost anonymity—never to make a big name for themselves. They gave all and remain to this day the lesser-known disciples.

Perhaps it will be said of us one day: they served quietly and faithfully.

Prayer: This Day I will gladly be a lesser-known disciple. Today, I will wear the robe of quiet anonymity with joy.

> *See what they spew from their mouths—*
> *they spew out swords from their lips . . .*
>
> —Psalm 59:7

Words matter. What we say is the outward expression of what is inside. The words we choose reflect the spirit within us. There is no shred of validity in calling someone a bigoted name and then saying, "I didn't mean anything by that." There is no truth in saying, "It is just a word." The words we choose matter, because they reveal the spirit within us.

Words reflect more than prejudice and bias. Consider the verbs we use to promote a good cause. We want to declare war on poverty. We propose to stamp out crime. We are going to fight back against domestic violence. We have a Drug Czar who is in charge of the war on drugs. We take a bite out of crime, fight tooth decay, kick the habit, attack injustice, fight racism, stomp out classism, break down social barriers, and strangle unemployment. These are brutal verbs. They reflect hostility within, which is a mismatch with the good we promote.

Mark Twain once commented on the use of words. He told the story of a bishop who stood on the ramparts of a castle and gave a blessing to the Crusaders as they left to fight the infidels. The Bishop prayed:

> "Oh Lord, be with us as we go to fight the scum who have desecrated your land. Be with us as we pillage his land, burn his granary, kill his ox, and enslave his people. Help us to drive a stake deep into the chest of evil and to scourge the land of Satan that it might never again bear fruit. We pray in the name of the Prince of Peace, our Lord and Savior, Jesus Christ."

The words of our mouths and the good we promote need to be congruous.

Prayer: This Day I will choose my words carefully. Today, I will listen to what flows from my lips so I might better know what dwells within me.

> Work as if you would live a hundred years,
> *pray as if you were to die tomorrow.*
> —Benjamin Franklin.

The Calvinist work ethic is one that understands all work as a glorification of God. Hard work, honest sweat, and good craftsmanship are all silent prayers. Therefore, our labor is a conversation with God.

I must admit that I have been a life-long, chronic workaholic. There have been times when that disease has been more acute than others. At its best, I am just busy. When it flares up at its worst, I become overwhelmed. Several dear friends, a mentor or two, a loving spouse, and more than one physician have tried to help from time to time. Usually, the relief is short-lived and a relapse is imminent. This is not a badge I wear with pride. Neither is it a condition for which I expect any sympathy. It is just who I am, and I can live with that.

I have made sincere efforts on a number of occasions to streamline my life and deliberately learn how to say, "No!" Every time I have found some spare time, I soon fill it up with new busyness. Perhaps I am a true Calvinist at heart.

My guess is that I am not alone in this. In fact, as pastor and counselor, I am well aware that many men and women have the workaholic disease. What can be done? Is there no cure? Is this a road to self-destruction that has no rest plaza? Is there no hope of normalcy?

I think there is hope. I have found that I pursue my meditation and my prayer life with the same intensity that I work. But, contrary to work, meditation and prayer rests the spirit, gives new strength, and brings a renewed sense of calm. Ambitious prayer and meditation fosters tranquility.

So, if you are a workaholic, then pray hard. The life you save may be your own!

Prayer: This Day I seek a calm spirit. Today, I will press less and ponder more.

Do not store up for yourselves treasures on earth, where moth and rust destroy, and where thieves break in and steal. But store up for yourselves treasures in heaven, where moth and rust do not destroy, and thieves do not break in and steal. For where your treasure is, there your heart will be also.
—The words of Jesus as recorded in Matthew 6:19–20

A friend once pointed out that a hearse does not have a trailer hitch, and no one has ever seen a hearse pulling an U-haul. The message seems simple. We are not to be fully consumed with earthly, material wealth. Rather, according to Jesus, we need to seek spiritual and eternal treasures. That is not new or revolutionary to traditional Christian understanding. Yet, there is something that is often missed in this passage.

It might shock you, but Jesus is promoting selfishness. He is saying, "You need to look after you. Your well-being and your eternal hope is your business. And, you need to build your own stockpile of heavenly treasures."

No doubt, that has rocked you back a bit. Maybe, it has caused you to blink once or twice and read the passage again. Jesus did not say, "Just settle back and all will be well." He said, "Continue to store up, but in a different realm." Jesus was clearly saying that the human hunger to have, to hoard, and get ahead is best satisfied with spiritual treasures. Stuff comes and goes. Moths, rust, and thieves always threaten, and its value wanes. But, work with the same intensity, the same diligence, the same passion, and in the same competitive spirit for heavenly goods, and you will have lasting wealth.

Jesus is saying that the Christian life does not mean lie down and die, be a pauper, or live without passion. Jesus is saying, "Get to it with every ounce of energy you have, but be sure that what you are pursuing really matters!"

Prayer: This Day I will pay attention to what captures my interest. Today, I will inventory my treasures and see how many have moth holes, flakes of rust, or are a robber's loot.

*Suddenly a great company of the heavenly host appeared with an angel,
praising God and saying: Glory to God in the
highest, and on earth peace to men on whom his
favor rests.*

—Luke 2:13–14

Today is Armistice Day. On the eleventh hour, of the eleventh day, of the eleventh month in 1918, the accords of peace were signed that brought an end to WWI. The date was chosen so that every school child in the world could remember the end of all wars. It was believed that this was the war to end all wars. The carnage of this war, its global consequence, and the suffering that civilians endured were like no other conflict ever waged before. Bigger and faster engines of destruction, lethal chemical gas, aerial bombing, and death beyond anyone's imagination gave the world new resolve to live in peace.

Tragically, we now know the rest of the story (or at least part of the rest of the story). Another world war and dozens of other conflicts have come our way since that November day in 1918. Even grimmer is the reality that our current ability to destroy life and all creation makes the machines of war in 1918 look primitive and rather harmless. This insanity has to stop, but how?

Peace is not the responsibility of a president, a king, a general, or the United Nations. The responsibility for peace belongs to every citizen on this planet. It begins in our homes and in the work place. It is how we treat our spouse, our children, and our parents. It is how we treat one another in the supermarket checkout line and our neighbor across the backyard fence. It is how we drive on the highways and how we behave as fans at a football game. It is how we treat our elderly, our infirmed, and our poor. Peace is a matter of personal responsibility that has its nucleus in individual lives.

Remember, the angel that brought the good news of Christ's birth and the promise of peace on earth spoke to a bunch of shepherds in a pasture, and not to a prince in the palace.

Prayer: This Day I will do my part to bring global peace. If just for this day all 7 billion of us work for peace, then the angel's promise continues to thrive.

This then is how you should pray:
"Our Father in heaven,
hallowed be your name,
your kingdom come,
your will be done
on earth as it is in heaven.
Give us today our daily bread.
Forgive us our debts,
as we also have forgiven our debtors.
And lead us not into temptation,
but deliver us from the evil one.
For yours is the kingdom, and the power,
and the glory forever.
—The words of Jesus as recorded
in Matthew 6:9–13

There are two almost universal fears. One is to be asked to read publicly, and the other is to pray publicly. People do not like to read or to pray in front of a gathering. No doubt, there is a fear of looking foolish if a word is mispronounced. Maybe, it is fear of getting stuck with nothing to say. Or, perhaps it is fear of ridicule. Suppose someone said, "That was a stupid prayer." Jesus must have known how hard it is for us to pray publicly. That is why He said, "Here is how it goes folks . . ."

Yet, I find it curious that we are intimidated to speak publicly about our relationship with our Creator. If God has really made a difference in your life, then it would seem that you would be anxious to tell the world about it. Ought that not be an easy conversation?

If you think your prayers are insufficient, somehow inferior, and not worthy of public display, then consider this. When you pray, you are speaking to your oldest and dearest friend. That ought to make it easier. And, if you still think you cannot pray and that you have no experience, then remember a time when you had a sick child. Ever had a sick child? Then you know how to pray.

Prayer: This Day my prayer is to my oldest and dearest friend. It is to the One who knows me best, loves me most, and wants to hear what I have to say.

Give and it will be given to you. A good measure, pressed down, shaken together and running over, will be poured into your lap. For with the measure you use, it will be measured to you.
—The words of Jesus as recorded
in Luke 6:38

I stopped at a roadside stand one fall day and bought a half-bushel of apples. The apples were big, round, and bright red. I could almost taste their tart crispness as I looked at the half-bushel basket filled with the beautiful fruit. The clerk took the basket and poured the apples into a brown paper sack. I paid my bill and proudly brought my purchase home. You can imagine my surprise when I opened the grocery sack and saw only small, wormy apples on the top of the sack. The vendor had put a half-bushel of wormy, puny apples in a basket and then put a few big, round, bright red beauties on top of the junk fruit. It was both times that I will buy apples from that roadside stand—the first and the last!

Jesus talks about a good measure. It is one that is pressed down and shaken together. It is a measure that is filled to the brim. Not another ounce could be heaped into this measure. God's measure is a full measure and then some. There are no rotten, wormy, inferior apples in the bottom of God's measure.

With God, what you get is what you see—*and then some!*

Prayer: This Day I will give with good measure as I receive with good measure. Today, I will thank the Great Vendor of Good Measure.

> *The manner of giving is worth more than the gift.*
> —Pierre Corneille

I know a man, whose name is unimportant, who has made a life-long practice of giving. He has prospered beyond his imagination. Before his retirement, he had gone to a top management position in the corporation he served. The man's salary was well into the six-figure bracket.

The man's wife also worked for the same company, but she worked in production rather than management. As you can imagine, there was a significant difference in the husband's salary and wife's check. The wife had no reason to work, because the husband's income was more than sufficient for their life-style. However, she worked because the couple had decided they wanted to do something special for those who were not as fortunate as they. They gave away every penny the wife made and lived on the man's salary. They helped family members, friends, church missions, and total strangers. The giving brought the couple much satisfaction, and they seemed to feel no pinch from their generosity.

One day at the supper table, the man said to his wife, "You know, we have more than we need. Our house is paid for. We have two cars, a boat, and a cottage. In fact we have far more than we need. Let's give away my salary and live on yours."

That is exactly what they did. They gave away more than $100,000 a year and lived on less than one-third of that amount. That is giving!

Prayer: This Day I am keenly aware that I can never match the model of giving, or the same measure, that God has given to me. But, today I will quietly do my best.

*The measure of true Christians is how they
act when no one is looking.*

—Unknown

Elwood was an elderly caretaker of the local Humane Society shelter. He was a retired man who volunteered most of his time. The animal shelter was always hard pressed for funds, so Elwood's volunteerism was surely welcome.

One day a huge ice storm plummeted Elwood's community. There were broken tree limbs, downed power poles, and the lines were in disarray. The roads were no better than hazardous skating rinks. You can imagine how tough such a storm was on birds and animals that were caught in its grip.

Somehow Elwood got his old car out of the garage and slipped into the animal shelter to feed and care for the dogs and cats that terrible day. There were no customers that day at the shelter—the roads were too bad. Since the phone lines were down, there were no calls, either. Along toward evening, as Elwood was about to lock up and go home, there was a knock on the door. A man stood in the icy entryway with a small bird he had found that had been pelleted nearly to death by the storm. Elwood invited the man in. He took the bird and warmed it by the fire, then carefully and lovingly put it in a warm box filled with straw. The man who brought in the bird thanked Elwood for his kindness and left.

About six months later, the Humane Society received a letter from a lawyer in California. The letter explained that the lawyer represented a man who had been visiting family in the north when a huge ice storm raged through the area. His client had found an injured bird, and an elderly man at the shelter had lovingly cared for the bird. The man had since died and he wanted the Humane Society to have a check for $25,000 as a tribute to Elwood's kindness.

Prayer: This Day I will welcome every opportunity to quietly help with no expectation of return. Today, I will show that I care with more than just words.

*Every heart that has beat strong and cheerfully has left a hopeful impulse
behind it in the world, and bettered
the tradition of mankind.*
—Robert Louis Stevenson

I would be surprised if the old, yellow bowl cost more than $2.98 when
it was new back in the 1950s. It is surely not made of crystal, fine
china, or delicate porcelain. It is just an old, yellow serving bowl. Probably in flea market prices, on a good day, it might fetch $25.00.

My grandmother bought the old, yellow bowl from one of the tea
and coffee companies that made the rounds selling all manner of household goods. Every month the company representative would bring a
new piece of a matching set of dishes. For a few dollars, a homemaker
could assemble a new set of dishes over a year or so of careful spending. Probably every home in America has one or two of these dishes
tucked away in some closet. The bowl is far from rare. It is an unremarkable bowl, yet it is a priceless family heirloom.

Why such value? Because at every family gathering the old, yellow
bowl graced our table. It was there at Thanksgiving filled with cran-
berry relish. On Christmas it was heaped with a colorful Jell-O. At
Easter the old, yellow bowl held mashed potatoes. Time and again at
a summer picnic it held potato salad or macaroni salad. The old, yellow bowl was present when we came home after saying a final good-
bye to a loved one. It was there when a baby was baptized. It was
present at our weddings, graduations, or when company came. It never
missed a birthday. It was with us in good times and in bad times.

In some ways that old, yellow bowl is a living memory and a constant presence. It is my grandmother saying, "Here, have some more.
I made it just for you, and besides it is good for what ails you!"

Prayer: This Day I will embrace tradition. Today, I will do my part in
keeping alive that which has been so freely, lovingly, and
graciously given to me.

*"Or suppose a woman has ten silver coins and loses one. Does she not
light a lamp, sweep the house and search carefully until she finds it? And
when she finds it, she calls her friends and neighbors together and says,
'Rejoice with me; I have found
my lost coin.' In the same way, I tell you, there is rejoicing
in the presence of the angels of God over one sinner who repents."*
—The words of Jesus as recorded
in Luke 15:8–10

A story of the importance of personal prayer and heavenly rejoicing
has been passed down through the recovery group, Alcoholics
Anonymous. In the mid-1930s, when A.A. was founded, there were
no detoxification centers. There were no trained counselors. The
medical community had only a primitive understanding of addictions
and recovery. In those early days, it was truly trial and error with an
occasional success thrown in to keep them trying. The main work
force was one recovering person helping another mainly through moral
support and encouragement.

St. Thomas Hospital in Akron, Ohio, offered a couple of rooms
and dedicated one nurse, Sister Ignatius, to help recovering alcoholics
and drug addicts in those first days of sobriety. One day, a man who
was deep in the throes of withdrawal said, "Oh, Sister, I am so sick.
Please pray for me."

The kindly nun said, "I will gladly pray for you. But you pray for
yourself, also. Because if there is one thing God loves to hear, it is a
stranger's voice."

Prayer: This Day I will keep my voice familiar to God's ear.

Therefore my heart is glad and my tongue rejoices;
my body also will rest secure, because you will
not abandon me at the grave, nor will you let
your Holy One see decay.

—Psalm 16:9

We tend to use happiness and joy unchangeably. The two work well as synonyms in everyday usage. Yet, in God's Word joy and happiness are not the same.

Happiness is fleeting. It comes for a while and then leaves. A new car makes us happy, but when it begins to rust and becomes our local mechanic's best friend, the happiness begins to ebb. A good movie, book, or dinner out makes us happy—for the moment. The latest fashions make us happy (at least for that season). Happiness is always based on circumstances, external happenings, and is temporal.

Joy, on the other hand, is not about external happening. Joy is an inwardly held grace. As the psalmist, David, points out, joy is a gladdened heart. Joy is an internal calm that can be with us even when we are not happy. It is the tranquil knowing that nothing will ever separate us from God's love. Joy is knowing you will never be abandoned. Joy is not seasonal and never goes out of fashion.

It is possible to have both joy and happiness. If you relentlessly pursue happiness, you might be a joyless person. However, if you base your life on joy, happiness will surely follow. Even in times when happiness seems like a distant memory, you can still have joy.

One other difference between happiness and joy is that joy usually costs less. Happiness always seems to come at a cost, but joy is free!

Prayer: This Day I will rejoice in the happiness that I savor, as I thank God for the joy I have found in Christ. Today, I will understand that happiness is a fleeting gift, while joy is God's lasting love.

It is a riddle wrapped in a mystery inside an enigma.
—Winston Churchill

This is about the time of year when caterpillars wrap themselves in cocoons and begin their final metamorphosis. Next spring, butterflies will emerge from those fuzzy blobs of fibrous stuff that are now attached to tree limbs.

I well remember the first time I heard the story of this remarkable transformation. One autumn day, my grandfather and I were making our last trip to Black Creek to catch some suckers when we came upon a cocoon attached to a low branch. He told me it held a caterpillar and next spring a butterfly would come out of this papery capsule.

Now why would he lie to me like that? I was no newcomer to this world. I was a six-year-old farm boy who understood that hens' eggs held baby chicks, cows had calves, and piglets were just smaller versions of their sow mothers. I knew soybeans grew from soybean seed, and corn the same. Life begets like life. Now, one of my most trusted mentors was telling me that an ugly, old, creepy caterpillar was going to become a butterfly. It was just too much!

Next spring, Grandfather and I were on our way down the little path that led to Black Creek to begin another season of catching suckers and rock bass, when he paused for a minute where the cocoon had been last fall. It now had a slit in one side and was just an empty shell of fibrous material. "See there, Jerry, the butterfly has emerged."

I was still unconvinced, and, to be honest, I still am a bit skeptical. Oh, I know in my mind the process of metamorphosis. But, in my heart it still does not make sense. But then, how a sinner is redeemed, set free, and finds eternal hope is also beyond my comprehension.

Some things in life do not have to be fully understood to be real. Caterpillars that become butterflies and lives made anew in Christ are just two of them.

Prayer: This Day I will simply and gladly take ownership of God's grace. Today, I will not try to understand it. I will just relish it.

> *Be joyful always; pray continually; give*
> *thanks in all circumstance . . .*
> —1 Thessalonians 5:16

As Thanksgiving draws near, we retell the story of the pilgrims and their spirit of thankfulness. Part of the Thanksgiving story has become more legend than truth. No doubt they dined on venison, lobster, and fish rather than turkey and cranberries. Probably the pilgrims were not a dowdy bunch of zealots, but were delighted in a robust meal and a grand party.

You probably have not heard of the *Speedwell*. When the pilgrims left England, there were about 150 passengers signed up for the journey. There were two boats, the *Mayflower* and the *Speedwell*. Both ships were miserable old tubs that were barely seaworthy. The seamen were fearful about what lay before them because it was too late in the season for a North Atlantic crossing. The old salts knew the hazards of a late departure, but the innocent band of pilgrims was insistent. So, the two ships set sail for Virginia.

A day or two out of port, the *Speedwell* began to take on water. They decided to return to port to repair the leaking ship. When the *Speedwell* was patched, once more they set sail for the New World. Again the leaky old wreck took on water. It was decided that the ship was too unsound to make the crossing. They returned to England a second time and some saw this as God's warning not to be foolhardy. A few—one hundred and one—were determined to sail to a new life in Plymouth Bay. So, they packed on the *Mayflower* and set sail. The *Speedwell's* crew and fifty or so pilgrims bid them God's speed.

Many years later, it was learned that the crew of the *Speedwell* sabotaged the ship. They knew that the main mast that was secured in the lower hold of the ship would allow the ship to leak if too much sail was rigged. The crew deliberately put on too much sail so the ship would take on water. For another half century after the *Mayflower's* crossing, the *Speedwell* continued as a prosperous merchant vessel. The *Mayflower* made one more trip across the sea—back to England in the spring of 1621.

Prayer: This Day I will live in a spirit of Thanksgiving. Today, I will fully acknowledge who I am and who looks out for me.

"I tell you that this man, rather than the other, went home justified before God. For everyone who exalts himself will be humbled, and he who humbles himself will be exalted."
—The words of Jesus as recorded in Luke 18:14

There is a huge difference between humility and humiliation. Though the two are often side-by-side in a *Webster's Dictionary*, they are worlds apart in meaning. Tragically, the two are sometimes confused and disaster results.

Humility is a spirit of calm. It is the void left when selfishness has been fully spewed from one's soul. Humility is a meekness that deplores the haughty. It is the spirit of modesty. Humility can be overdone. To become overtly humble is akin to living lowly and downtrodden. Benjamin Franklin once said that humility was impossible to achieve, because of the pride one has in having become more humble. Even though perfect humility is an oxymoron, a spirit of humility is desirable.

Humiliation is a whole other matter. Humiliation is to have one's dignity ripped apart. It is your sense of well-being and worthiness torn from your soul. Humiliation is to stand in total spiritual disrepair. Though we can, and occasionally do, bring humiliation upon ourselves, it is more often a matter of victimhood. There seems to be a few who delight in humiliating others. They are sorry soul-wreckers who cannot bear to see another's bliss.

In a perfect world, there would be more humility and no humiliation. Jesus had a lot to say about humility and relatively little to say about humiliation. But, I think Jesus was well aware of the pain of humiliation. I think he championed human dignity. After all, the Good News is about how to be humble, without the expense of humiliation.

Prayer: This Day I will try to be more humble and, at the same time, I will avoid bragging about my humility. Today, I will do my part to rid my little corner of the world of humiliation.

*From everyone who has been given much, much will be demanded; and
from the one who has been entrusted with
much, much more will be asked.*
—The words of Jesus as recorded
in Luke 12:48

Orville was from a family of thirteen. He was born poor, and by his early adulthood he had become even poorer. He worked as an apprentice carpenter, and he and his wife lived in a small rented house.

Orville's work was seasonal, and it was not unusual to be unemployed during the winter months. One winter lull, Orville told his landlord he was short of cash and he would like to trade work for rent. The landlord was agreeable. So, Orville gathered up some scrap lumber and built a set of kitchen cupboards for the house. The landlord was so impressed with the young man's workmanship that he hired Orville to build cabinets for some of his other rentals. Others saw his cabinets and they, also, wanted him to help remodel their kitchens.

The next spring, Orville set up a shop in his garage and began building cabinets after working for his landlord and friends. Soon, the orders were more than a part-time, after-work hobby. Orville quit his regular job and began to build cabinets full time.

That is the story of the beginning of Merillat Industries. America's largest cabinetry company began as a part time-hobby by an unemployed man who was looking for a way to pay his rent.

Orville Merillat was a man of deep faith. He made a fortune and gave millions to charities. This simple man, who began life with so little, became one of this nation's most generous hearts. Toward the end of his life, he was asked what he thought was the secret of his success. Orville said, "I think God knew that He could trust me to do some good with wealth."

Prayer: This Day I will do whatever it takes to be trustworthy in the eyes of God. Not merely to have much and to know wealth, but to be so positioned in life that I can be capable of doing his work.

If you believe, you will receive whatever you ask for in prayer.
—The words of Jesus as recorded
in Matthew 21:22

A woman went to a Wednesday-evening prayer service. The pastor asked, "Does anyone have any special prayer requests?"

The woman raised her hand and said, "I have six grandchildren who live a long distance away. I would like to see my grandchildren more often, so my prayer is for my son and his family to relocate."

The next morning the woman's son called his mother. "I have great news! My company is sending me overseas for eight months. My wife and six children will be moving in with you and Dad until next summer."

The woman's husband said, "The next time, you better be more careful what you pray for."

Indeed, God does answer all our prayers. There are three answers to Prayer: yes, no, and not now. Some say there may even be a fourth possible answer—you have to be kidding!

The fact is that God does answer our prayers. However, sometimes what we think we need is not part of God's greater plan. Sometimes, what we want may not be what we want at all. And, sometimes, what we think is vital to our lives is just trivial to the overall scheme of things. All you really need to know about prayer is that God listens, the heart of God is moved, and God responds. The listening and the moving are certain. The response can be a surprise.

Prayer: This Day I will see my prayer as an unending conversation with the One who knows what is best for me. Today, I will carry my needs to God and patiently await his response.

"Everything they do is done for men to see."
—The words of Jesus as recorded
in Matthew 23:5

A common, though seldom discussed, practice in CornBelt farming communities is to present a good appearance. Most would be embarrassed to admit it, but if there is a bit of fertilizer left in the cart after the field has been covered, the farmer will spread that extra fertilizer near the end rows along the road. It gives the appearance of a better crop. It may not yield any better, but the crop looks more robust all summer.

There is a name for that practice. It is called "bankers' rows." The notion is that a banker, who has invested in the crop, will be pleased with the crop's progress if he should drive past the field. The practice is also based on the assumption the banker will not leave the comfort of his car and get mud on his shoes to check beyond the outside rows of the field.

It is a sleazy and dishonest practice that fools no one. The end result at harvest time is what matters. Regardless of how things look all summer, there comes a day of reckoning.

Life can be like "bankers' rows." We can put on good appearances and still not be prepared for harvest time. A life lived in Christ is one that can be transparent, stands up to deeper scrutiny, and holds no surprises at harvest time. A life lived in Christ is one that looks the same on the inside as it appears to others on the outside. You will not find "bankers'-rows" Christians in heaven.

Prayer: This Day I will be willing to be transparent. Today, I will bravely endeavor to really be as others see me.

*And we also assume the responsibility for bringing to the house of the
LORD each year the firstfruits of our crops and
of every fruit tree.*

—Nehemiah 10:35

A young lad, seated at the supper table, was busily cutting his portion of meat. He delicately carved around the bone and whisked
off a bit of fat. He sliced the meat into small bite-sized pieces, then
divided the pieces into two piles. His father asked, "What are you
doing?"

"I'm cutting up my meat so I can share my supper with my dog,
Bing."

"You will not feed that to Bing. Let the dog have the scraps that
are left over."

"Please, Dad," begged the boy, "let me give Bing some of the best."

"No, and that's final. The dog gets scraps."

The boy finished his supper and gathered up the odds and ends of
table scraps, and took the miserable lot of waste out to the dog's pen.
He dumped the castoffs into the dog's dish and said, "Here is your
supper, Bing. I had hoped to bring you an offering, but all I have is a
collection."

Too often, we give God a collection of what is left, when God
really deserves the best we have to offer.

Prayer: This Day God gets my good portion. Today, there will be no
collection of leftovers. Because God has given me his best,
he deserves the same in return.

*. . . all the finest olive oil and all the finest new wine and
grain they give the LORD as the first fruits of
harvest.*

—Numbers 18:12

For some reason, roasting a turkey challenges some cooks. Perhaps it is because of lack of familiarity, since the event only comes once a year in some homes. Or, maybe some of these reluctant cooks feel the pressure of preparing a big meal for a dozen or more guests. One thing for certain, Thanksgiving brings with it a turkey-roasting anxiety to many kitchens.

The Butterball Turkey people understand this anxiety. Beginning several years ago, the Butterball Company set up a turkey hotline. Reluctant and anxious cooks could call in their turkey prep questions and get an expert's advice on the matter.

One woman called the Butterball hotline and said, "I have a turkey that has been in my freezer for eleven years, and I am wondering if it is still safe to eat?"

The Butterball expert said, "If you can be absolutely certain the turkey has never been thawed, it is still safe to eat. However, it is likely to be freezer burned and probably has lost much of its moisture. I would suggest you would be much more satisfied with a newer turkey."

The caller thought for a moment and said, "Well, in that case, I guess I'll just give this one to the church and get a new one for my guests."

In this season of Thanksgiving, it is good to remember that God gave us his very best.

Prayer: This Day God will know my thankfulness firsthand. Today, God gets the best I have to give.

---

*You will be ever hearing but never understanding; you will be ever seeing
but never perceiving. For this people's heart has become calloused; they
hardly hear with their ears,
and they have closed their eyes. Otherwise they
might see with their eyes, hear with their ears,
and understand with their hearts
and turn, I would heal them.*

—The words of Jesus as recorded
in Matthew 13:14–15

A father wanted to spend a quiet Sunday morning reading the Sunday
newspaper and having a leisurely cup of coffee. His young daughter
awakened early that morning and came into the kitchen. She began to
ask a long line of a six-year-old's questions. Wanting to sip his coffee and
read the paper, the disinterested father tried to think of something that
would occupy his inquisitive daughter's attention. He noticed a map of
the world on the paper's front page. He tore that page from the paper,
took out a pair of scissors from a cabinet drawer, and clipped the paper
into what looked like a jigsaw puzzle. "Here, Sweetheart. Here is a map
of the world. See if you can piece it together," the father said.

He went back to sipping his coffee, knowing his daughter would be
busy for the next couple of hours. Much to his surprise, she came to him
saying, "Look, Daddy, I am all done!"

The map was flawlessly assembled. Every continent, ocean, mountain range, and nation (even the tiny ones no one can spell or pro-
nounce) were all in place. "How in heaven's name did you do that so
quickly?" asked the surprised father.

"I looked at the back of the pictures and saw the face of a person.
When I put the person back together, the world came together."

That is what Jesus had to say also—heal the person, and the world
is put back together.

Prayer: This Day is a day of kingdom-building—one soul at a time.

*People were bringing babies to Jesus to have him touch them. When the
disciples saw this, they rebuked them. But Jesus
called the children to him and said, "Let the children
come to me, and do not hinder them, for the kingdom
of God belongs to each of these. I tell you the truth,
anyone who will not receive the kingdom of
God like a little child will never enter.*
—The words of Jesus as recorded
in Luke 18:15–17

Consider the word, *"Important."* Note that it begins with IM—I'm important. That is the message Jesus was teaching to his disciples. A child is important to God.

Sometimes we hear well-meaning people talk about children as the church of the future. That is wholly nonsense! Children are the church of today. They are vital to the church and important to God. Importance is not a matter of maturity. There are no board exams we must pass. There is no magical or mystical age one must attain to be important to God. Every soul matters regardless of age.

The kingdom of God is not like a ride at Disney World where a silhouette of Mickey Mouse says, "You have to be this tall to ride this ride."

In fact, Jesus is so adamant about childlike innocence that he said we all must enter the kingdom like a child. What does that mean? I think it means with enthusiasm. It means without reservation, pre-conceived ideas, or for political gain. A child enters with trust, innocence, and unquestioning faith. A child enters because, like all God's children, they matter to God.

Prayer: This Day I'm delighted to be important to God. Today, I will practice my childlike faith because that is especially important to God.

*Therefore go and make disciples of all nations, baptizing them in the
name of the Father and of the Son and of the
Holy Spirit, and teaching them to obey everything
I have commanded of you. And surely I am with
you always, to the very end of the age.*
—The words of Jesus as recorded
in Matthew 28:19–20

Cartoonists show them as a light bulb connected by dots to the
person's head. Teachers call them teachable moments. I call them
"head-slappers." No doubt, at some time, you have slapped your forehead and said, "Wow! Now I see what you mean." A teachable moment is when it all seems to fall together. Call them head-slappers,
teachable moments, or light bulbs, they are unforgettable moments
when we come to a sudden and new realization.

A friend of mine says that this sudden breakthrough of awareness
is not accidental. My friend puts it this way: **When the student is ready,
the teacher will appear.**

There have been many times in my pastoral life when someone
tells me that something I said changed his or her life. Often, when they
repeat what I had supposedly said, for the life of me I cannot recall
ever having said that. In fact, the opposite seems to be true. Whenever
I try to be profound, I usually have nothing of benefit to say. When I
deliberately try to orchestrate a head-slapper moment, it usually ends
in failure. When I feel the least helpful, the least profound, and the
poorest prepared to advise is when another often hears the Good News.

The message seems simple. We are not in charge of teachable
moments. We cannot fashion a head slapper. Light bulbs are only for
the comics. The epiphanies of life, those life-changing, and the breakthrough moments, when we are changed in an instant, are the Holy
Spirit at work through another. Indeed, it is as my friend says, "When
the student is ready, the teacher will appear."

Prayer: This Day I will willingly be the teacher if so called. But to-
day, I will understand it is not my brilliance that teaches.
Rather, it is the Holy Spirit speaking through me. For that
I will be grateful.

The best is yet to be.

—Robert Browning

A woman who had been diagnosed with a terminal illness was well aware that her time on this earth was short. As she was getting her final affairs "in order," she contacted her pastor and had him come to her home to discuss her funeral arrangements. She had given the matter much thought and was quite specific about which songs she wanted sung at the service, which Scriptures she would like read, and even which dress she wished to be wearing. The woman also requested to be buried with her favorite Bible.

Everything was in order, and, as the pastor was prepared to leave, the woman suddenly remembered something very important to her. "There's one more thing," she said excitedly.

"What is that?" asked the pastor.

"This is very important," the woman continued, "I want to be buried with a fork in my right hand." The pastor stood looking at the woman, not knowing what to say.

"That surprises you doesn't it?" the woman asked.

"Well, to be honest, I am a bit puzzled by the request." He said.

The woman explained, "In all my years of attending church socials and potluck dinners, I always remember that when the dishes of the main course were being cleared away, someone would say, "Keep your fork." It was always my favorite part of the meal. I knew that something wonderful was about to come. It might be a deep-dish apple pie, a chocolate cake, or some other delightful treat. When I saved my fork, I knew that the best was yet to come."

The woman paused for a moment and then said, "I want everyone to know when they see that fork, that I fully expect that the best is yet to come!"

Prayer: This Day I will cherish this life with the knowledge that it is but of glimpse of the best that is yet to come.

December 1

*He called a little child and had him stand among them. And he said, "I
tell you the truth, unless you change and become like little children you
will never enter the kingdom of heaven.
Therefore, whoever humbles himself like this child
is the greatest in the kingdom of heaven.*
—The words of Jesus as recorded
in Matthew 18:2–4

Everyone called her Aunt Vera. The title was more a matter of respect than genealogy. Every year around Christmas time it became clear why all who knew her fondly called this quiet and gentle
soul "Aunt."

It would begin early in December. Aunt Vera had a huge Blue
Spruce tree in her front yard that she decorated with hundreds of
bright lights. This simple act may not seem remarkable by today's
standards, but her tree was the delight of the neighborhood. First,
there were few spruce trees in this land of hardwoods. Second, no one
could afford to purchase the necessary strings of outdoor lights or the
electricity to operate them. It became a December ritual for me to
press my face against my frosty upstairs bedroom window and look
across the half-mile of flatland fields to see if Aunt Vera had her tree
decorated. Her tree stood as the official herald of the season to come,
and it seemed to belong to all of us.

Around the middle of December, Aunt Vera would call all the
neighborhood children to tell each of us to remind our parents that a
special treat would be awaiting us on Christmas Eve at her house. She
always baked some out-of-the-ordinary goody for each of us. Perhaps
it was an intricately decorated gingerbread man, or a snowman made
out of colored popcorn, or maybe a pair of hand-knit mittens. I thought
Aunt Vera had to be the wealthiest woman in the world. Imagine having a lighted outdoor tree and giving gifts to dozens of children. To
this child's mind, she was enormously rich!

It was many Christmases later that I learned it was not wealth that
earned Vera her well-deserved forename. It had nothing to do with
earnings, holdings, or dividends. Vera became Aunt Vera not by fortune, social status, or by political sway. She became aunt to all simply
by giving the most lasting of all gifts—her love.

Prayer: This Day my prayer is to give the only gift that really matters—love. Today, I will begin to do whatever it takes to
make it a year around gift.

*Do not be afraid. I bring you good news of great joy
that will be for all people. Today in the town of David,
a Savior has been born to you; he is Christ the Lord.*
—Luke 2:10-11

On a recent news telecast, several market-watchers made their predictions about the economic outlook for the upcoming Christmas-shopping season. Their verdict was unanimous. It was also grimly unanimous. The economists' outlook was for a dreary and dismal shopping season.

They cited the usual negative markers such as uncertain fuel prices, high credit card debt, and a general concern over dwindling stock market averages. One of the economists mentioned that the season's biggest problem was the lack of what she called a "zinger." She said, "This shopping season we do not have an Elmo, a Cabbage Patch, a Furbee, or a Pokemon to incite interest and create a buying frenzy among the shoppers."

What a sorry world! No doll to incite a buying frenzy is like no dried cherries in the fruitcake! Big deal! What happened to the Child in the manger? Why is that not excitement enough? Is there no "zinger" in Bethlehem?

We may not have to wait in line or suffer a Cabbage Patch shortage as we endure a "zinger-less" Christmas. So, let's just focus on the only frenzy that really matters this Christmas. Why not rejoice in the one "zinger" that never goes out of style? The one that still changes lives, brings hope, and offers peace.

Let's stand in line at the manger. It may not be as crowded, but Jesus is all the "zinger" we will ever need.

Prayer: This Day I will refocus on the reason for this season of hope. Today, I will rejoice in the grandest gift of all.

> *So Joseph also went up from Nazareth in Galilee to Bethlehem. . . . While*
> *they were there, the time came for the baby to be born, and she gave*
> *birth to her firstborn, a son.*
>
> —Luke 2:4–6

When I was a child, my family had a well-worn nativity scene. Each year it came out of the box and was assembled with great care. As nativity scenes go, it was not much of a piece of art. It was old and made out of cardboard. It featured a donkey with a broken off ear and a lamb with a missing leg. It showed signs of having been much-handled on many a Christmas past.

There was the manger that held baby Jesus and the stable with a light bulb that looked like a Star of Bethlehem. There were Mary, Joseph, and angels. There were several robed men with long shepherd staffs, a lamb or two, a cow, and the donkey with a broken off ear. It has been a long time since that nativity scene has been hauled out and set up. The Lord only knows what has become of it. Maybe it rests in the bottom of some landfill? Maybe it is tucked away in someone's attic? Maybe another family member has it? I just don't know.

Yet, one place it still exists is in my mind's eye. That worn-out cardboard scene still informs my view of Christ's birth. Since I was a child looking at that pathetic donkey with the broken-off ear, I have read and studied that story more than a few times. I have had the opportunity to visit Bethlehem. I have read the commentaries and heard the seminary professors' lectures. I know that the nativity scene has some factual flaws.

The fact is that Mary and Joseph were probably too poor to own a donkey. Yet, I rather liked the idea that poor, pregnant Mary rode a donkey from Galilee to Bethlehem. Maybe some kindhearted soul came to Joseph and said, "Would you like to borrow my donkey—being that Mary is in no condition to walk? My donkey does not hear too well, but you are welcome to borrow it." Maybe that happened. Maybe it did not. Either way, I think I'll keep the donkey in my nativity scene, because it is a reminder of some kindhearted person who was willing to share. I'll keep it because who wants a donkey with a broken off ear?

Prayer: This Day I will look squarely at the factual truth. And the fact is this: God has used the lowly and the ordinary to bring forth the glorious and the extraordinary.

A truth that's told with bad intent
Beats all the lies you can invent.

—William Blake

I had the good fortune of playing on a strong eighth-grade basketball team. As we prepared for our final game, we knew that our undefeated eighth-grade season, combined with our 15–0 seventh-grade season, would give us a perfect Middle School record of 30 and 0. It had never been done before.

The pressure was not great. Remember, these were eighth-grade boys who knew no fear. These were boys who were not yet men and surely not children. We were young boys who compensated for our fear with arrogance. We were a confident and a cocky lot!

One of the five starters got a bright idea. He suggested that the first string was the reason for the remarkable success. The five of us ought to do something to stand out from the others. We should dress slightly different from rest of the team. But how? How could we stand out and yet not be too outrageous? How could we be arrogant, but not too arrogant? How could we be cocky, but not too cocky? I know it sounds silly, and if you were never an eighth-grade boy, it may be hard for you to understand.

Here was his idea: We would go down to Leo Brink's shoe repair and buy five pairs of florescent orange shoelaces. Those orange shoelaces made us stand out as special. We were unique. We stood out from the rest, but not for long. As we huddled up before the opening tip-off, the coach said, "You five with the orange shoe laces go sit down. If we need you, we will call. But, don't hold your breath waiting for a call."

My heart sank. Why had I done such a stupid thing? I sat there on the bench, and looked at those horrid orange shoelaces and loathed them. I was angry with the coach, the airhead who cooked up the florescent orange shoelace idea, but mostly, I was angry with myself for following along with such a dumb idea. I had not intended for it to end like this. I learned an important lesson that day: **We are known by our actions and not by our intentions.**

Prayer: This Day I will carefully consider my actions and intentions and make every effort to make them be a good match.

After Jesus was born in Bethlehem in Judea, during the time of King Herod, Magi from the east came to Jerusalem and asked, "Where is the one who has been born king of Jews?
We saw his star in the east and have
come to worship him."

—Matthew 2:1–2

Humorist, Lila Hangartner, of Finland, Minnesota, asks, "Do you know what would have happed if it had been three wise women instead of three wise men who visited the Baby Jesus?"

"First, they would have stopped and asked directions. Second, they would have gotten there on time. Third, they would have helped deliver the baby. Fourth, they would have helped clean the stable. Fifth, they would have made a casserole. And finally, they would have brought practical gifts, like Pampers or a teething ring."

It is true that God's choice of wise men coming from the Far East did have its flaws. They arrived late and could have been more helpful. And who would bring embalming spices to a baby shower?

So, the story begins with curiosity and wonder, and grows even more curious and wonderful. Simply because God uses us in our flawed-ness, our less than prefect response, and even our bewilderment, the story of the Incarnation is even more amazing.

Prayer: This Day is a good day to not take myself too seriously. Today, the wonder of all of us less-than-perfect souls, who are perfected by Christ, is enough to ponder for one day.

> *Do not be too wise, nor too foolish,*
> *Do not be too conceited, nor too retiring,*
> *Do not be too haughty, nor too humble,*
> *Do not be too talkative, nor too silent,*
> *Do not be too hard, nor too weak.*
> —The ancient instructions of
> Irish King Cormac

M oderation is not a given for most of us. Our rationale is often flawed with the idea that if anything is worth doing, then doing it in excess must be better. Of course, that can lead to destruction. Yet, finding that delicate balance we call moderation is elusive. Think of it in terms of eating just one potato chip. One is too many, and ten thousand are not nearly enough.

So, how do we pursue moderation? How do we keep the "too" out of our lives?

One test is to honestly examine our motives. Whose needs are being met? Why do we do what we do? Is it to look good before others? Is it to win their applause? Is it to fulfill the expectations of a parent, a spouse, a friend, or an employer? Is it to look good to God?

Another test of moderation is to ask if it is destructive to others or to myself? Destructive does not always mean the obvious. Drinking, drugging, eating, gambling, working, or loving to excess can obviously be destructive. Have you ever met someone who was an enormous bore because all they wanted to talk about was their work or a favorite hobby? Their excessive passion had become destructive to the relationship.

A third test for moderation is to take the energy you put into your passion and funnel it into its antithesis. If you work too hard, try to play just as hard. If you whine too much, laugh more. If you complain excessively, compliment more. If you argue too much, affirm just as vigorously.

Going against your natural grain is a guaranteed way to soon learn moderation.

Prayer: This Day I pray, "Slow me down, Lord! Help me to strive for moderation in all things.

Forgive us our debts, as we also have forgiven our debtors.
—The words of Jesus as recorded
in Matthew 6:12

Forgiveness is a two-way street. We are forgiven in the same measure, and at the precise moment, that we forgive another. To withhold forgiveness for another keeps our own forgiven state unattained.

When another has wronged us, there is a twinge of satisfaction in wearing that bandaged wound where the whole world can see. Finding bliss in carrying the scars of unresolved blame is the gruel that nourishes a puny soul. The wronged is shackled to the wrong doer. The only cure is mutual forgiveness.

Sometimes, all we can do is exit the situation. Forgiveness is impossible. As author Caitlin Matthews says, "To forgive does not mean to condone, but it does mean to end the condemnation."

Have you ever had an overdue library book? Every day your intentions were to take the book back to the library and pay the fines. Every day you set the book out where you would not forget to take it back. Every day you got busy, went the other direction, were too preoccupied, or just plain forgot. The fines piled up and the penalty got worse. Then one day, there was an article in the newspaper that said the library had a one-day amnesty for all overdue books. That day you remembered the book. That day you felt the blessed relief of having been forgiven. The librarian was also happy.

To be forgiven is to be liberated. To be the forgiver is just as liberating.

Prayer: This Day I pray that I can be forgiving so that I may be forgiven. Today, I will cut the cords that bind me to blame or keep me bound as blamer.

Prosperity doth discover vice, but adversity doth best discover virtue.
—Francis Bacon

It has been said that adversity does not make us better people. Adversity just reveals what has always been within us. It is true.

Somewhere we came up with the notion that God likes to give us a bunch of misery now and then, and that is supposed to make us better. It is like football training camp theology—heap on the hurt, because it makes you stronger. That is a harsh understanding of God. It is wholly incongruent with a God of mercy and grace. In fact, it makes God look a bit psychotic. It sounds like God would both set fire to our house, and then drive the pumper truck to put out the flames. What kind of God is that?

No, God does not heap on hurt to make us better. Rather, God has instilled within us far more resolve, more strength to endure, and more wherewithal than most of us can ever guess. It is in the harsh times of life that we get a glimpse of our inner self. It is when life is at its toughest that we get an inkling of the magnitude of what God can do through us.

We come out the other side of those ugly times of life with a new sense of self. It may look like toughness has been added. We may think we are better for the experience. But, the truth is, we have just gotten a glimpse of our inner self.

Next time you hear someone say, "These things make us stronger," tell them, "You had it in you all the time!"

Prayer: This Day I will reach deeply within if necessary. Today, I know there is nothing that can come my way that God and I cannot handle together. Sometimes it just takes more God than others.

December 9

> *Cast all your cares on God; that anchor holds.*
> —Alfred Lord Tennyson

Jack was an avid outdoorsman. He loved to hunt, fish, and trap. If it ran, flew, or swam, Jack loved the chase. But, Jack's life had come to a tough juncture. Bankrupt is the word. He was bankrupt spiritually, physically, emotionally, financially, and maritally. He had nothing. Zip! All gone! Jack had drunk himself into bankruptcy.

Jack made a decision. He would take his fishing rod, his traps, and his deer rifle and escape into the wilderness. He would head north—maybe Canada, or maybe he would keep going north until there was no more north. There, he would no longer be hurting the ones he loved. His bankrupt role as husband, father, and son would no longer bring shame to his family. And, if his escape to the north woods did not work, he could turn the deer rifle on himself. That is just how bankrupt Jack had become.

But, just before he headed for the woods, Jack tried a desperate prayer that went something like this:

> Dear God, I have made a horrible mess of things. The wreckage that I now endure is the handiwork of my own doing. And, I know that it has been a long time since we have talked, but please take this scourge from me and take it to the farthest reaches of your realm where I never, ever have to see it again.

Almost as an after thought, Jack added:

> "I'll do whatever you ask. If there is anything that can be salvaged from this life, it is yours to do with as you will. Please, please, please help me to never drink again."

God heard his prayer. Jack unpacked his bags.

Prayer: This Day is a good day to take any part of my bankrupt life to God. There it can be restored, renewed, and set free.

"Classic." A book which people praise and don't read.
—Mark Twain

As often is the case, Mark Twain points out a universal human flaw in a friendly way. We love to, either knowingly or unknowingly, quote from the great authors. We rely on their nuggets of wisdom and unwittingly turn classic quotes into clichés.

What about the one, true classic that underpins our faith? What about quoting from, but failing to read God's Word? Could that possibly happen?

You have likely heard it said, "I just don't have time to read the Bible. Besides, the Bible is written in such a stuffy way that I cannot understand it. *Webster's Dictionary* or the *Yellow Pages* is about as readable as the Bible."

Tell your spouse, your child, your employer, or your favorite hobby, "I don't have time for you." See how they respond to your stinginess of time. There is time for anything you want to do. A more honest answer would be, "I don't want to take time away from other interests."

What's this about God's Word being impossible to understand? Did you understand how to read page one in your first reader on your first day of school? Of course not! You persisted, and eventually you learned how to read. Grasping the meaning of the Bible is no different. You begin to understand God's Word by keeping on keeping on.

If time and comprehension are not the issue, then what is stopping you from daily Bible reading? God has something to say to you. You begin to hear what God has to say when you pick up God's Word.

God is aching to tell you his story. If you are going to quote God's Word, a good place to begin is by first reading it.

Prayer: This Day I will do what I have been putting off for a long time. Today, I will begin my conversation with God through his Word. This is not going to be easy and it may take away from my busy life, but I know in my heart that God has something to say to me.

If we live, we live to the Lord; and if we die, we die to the Lord. So,
whether we live or die, we belong to the Lord.

—Romans 14:8

It was the heart of the busy Christmas-shopping season. Charlotte, my then eleven-year-old granddaughter, and I were sitting on a mall bench. We were resting from the rigors of shopping and doing a bit of people-watching.

However, this was no ordinary shopping excursion. There was something else that preoccupied our minds on this day. My father was critically ill. In fact, he was dying. So, our shopping venture was a welcome respite from the transition that was unfolding in our family during this Christmas season.

As we sat on the bench in the midst of much merriment and hurry, I was wondering how Charlotte was coping with her great-grandfather's impending death. I asked, "Well Char, what do you think? Do you think Papa is going to make it?"

"I don't know. What do you think?" she replied.

"I think Papa is going to spend Christmas with Jesus this year." I said.

Charlotte's reply was simple, reassuring, and wise beyond her years. She said, "We always spend Christmas with Jesus!"

The child had grasped the essence of God's enduring nature that is ours in Jesus Christ. Once we are alive in Christ, we are alive forever. In her child-like way she had said that life begins here and now and lasts forever. If we live, or if we die, nothing really changes for the one who lives in Christ.

Prayer: This Day I will need your help to be fully alive as I drink in the wonder of this world and prepare for the next. Comfort me in the hope of Christmas, and in knowing that a life lived in Christ has no ending.

I realize that patriotism is not enough.
I must have no hatred or bitterness towards anyone.
—Edith Cavell

What was left of the nineteen-year-old farm boy from Iowa lay on a cot in a battlefield tent. A German grenade had severed his left arm near the shoulder. The blow had ripped his youthful body like some violent tornado out of the Midwest hurling a farmer's spike tooth drag through the air. The lad's life hung by a thin gossamer thread.

A few days later, the young soldier's physical condition showed signs of improvement. It looked like he would defy death. A battlefield miracle was in process. However, his spirit was broken. He was a shattered wreck of emotional discontent. He was filled with anger, self-pity, and bitterness. He just lay on the cot, looked at the canvas tent ceiling with an unblinking blank stare, and wept.

An Army chaplain made his rounds one day and saw the youthful soldier with the blank stare. He came over to the young man's cot and stood silently for a time. Then the chaplain said, "Son, you can stay bitter or you can get better. But, you cannot get better being bitter."

Today, that Iowa farm boy is a man nearing his eighties. He is retired. The boy healed, became a pastoral counselor and author. He wrote and lectured on how to live beyond tragedy. His advice was always the same: You cannot get better being bitter.

In the aftermath of September 11, 2001, this nation has had to learn how to heal without the bile of bitterness. To lash out at the government, the airlines, the Muslim world, or any other institution will never heal the tears in our national soul. Only living beyond the tragedy will rebind us. We, too, cannot get better being bitter.

Prayer: This Day my bitterness will give way that better-ness may flow into its place. Today the wounds will be cleansed of bitterness.

"It's no good, it's no good!" says the buyer;
then off he goes and boasts about
his purchase.

—Proverbs 20:14

As the year draws to an end, we begin to get year-end market-analysis reports. When we review our decisions, we may compliment ourselves on our brilliance and our foresightedness. Or, if the market has treated us poorly, we may wish we had put our money in a Mason jar and buried it in the back yard. Such is capital risk!

A troubling market trend has begun to emerge. What market people crudely call "sin stocks" have been amazingly consistent. Investments in tobacco, alcohol, casinos, and military weapons have been big winners. According to the S & P 500 report, in the five year period between 1997 and 2002, these sin stocks have had a 53% increase, while the balance of Standard & Poors 500 stocks have shown a paltry 12% increase.

For the investor who wants to be morally and socially responsible, this is hard to ignore. Underwriting funds that bring harm, add to suffering, and increase human indignity is not a comfortable place for most of us. We ask, how can we pray for peace and invest in missile makers?

When you consider your portfolio, instead of asking, "Who cares anyway?" or, "What difference does my little bit of change make to the world?" ask, "How can I begin to make a difference?"

Prayer: This day I will see my tiny contribution to the whole as important. Today, I will see right profit above big profit.

". . . all things are possible with God."
—The words of Jesus as recorded
in Mark 10:27

Optimistic. It is a good word. It is good, because it points to the way the world is and sees how the world could be. The optimistic person is not merely a dreamer, a romanticist, or foolhardy. The optimist is a visionary who is in love with life and embraces its possibilities.

The most optimistic people you will ever meet are farmers. They deal with uncertain weather, unpredictable markets, spiraling costs, disease, insects, and bureaucracy, yet they remain optimistic. A farmer friend once said, "I have farmed for nearly thirty years. In all that time I have had only two what you would call "good years." The first one was about twenty-five years ago, and the other one is next year!" That is optimism.

God must be an optimist. God saw the world as it was and optimistically saw how it could be. God was an optimist in a cow shed in Bethlehem. He was optimistic on a hillside in Galilee. God was an optimist at another hill called Calvary.

God looks at a smoldering heap of what was once a skyscraper and is optimistic. God hears war rhetoric, racial slurs, and a child told that he or she is unwanted, and yet, God remains optimistic. God sees hungry people, a mother living with HIV/AIDS, an unfaithful spouse, an addicted man on the streets, a business fold, and a mere child flashing a gang sign, and is still optimistic. God sees the world as it is and God says, "It will get better."

It really is quite simple. Because God is an optimist, we call it the Good News.

Prayer: This Day I will look at my corner of the world and try to see beyond the way it is. Today, I will do my part to make it the way it could be.

It takes a heap o' livin' in a house t' make it home . . .
—Edgar A. Guest

A house comes as close to having a soul as any inanimate structure can. It is almost as if this heap of boards, shingles, and concrete is a living, breathing entity. Have you ever noticed that a vacant house falls apart quickly? It seems that a house thrives on occupancy. One that is without tenant is unloved and soon falls into disrepair.

You can say, "It stands to reason that an empty house would fall apart. There is much maintenance to be done. If a shingle blows off, the water will run in. If the water leaks in, the rafter will rot. If the rafters decay, the roof will soon collapse. It is a matter of maintenance and not about a structure with a soul."

Yet, there is more than mere maintenance that keeps a house alive. A house with children usually has pleasant disarray to it. One that is home to a single person is uncluttered, but can be sterile and formal. One that has a cat or dog has friendliness about it. One that has a hospice bed in the front bedroom has a quiet solemnity. One that has a decorated spruce tree in the corner has a gaiety. One where the smell of baking bread drifts from the kitchen has a sense of hospitality to it. One with a fire in the hearth has physical heat and warmth for the soul. One where love calls home has a living, breathing, and almost-person quality to it. Such a place is far more than a heap of boards, a thirty-year mortgage, or an address.

When God's goodness dwells there, a house becomes a home.

Prayer: This Day I will value home above house. I will try to begin to understand the mystery of God's presence in my present place.

Your attitude should be the same as that of Christ Jesus: Who being in very nature God, did not consider equality with God something to be grasped, but made himself nothing, taking on the very nature of a servant, being made in human likeness. And being found in appearance as a man, he humbled himself and became obedient to death—even death on a cross! Therefore God exalted him to the highest place and gave him the name that is above every name, that at the name of Jesus every knee should bow, in heaven and on earth and under earth, and every tongue should confess that Jesus Christ is Lord, to the glory of God the Father.
—Philippians 2:5–11

If you look through the automotive section in the classified-advertisements section in a newspaper, you begin to notice an abbreviated language. Air conditioner is AC. PW and PD means power windows and power door locks. Ex. Cond. is short for excellent condition. PS & PB tells the reader that the car has power steering and power brakes. Often, a car or truck will have the asking price and OBO. OBO in classified language means "or best offer."

OBO invites the idea that the price is negotiable. It seems to say, "I know I am asking too much, but what are you willing to give?" Probably, OBO does move some casual classified readers to become serious lookers. It takes lookers to have buyers. So, OBO is a welcome mat for buyers and a clever ploy for sellers.

In some ways, Christmas is God's OBO. The birth of Jesus is God's best offer. If you long for a better deal, it will not come. You will not find a flashier Savior, a more modern invitation, or one with fewer miles. Since Jesus Christ is God's OBO, we would do well to take His OBO and run!

Prayer: This Day is a day of quiet reflection in the midst of Christmas rush. Today, I quietly consider what God has done for me in the gift of Jesus Christ. Christ is truly the best offer I've ever received!

> *Winning isn't everything, but wanting to win is.*
> —Vince Lombardi

It all began last July. In the summer heat, thirty-two professional football teams put on their pads, groaned under the hot July sun, pushed the blocking sled through mud and dust, ate hearty meals, and worked on playbooks. Every one of those thirty-two teams had a single vision—win the Super Bowl.

Soon, the thirty-two teams will be down to two. Then, in late January, only one team will emerge as Super Bowl Champion. There will be one winner and thirty-one losers.

In many of those thirty-one "also ran" communities, local sports writers will write scathing editorials that claim their town's team just cannot seem to win the big one. Quarterbacks will be traded, high salaried players will be released on waivers, new recruits will be courted, old bruised-up players will be retired, and coaches will be fired. The common cry in those thirty-one towns will be, "Just wait until next year!"

Those are poor odds—one winner and thirty-one losers who cannot win the big one.

Consider the church of Jesus Christ. It is where all can be winners, because it is where every loser can become a winner!

Prayer: This Day I will rejoice in my victory in Christ. Today, I will fully see this is the only Super Bowl that really matters.

> *"He is looking good and living large!"*
> —Quoted from a man whose child was born
> with a serious physical condition

Living large is the goal, but tragically, too many settle for largely living. To live large is to live with confidence and enthusiasm. It is to live with a sense of faith and assurance that is free from fear. To live large is to live with a sense of excitement in the face of challenge. It means to have immeasurable limits that define the possibilities that life may offer. Living large is living with boldness.

To largely live is to merely exist. It is to think small, set low goals, and accept whatever life brings to your door. Largely living settles for the norm, expects little joy, and holds few celebrations. Admittedly, those who largely live have few disappointments. They effectively factor few disappointments into life by setting low expectations. Those who largely live perish spiritually long before physical death. They seem to wither and die from lack of imagination.

The father of the child who was born with a serious condition seemed to glow when he said, "Looking good and living large!"

Could it be that the child's largeness was in any way connected to the father's enthusiasm, faith, and positive attitude?

What do you think?

Prayer: This day is a good day to live large by surprising the world with the possibilities that God and I can accomplish together. Whatever today brings to my door, I will not settle for merely largely living.

> *For nothing is impossible with God.*
> —Luke 1:37

Have you ever known a "What-if'er?"

What is a "What-if'er?" It is a person who only sees the negative possibilities of life. They are constantly saying, "Yes, but what if?" Everything is questioned from the perspective of a negative outcome. A world class "What-if'er" lives with a gripping fear of the minute possibility that something could go wrong. What if the market crashes? What if my health fails? What if it rains? What if the car won't start? What if the furnace conks out on a cold night? What if I have a party and no one comes? What will I do with all the food? What if I have a party and everyone comes? Will there be enough food?

Of course, there are matters that deserve our healthy concern. But, the "What-if'er" sees only the worst possible outcome.

There is a strange energy that flows from the "What-if'er" to the questioned possibility. The insistent questioning has a mysterious way of draining the certain out of certainty. It is as if the "What-if'er" has put some dark spell on the absolute. The "What-if'er's" joy is now complete when he or she can say, "See, I told you so! I just knew that was going to happen!"

The heart of the "What-if'er's" dilemma is that he or she overlooks the possibility of God. Faith in God excludes impossibility. Oh, sure, not every undertaking ends in success, but with God, nothing is beyond possibility. To express constant and unyielding doubt only weakens and withdraws God's presence. Every time the "What-if'er" says, "What if?" a bit of God is denied.

What do you do with "What-if'ers?" Probably the best you can do is not add to their number!

Prayer: This Day I will shape my question as "why not?" instead of "why me?" or "what if?' Today, I will see the extraordinary possibility and treat the impossible with indifference.

Most of the change we think we see in life
Is due to truths being in and out of favor.
—Robert Frost

A number of surveys have been designed to try to discover the secrets of success for couples who have been married more than sixty years. All have come to the same conclusion. People who stay together are people who are capable of living with change. The same is true for longevity. Persons who have lived past their one-hundredth birthday overwhelmingly are able to cope with change.

Change is inevitable. Nothing is static. The weather changes, markets change, neighborhoods change, and cultural choices change. We grow older, and our children grow older. That is good. If children never changed, we would only know them as infants. Though most of us would like to slow the aging process, we have to agree that the journey through life would be awkward or impossible if lived without change.

We are powerless to stop change, yet understand how vital it is to live in harmony with it. So, how do we live alongside of change?

First, we need to see change as a friend. If the weather never changed, we would have either continuous flood or ever-present drought. If our children did not mature, the species would soon become extinct.

Second, understand that change may be for the better. We fear growing old, but maturity does bring its advantages. We need to develop a spirit of acceptance and interest in change, rather than fear and trepidation.

And finally, take heart in knowing that in this ever-changing world, there is one thing that never changes. God is unchanging. The God of yesterday, today, and tomorrow is always and forever.

In an ever-changing world, that is comforting to know.

Prayer: This Day my joy is bigger than my fears. I will not have to replicate the past, reinvent how I must live today, or worry about tomorrow. This Day, God is God and all is well.

---

*In him was life, and that life was the light of men. The light shines in the
darkness, but the darkness has not
understood.*

—John 1:4

Today is Midwinter Day. Tomorrow is the first full day of winter.
Midwinter Day is the inverse of Midsummer Day (see June 21).

Today is the shortest day of sunlight and the longest night of the
year. If you live north of the equator, your shadow at noon today will
be the longest it is any time of the year. It has ominous possibilities to
think that today you cast a long shadow.

Take a moment to think about your long shadow. Pause and consider the places your shadow has fallen on the earth. What markers
have you left of your having passed through this life? What are the
deeds, the significances, and the lasting marks you have made?

Your shadow means nothing. It flows around you, and you have
no control of its length, its shape, or its shade. It is merely there.
However, you can control in whose life your light and presence brings
life.

The shadow you cast is transient and insignificant. The light you
shed is eternal.

Prayer: This Day I pray that the light of Christ shines through me.
Grant that I might illumine some dark corner, add warmth
to another, or be a reflection of God's lasting goodness.

You better watch out
You better not cry.
You better not pout.
I'm telling you why.
Santa Claus is coming to town.
He is making a list and checking it twice.
Gonna find out who is naughty and nice.
He sees you when you are sleeping.
He knows when you are awake.
He knows if you've been bad or good,
So, be good for goodness sake!
Oh! You better watch out.
Cause Santa Claus is coming to town.
—From the song, Santa Claus is Coming to Town

You have seen the "What would Jesus do? (WWJD) bracelets. A new twist on the same idea is, What if Jesus is looking? (WIJIL)

The "What if Jesus is looking?" is one of fear and trepidation. It is a theology that promotes a God who is watching for an opportunity to smash you like a bug unless you behave. So, which is the better of the two WWJD? or WIJIL? Which is most realistic? Which best speaks to the mission of Jesus Christ? Is it one that says, "I know you are up to no good and I am watching you to keep you honest?" Or is it one that says, "Be Christlike in all your daily affairs?"

The answer to that is not too hard. It is "What would Jesus do?" It is surely not "What if Jesus is looking?"

Take a look at what Jesus did if you want to have any sense of what would Jesus do? Peter says Jesus did not retaliate. He made no threats. Instead, he entrusted himself to God. (1 Peter 2:23)

That sounds like a mild-mannered Savior and not one who is making a list and checking it twice.

Prayer: This Day will be lived as Christlike as possible. Today I will put away for good the fear-filled notion that I must behave because God is watching.

A Christmas prayer for all who have a loved one in heaven:

I'm Spending Christmas
with Jesus Christ this Year
I see the countless Christmas trees
Around the world below
With tiny lights, like heaven's stars,
Reflecting on the snow.

The sight is so spectacular,
Please wipe away that tear,
For I'm spending Christmas
With Jesus Christ this year.

I hear the many Christmas songs
That people hold so dear.
But the sounds of music can't compare
With the Christmas choir up here.

For I have no words to tell you
The joy their voices bring.
For it is beyond description
To hear as angels sing.

I know how much you miss me,
I see the pain inside your heart.
For I'm spending Christmas
With Jesus Christ this year.

I'll ask Him to light your spirit
As I tell Him of your love.
So then pray for one another
As you lift your eyes above.

So please let your hearts be joyful
And let your spirits sing.
For I'm spending Christmas in heaven
And I'm walking with the King!
—Author unknown

*I bring you good news of great joy that will be for all people. Today in
the town of David a Savior has been born to you;
he is Christ.*

—Luke 2:10–11

Every Christmas Eve, I am the most privileged man alive. This is the most magnificent and the most personally moving moment in my entire year. And each year, it grows with more intensity, more preciousness, and holds greater meaning for me. Tonight is one of my bright threads of life. This is a sweet moment.

As pastor, I get to look out on a community of people whom I love and see their faces bathed in the Christ candle. For a moment, as we sing *Silent Night*, I alone have the opportunity to look at the faces of the people. As I look out on the congregation I serve, I see the face of God as clearly as any moment in the entire year. There is a kind of instant replay. Each face holds a story.

There is the face of the man who came close to death, but miraculously lived. There are the faces of the newlywed couple, and the faces of the long married couple who worked so hard to put love back into their lives. There are the faces of the new parents, and the parents who just buried a child. There are the faces of ones who just found Jesus Christ for the first time, and those who cannot remember not knowing Christ. There are the faces of the recently widowed, the about to be widowed, and those healing from sorrow. There is the face of the new graduate who just landed a job, and the faces of ones who lost a job, and the ones whose unemployment payments are running out.

And the mystery of it all, the great paradox, is this: The same light of Christ bathes every face. The broken and the hopeful, the sick and the restored, the alone and the accompanied, the young, the old, the rich, the poor, the lost and the found, the righteous and the ones who are trying to do their best. In your finest moment, in your worst moment, and in your great in between moment, the same light of Christ is shed upon every one of God's children.

And that is the *real* Christmas story!

Prayer: This Day I will bask in the warming glow of the light of life. On this Christmas Eve, I will rejoice and thank God for the greatest of all gifts.

> *Suddenly a great company of the heavenly host appeared*
> *with the angel, praising God and saying,*
> *"Glory to God in the highest,*
> *And on earth peace to men on*
> *whom his favor rests."*
> —Luke 2:13–14

In the slaughterhouse days of the bloodiest of all American wars, the Civil War, a temporary quiet of sorts took place. General Picket and his Confederate troops locked horns with the Union troops outside of Richmond, Virginia. The two armies waged the cruelest of campaigns against each other. Then one night there was a lull in the action. Strangely, there were dozens of bonfires and singing that filled the air among the Confederate lines. The Union guards discovered that the Confederates had received news that General Picket's wife had given birth to a child.

General Grant was so moved by the event that he ordered the Union troops to light like bonfires as a symbol of shared joy and respect. The next day, under the white flag of truce, General Grant sent a letter of congratulation to his Confederate counterpart.

It happened again on Christmas Eve, 1914. An amazing and unplanned three-day armistice took place all along the entire Western front. You may have heard the stories of the Axis and the Allied troops who filled the Christmas Eve air over that moonscape "no man's land" with Christmas carols. For a time, on one cold December evening, in the midst of what was to be called "the war to end all wars," the two armies left their trenches and shook hands, sang songs, traded plugs of tobacco, and wished one another Merry Christmas. The quiet went on for three days, until their superiors ordered them back into the trenches to make war once more.

If war could cease once for three days, then peace on earth is possible.

Prayer:　This Day is a good day to begin world peace. May mutual respect fall like a pebble in a pool and radiate out to the entire world. May its ripple be a tidal wave of lasting peace.

"I will honor Christmas in my heart and try to keep it all the year."
—Ebenezer Scrooge from Charles Dickens'
A Christmas Carol

For some of you, Christmas is over. For others, you may have a Christmas or two to go yet. Many families are obligated to divide their holiday season with the various parts of their family. So, today finds some who are basking in the joy of a grand season, some who are still deeply engaged in the spirit, and others who have grown weary of the whole thing. Some are wondering why all the fuss for just a few hours of joy. Some might be questioning the mismatch between preparation and actual happening. Some might be pondering how long it is until the bills begin to arrive that were advertised as, "no payments until January."

Today is a mixed bag for many of us. The joy, the expectation, and the busyness of this season seem closest to us on the day after Christmas. It can mean that the expectation has waned, and it is not yet New Year's Day.

So, how do we capture a bit of this glow and carry it forward? How do we hold on to the warmth? How do we keep alive that extra measure of kindness that we gladly received and gave back so generously? Or, do we have to wait until next December 1?

We can unmix the mixed bag of Christmas spent. We have caught a glimpse of the best of the human condition in these past weeks. There is no earthly reason that we cannot keep it alive. The only possible way that the spirit of Christmas can slip from our midst is if we understand it as a single day in late December, or one that is between dinner at Aunt Minnie's and supper at our other Grandma's place. If Christmas is just the day of presents and gorging between Thanksgiving and New Year's Day's conviviality, then it is surely gone until another December 25. Keep Christmas alive twelve months a year. It is a season that is never out of season.

Prayer: This Day I will keep alive within me the life that has been so graciously given to me in Christ's birth. Help me, God, to live more fully, to love without condition, to be more caring, and to embrace the world's suffering in a way that never goes out of season.

In life, as in a football game, the principle to follow is:
Hit the line hard.

—Theodore Roosevelt

The hysteria of football bowl games is upon us. For those who love the crash of shoulder pads, the smell of a sweaty helmet, and the guttural grunts of men slamming into each other, this is as good as the gridiron gets. For those who see football as a primitive combat of masculine nonsense, just bear with us, because it soon will be over.

During the dozens of bowl games this week, you will hear many clichés. You will hear the commentators and coaches say, "Well, they are just like us. They put their pants on one leg at a time." Someone will surely say, "This one is for the fans." Predictably we will hear, "We will play them one game at a time." Of course, the classic of all clichés will once again be said: "We gotta step up and reach deep to win this one." Football clichés will run rampant for the next few days.

However, some clichés do have deep and profound meaning. For example: "Games are always won or lost in the trenches." It means that those interior linemen who tough it out with little glory are the ones who are the true heroes. The anonymous ones who open the way for the running backs are the ones to watch. The nameless, grass-stained, mud-covered behemoths that are on the bottom of the pile are the ones who shape the game.

Maybe football clichés are not so silly after all. Maybe they are metaphors for life. Perhaps in the end, the real winners are those who quietly labor without fame. If that is true for football, then just maybe we are relieved of having to be an All Star in God's eyes.

Could it be that playing with resolve, humility, and courage is what God is asking of us in the game of life?

Prayer: This Day let it be known that all who play on God's team are winners. This team plays without clichés, excuses, and roaring crowds. And at the game's end, it always brings home the trophy.

Nothing great was ever achieved without enthusiasm.
—Ralph Waldo Emerson

Louis Leakey's parents were missionaries who labored for the gospel in Kenya. Leakey and his wife, Mary, were renowned anthropologists. The Leakey's have made countless discoveries and have added greatly to our understanding of early human history. The couple spent a lifetime poking around in desert heat, sifting through tons of soil looking for fossils, tools, bone fragments, and other artifacts in Kenya, Africa.

Louis Leakey is best known for his work as an anthropologist. However, he was also a humanitarian, an explorer, an historian, and a devoted Christian lay minister. Louis Leakey was the first white person elected to the parliament in Kenya.

Over their illustrious careers, the Leakey's were awarded many citations and awards. No award, accolade, honor, or epitaph was more succinct and profound than the caption under Louis Leakey's picture in the Smithsonian Magazine. It simply said, "Louis Leakey was a man of many enthusiasms."

Would that we could live in such a way that it could be said of us, "He or she lived with many enthusiasms."

Prayer: This Day is a splendid day to multiply my enthusiasms. Let living with zest, passion, and gusto be the core of my being.

Dreams are the touchstones of our characters.
—Henry David Thoreau

What limits you? Is it money? Power? Education? Wit? Energy? Drive?

Chances are, none of these put a lid on your possibilities. The most limiting, and by far the most crippling, of all human endeavors is a puny imagination. The size of your dreams is in direct proportion to the size of your accomplishments. If you dream big, you do big. If you think puny, you invariably will harvest a scrawny crop. The inverse is just as true. If you imagine success, you will likely know success.

Our dreams and imagination underwrite our accomplishments.

There is a mysterious element to this notion. It is as if there is an unseen energy that emanates from positive thinking. Success is like an extension of our physical self that begins in our spiritual core. Accomplishment flows from the mind in some undeniable, though inexplicable way.

Another aspect of a healthy imagination is how it impacts others. Suppose you went to a political rally. The main speaker was a candidate for a high office. He or she said, "Well, I suppose we can expect a few votes. Maybe we can help the economy, but probably not. Maybe we can create jobs, though I doubt it. As far as crime goes, there is little we can do."

Would you vote for such a small-thinking and dreary candidate? Surely not! Big dreams, large imaginations, and great enthusiasm tear down the barriers that limit us.

Dream big, share them with others, and go change the world!

Prayer: This Day my dreams will drive my limits to new heights. Today, I will not settle for puny dreams or modest limits. Kingdom-building is a big job, so I will need all the barrier busters I can muster.

And they will live securely, for then his greatness
Will reach to the ends of the earth.
And he will be their peace.

—Micah 5:4–5

Christmas sometimes has its disappointments. Do you remember when you wanted an electric train and got slippers and a bathrobe instead? Some find Christmas a disappointment when they see the overt, blatant commercialism that displaces the reason for the season. Some find disappointment in the fact that we prove, for a brief moment, that we can be more caring, more giving, and kinder folk, but the spirit of compassion soon wanes.

What ought to be the most disappointing about the Christmas season is the fact that the words of the prophet, Micah, and the words of the angel—"Peace on earth, good will to all people"—are still unfulfilled. The promise of peace on earth is not realized, and that is what is most disappointing.

Our world has dozens of nations where thousands, if not tens of thousands, of missiles are pointed at each other. Every year, another culture faces genocide and suffers under an iron-fisted oppressor.

We believe that because of the gift of the Christ child, there will be "Peace on earth, good will to all people." We send the cards and we sing the songs that proclaim peace on earth, but the world is really not a peaceful place. After 2,000 years we still have not gotten it right. The promise goes unfulfilled.

It is not an idealist's dream that all that can change. We have the promise, and God keeps his promises. So, we need to pray for world peace. Praying together, we can make this the best Christmas ever. We can fulfill that promise in our time!

Prayer: This Day may the world know the promise of world peace. May it begin with each of us who pray together for that end.

Never tell your resolution beforehand.

—John Selden

Today, we stand at an ending and peer over the threshold of a new beginning. The tendency is to hurriedly make a list of resolutions for the coming year. We seem to have an innate desire to shackle ourselves with a self-imposed list of "Thou shall nots." Our hope is to rid ourselves of some bad habit or to remake our image. Since we are never at a loss for resolution ideas, we must be generally unsatisfied with our performance.

Here are two ideas about resolution-making that you might find helpful: First, take a long and careful look backward. Instead of thinking about next year, use today to inventory the time that is in your immediate wake. What do you see that you liked? What gave your life meaning? What bliss and what zest do you want to take with you? Instead of compiling what am I going to quit doing, why not think in terms of what am I going to keep doing. Your chances of success put into positive terms will increase exponentially if you just keep on keeping on with what you like.

Second, it always helps to set the bar low enough so that you are certain of some success. Sure, go ahead and give yourself a tough resolution to follow. Make it one that is going to demand every ounce of energy you can muster. But, balance that tough one with a no brainer! Set the bar high and balance it off with one that is highly doable. A few years ago, I resolved that I would not use a semi colon for the next twelve months. Guess what? I made it!

This year, I resolve that I will keep on doing what adds zest to my life. I will also resolve to not eat any hippopotamus meat for an entire year.

Prayer: This Day brings the year to a close as it stands in hopeful expectation for the year ahead. My prayer for today is, "Thank you, Lord, for that which you have given and that which I am about to receive."

Index

C

Calling	Mar. 17; Oct 14, 27.
Caring	Mar. 19, April 23, 27, 28;
	May 20; June 6, 9;
	Dec. 21.
Change	Mar. 26–28; April 22, 24;
	May 14; June 24, 28; Oct. 12, 23; Nov. 29;
	Dec. 20, 31.

Christian Living

Jan. 1,19; Feb.1, 4, 5, 9, 12, 18, 19, 22, 23, 26; Mar. 3, 6, 7, 9, 10;
April 3, 14, 17; May 7, 8, 11, 15–17, 21, 22, 24, 27;
June 11, 19, 21, 25; July 5–7, 9, 11, 13, 19;
Aug. 1, 7, 8, 10, 12, 13, 15, 17,

Christian Living Cont.

Aug. 20, 21, 24, 28; Sept. 3, 10, 13, 18, 21, 25, 28, 29; Oct. 5, 6, 11, 16; Nov. 10, 11, 21; Dec. 1.

Church	Jan. 10; Mar. 3, 4, 5, 8, 15, 20; April 12, 26, 27;
	May 14, 18; June 18, 23, 26; July 5, 30; Aug. 2,
	16, 31; Sept. 2, 6, 26; Nov. 27, 28.
Comfort	Mar. 1; April 7, 28;
	July 19, 26–31; Sept. 11, 17, 19.
Community	April 10, 19, 21, 27, 29; May 19; June 12, 17;
	July 16; Aug. 6; Oct. 18; Dec. 13, 24.

Complaining

Jan. 8, 20, 21, 24, 27; Feb. 28; April 7; Sept. 28.

Confidence	Sept. 24, 29.
Courage	Jan. 1; Mar. 21; April 24; May 26; Dec. 27.
Creation	Feb. 9, 14; Mar. 29; May 8, 23, 28; June 6, 21;
	Aug. 6; Sept. 5, 25,
	Oct. 8, 22; Nov. 1; Dec. 21.
Cross	Jan. 4; April 12; June 24; July 8, 12, 27, 28, 31;
	Oct. 2.

D

E

F

G

H

I

Imagination	April 1, 15; Sept. 8, 9.
Inclusiveness	Feb. 15; Aug. 14; Sept. 5.
Inconsistency	Jan. 17

J

Joy	Jan 2; May 1, 25; June 18, 30; July 15, 17; Aug. 22; Sept. 2; Nov. 18; Dec. 2, 18, 24, 28.
Justice	Feb. 10; April 9.

K

Kindness	Aug. 10

L

Love	Jan. 29; Mar. 10; April 12; July 12, 15, 25; Aug. 26; Sept. 16; Oct. 31.

M

Marriage	April 11.
Ministry	Jan. 19; July 5.
Miracles	Jan. 14; July 15; Oct. 21, 22.
Moderation	July 11; Dec. 6.
Moses	Dec. 18.

O

Overcoming	Jan. 14, 24; Mar. 21, 24, 26, 27, 28; May 24, 25; June 1; Dec. 8, 9, 12.

P

Paradox	Feb. 11; July 20; Sept. 1; Dec. 24.
Parenting	May 31; June 20; Aug. 8; Nov. 6; Dec. 12.
Patience	Mar. 25; May 15, 16, 17; Sept. 11, 12; Oct. 4; Nov. 6.

To order additional copies of

This Day . . .
A Daily Guide to Living

Have your credit card ready and call:

1-877-421-READ (7323)

or please visit our web site at
www.pleasantword.com

Also available at: www.amazon.com